KT-520-936

The VOGUE

Winter

COOKBOOK

The VOGUE

Winter
COOKBOOK

Arabella Boxer and Tessa Traeger

Mitchell Beazley

Editor	*Fiona Grafton*
Art Editor	*Val Hobson*
Assistant Editors	*Jane Garton*
	Helen Scott-Harman
Assistant Art Editor	*Ingrid Mason*
Art Assistant	*Flick Ekins*
Executive Editor	*Alexandra Towle*

The Vogue Summer and Winter Cookbook was edited
and designed by Mitchell Beazley Publishers Limited,
Mill House, 87-89 Shaftesbury Avenue, London W1V 7AD

© Mitchell Beazley Publishers Limited 1980
Text © Arabella Boxer   Photographs © Tessa Traeger and
Condé Nast Publications Limited
All rights reserved
No part of this work may be reproduced or utilized in any
form by any means, electronic or mechanical, including photo-
copying, recording or by any information storage or retrieval
system, without the prior written consent of the publisher

ISBN 0 85533 216 6

Typeset by Pierson LeVesley Ltd
Reproduction by Gilchrist Bros Ltd, Leeds
Printed in Great Britain by Morrison and Gibb Ltd

The publishers and authors would like to thank the following:
Vicarage Herbs, East Claydon, Buckinghamshire;
Mr Vincent at Enton Hall Health Centre, Godalming, Surrey;
Stephen Long, 348 Fulham Road, London SW10; Pat
Walker of the Doll Shop and all the stallholders of
Antiquarius, King's Road, London SW3; Elizabeth David of
46 Bourne Street, London SW1; Elijah Allen and Son and
J.W. Cockett, Butchers, of Hawes, Yorkshire; Justin de
Blank Provisions, 42 Elizabeth Street, London SW1; Justin
de Blank Herbs, Plants and Flowers, 114 Ebury Street,
London SW6; L'Herbier de Provence, 341 Fulham Road,
London SW6; Still Too Few, 300 Westbourne Grove,
London W11; Anglers' Retreat, Stall 93, Chelsea Antique
Market, King's Road, London SW3; Giovanni Filippi of
Lina Stores Ltd, 18 Brewer Street, London W1; Chattels,
53 Chalk Farm Road, London NW1; Bernard Gaume of the
Carlton Tower Hotel, Cadogan Place, London SW3.
Our special thanks to Jan Baldwin, Tessa Traeger's assistant,
and to Oula Jones who compiled the indexes.

Contents

How to use this book . . . . .

The Summer and Winter Cookbook is presented as two books
bound together under one cover. Each book is divided into two sections.
The illustrated text on seasonal cookery themes is cross-referenced to the recipe section.
The index for the Winter Cookbook begins on page 127.

Introduction

During the winter months we become more than ever dependent on our food. It helps us to keep warm and is of course essential to provide the energy to do any sort of work, whether mental or physical. During the enervating winter months even vegetable lovers like myself feel the need for more protein, usually in the form of meat. Stews and roasts, that might seem too heavy at other times of the year, are especially welcome in cold weather, as are the filling winter soups made with combinations of fresh and dried vegetables, grains and pasta.

In contrast to these substantial dishes, we have shellfish, rich in iodine and mineral salts, at their best during the cooler months. Moules marinières, clam chowder, grilled Dublin Bay prawns, seviche of scallops, oyster stew, stuffed mussels and clams in aspic all make appetizing and nutritious dishes, either as first courses or as less filling alternatives to the meat dishes.

Smoked fish is also excellent during the winter, since autumn is the customary time for smoking. Scottish kippers and Arbroath smokies, buckling, mackerel, haddock and cod are all readily available for making into delicious smooth pâtés, or for serving in conjunction with poached or scrambled eggs. The more expensive smoked salmon, sturgeon, halibut and eel are best eaten simply with fresh lemons and brown bread and butter.

Roasts of beef and tender grilled steaks are among our favourite winter dishes for festive occasions, while stews, casseroles and pies make sustaining dishes for everyday meals. Lamb provides a wide range of good dishes, like roast leg of lamb, braised shoulder of lamb and grilled lamb chops, as well as stews like Lancashire hot pot, Irish stew and the French *navarin d'agneau*. Roast pork with apple sauce, sometimes with sage and onion stuffing, is a popular Sunday luncheon dish in England. We have our black Bradenham hams and Alderton gammons which rival for flavour the delicious sweet-cured hams of the southern United States. Small cuts of gammon or bacon make simpler dishes, often combined with dried beans or peas, or served with fried eggs.

Game makes a welcome appearance during the winter months; grouse and pheasant remain two of the favourite luxuries in Britain and quail are now farmed domestically and obtainable all the year round. Sadly, we have no equivalent to the delicious American squab; our wild pigeons are much coarser and tougher and no one has yet started to breed them especially for the table. Venison is much loved by some, as is hare. I find both these a bit strong for my taste and much prefer the milder flavour of farm-reared rabbit, cooked in the Provençal fashion.

Dried vegetables are immediately useful in wintertime, for they provide a valuable source of protein. Dried beans, peas and lentils can all be made into purées, soups and vinaigrettes; chick-peas are extremely good when used in this way. Root vegetables are at their best in the cold months, especially parsnips, which actually benefit from the frost. Turnips, swedes, celeriac and kohlrabi are all delicious when cooked in the minimum of water, well drained and served with generous additions of butter, cream and freshly ground black pepper. Brussels sprouts, leeks and the various sorts of green cabbage are all welcome after their long absence. Salads are somewhat limited at this time of year but there is watercress to liven them up and, when hot-house lettuces become too limp and costly, we can turn to shredded white cabbage with grated carrot, apple or celery. Home-grown apples and pears last through the winter and exotic fruits from tropical countries add interest to our meals in mid-winter. Imported plums, also frequently in the shops during our coldest months, are useful for making fruit sauces for game, as well as puddings.

Spices are at hand all winter for adding variety to what may tend to be a slightly bland diet; the warm flavours of cumin and coriander give an exotic touch to dishes of courgettes and cabbage, and juniper berries or caraway seeds enhance dishes of sauerkraut and game. Curry powder, whether bought or made at home, is good with chicken, fish, or hard-boiled eggs and even fruit.

In November, just as we get well into winter, the preparations for Christmas begin. It is surely no accident that the celebrations of Christmas and New Year, with origins going back all the way to pagan times, should come just at the solstice, when the sun is farthest away from us. The feasts must have helped our ancestors to endure the long dark months. For us it is the season of lists and endless shopping. It is sad that modern life should have overlaid these holidays with such commercial frenzy. But even in the midst of list writing and present buying, as we search for silver sixpences for the plum pudding, for the plumpest turkey or goose, and the tangerines for filling stockings, we can look forward, through January and February to the coming of March, which always brings the first hints of spring. Until then we can indulge in the heartening foods that abound during the winter months.

Autumn soups

Lighter than the meat-based soups of deep winter, autumn soups combine the last of summer's fresh vegetables with the comforting nourishment of dried peas and beans

In early autumn, a whole range of new dishes come into season, some of which cannot be made at any other time of the year. These are vegetable soups, from Italy, France and Spain for the most part, and they combine the last of the summer's fresh vegetables with the first crop of dried vegetables, at their best at this time. They are full of flavour, yet less heavy than the meat-based soups of the true winter months.

One of the best of these soups is a bean soup from Tuscany, made with the new season's *cannellini* beans, fresh juicy garlic, and the first of the virgin oil, that aromatic green substance which results from the first pressing of the olives. Another is *ribollita*; the name means literally "reboiled", for it is traditionally made with the remains of yesterday's minestrone, reheated and poured over an unusual purple cabbage called *cavolo nero*, which comes into season in October in Tuscany and the surrounding region. Almost the best of all is the Genoese *zuppa al pesto*, a thick soup made with a mixture of fresh and dried beans, and imbued with a fragrant mixture of pounded basil, pine nuts and Parmesan. The Italians also make an excellent pumpkin soup in the autumn, for the pumpkin is at its best when combined with the sweet taste of fresh basil, a tender annual which perishes with the first frost. Another good soup which is not often seen outside its native Italy is *pasta e fagioli*, a combination of dried haricot beans with spaghetti, cooked with bacon and fresh vegetables, and flavoured with garlic.

An unusual soup is made from dried chick-peas; this is popular in Spain, in Italy and parts of Mediterranean France. A most delicious soup that is found all over Spain in varying forms is the *sopa de ajo*, or garlic soup. As served to me in a restaurant in Granada, it consisted of a thin garlic-flavoured broth poured over a poached egg and pieces of bread in a capacious bowl. Many of these continental soups have bread in them, and ideally they should be home-made. If this is not possible, try to buy an unsliced crusty white loaf and keep it for a day or two before using.

Many Italian soups also have an egg in them, and these make light, sustaining meals, easily digested even when one is tired. One of the best is *zuppa pavese*, where a whole egg is either poached in chicken stock, or simply placed raw in a warm bowl, and very lightly coddled in the heat of the chicken broth which is poured over it. Another, *stracciatella*, consists of chicken stock with a couple of raw eggs beaten and stirred into the soup while boiling. It is allowed to boil gently for a moment or two, stirring constantly, so that the egg is cooked in shreds. A similar soup is the Greek *avgolemono*; here the eggs are beaten with lemon juice and stirred into the soup below boiling point. The broth is thus enriched by the eggs, and flavoured with the lemon.

With the exception of *zuppa al pesto*, which needs fresh beans and basil, most of these soups can be made throughout the winter, but they are at their freshest and best in October and early November. Even the heavy French dishes like *potée* and *garbure* take on a lighter character when made with fresh, albeit elderly, peas and beans. The soups containing dried beans are very filling, and can be treated as a meal in themselves, possibly followed by a fresh salad and cheese. They take a long time to make, and I now use a pressure cooker, which works well. The base is a bit thin for prolonged frying, so I sometimes use a heavy sauté pan for the first stage, before transferring the contents to the pressure cooker for the lengthy simmering, which is thus cut by two-thirds. On the other hand, the lighter soups made with eggs and chicken stock are made in a matter of minutes, always providing you have a supply of good chicken stock already made, for these delicate soups are just not worth making with stock cubes. If I am alone, I often make a light meal of one of these, usually *zuppa pavese*, which is easily made for one person. They can serve as the first course for a conventional meal.

With the exception of *zuppa al pesto*, all these soups are improved by some last-minute addition. The bean soup and the *ribollita* should have a little fresh olive oil (ideally green Tuscan oil) added just before eating, although chopped parsley can be substituted by those who are not enamoured of olive oil. Freshly grated Parmesan is an important part of the Italian soups made with eggs and chicken stock, although when this is too expensive, I sometimes substitute Fontina or Pecorino, or even Gruyère or Emmental. All vegetable soups are improved by sea salt and coarsely ground black pepper, added by each individual to his own taste.

1 Tuscan bean soup
2 Vicchio Maggio, a classic Chianti
3 Italian bread
4 Garlic
5 Cannellini beans
6 Parsley

Favourite first courses

Delectable, pretty and colourful hors d'oeuvre can either make a meal on their own or give distinction to a meal by setting the tone for the rest of the dishes to follow

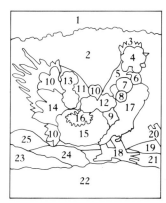

1 *Shredded iceberg lettuce*
2 *Sliced cucumber*
3 *Carrot*
4 *Snails, courgette, lemon*
5 *Salami*
6 *Onions*
7 *Goat cheese in chestnut leaves*
8 *Camembert cheese*
9 *Pepper goat cheese*
10 *Mussels*
11 *Dover sole*
12 *Baked oysters with sorrel and green peppercorn sauce*
13 *Baked oysters with vegetables*
14 *Red mullet*
15 *Crab*
16 *Parsley*
17 *Lobster*
18 *Runner beans, lemon and orange peel*
19 *Runner beans*
20 *Fennel*
21 *Fish pâté*
22 *Prosciutto ham, peas, beans, carrots, potato*
23 *Mangetout peas*
24 *Mixed shredded vegetables*
25 *Sliced courgette*

From a psychological point of view, the first course of a meal is the most important. If it is pretty and interesting and tastes delicious, it will set the tone for the whole meal and the rest can be relatively simple. If, on the other hand, it is dull and depressing, nothing that follows will redeem the meal. I take more trouble over the first course for a dinner than over any other, partly for the reasons given above, and partly because it is my favourite course.

Almost all the dishes I like best qualify as first courses; in restaurants I often find it hard to choose from so many appealing things, while the list of main courses does not tempt me at all. Little dishes made from combinations of pastry, pasta, pancakes or rice with vegetables, eggs or shellfish seem to me more attractive than the serious heavy dishes that in restaurant terms qualify as main courses. There is no reason why we should not have a series of first course dishes, either together or in sequence, as a complete meal at home. My favourite first courses are pretty and colourful, so that they provide a table decoration in themselves: little pastry cases filled with sliced mushrooms in a cream sauce; a gratin of hard-boiled eggs and onions in a creamy sauce; green pancakes rolled round fillings of chopped tomato in sour cream; a mixture of smoked and fresh haddock, flaked in a creamy cheese sauce; curried eggs; green gnocchi; stuffed tomatoes; or little skewers of firm white fish, basted with olive oil and lemon juice while grilling. Many of these dishes are quite a lot of trouble to prepare, although almost all are greatly accelerated by the food processor, as they are based on pastry,

batter, or purées of raw fish or meat. A few of them, like green gnocchi, skewers of fish and pancakes, must be made at the last moment; others, like the mushrooms in pastry cases, can be prepared in advance and assembled just before serving. Gratins can be made beforehand, and only reheated and browned before serving, while pâtés can, of course, be made several days in advance.

I like to have two or three different hot dishes for a first course, time permitting; I remember a small restaurant in Rome where, each evening, they served three different hot hors d'oeuvre. One could eat them separately if one wished, but they were always planned to complement each other; a small slice of onion quiche was served with a spoonful of vegetables stewed with oil, and a slice of hot fish pâté.

When serving a home-made pâté, I try to have some warm, freshly baked bread, with a dish of mixed vegetables, possibly sliced fennel and tomatoes, stewed in oil and served warm. Sometimes I make three different hot, or warm, vegetable dishes: string beans with chopped bacon, sliced mushrooms in sour cream, and grilled tomatoes with garlic and parsley butter melting over them. These dishes are greatly enhanced by home-made bread, possibly a slightly unusual one like onion bread, or saffron bread. After a series of dishes like this, only the simplest main course need follow, such as beef stew, a roast chicken or a whole fish, baked or poached, served with only a sauce; certainly no more vegetables are needed, nor even a great degree of choice.

Sustaining soups

Warming and restoring, a stout winter soup is a meal in its own right. With the right accompaniments, a good soup will rise to almost any occasion

If I had to choose one type of food to live on for the rest of my life, I would probably settle for soup. I can think of no other dish which covers such a wide range, and I am sure I could think up a different one for every day in the year if I put my mind to it; I made a list of over seventy without even trying.

I like almost all sorts of soup: thick hearty broth; creamy vegetable purées; clear consommés, either hot or jellied; chowders made from fish or vegetables; and iced summer soups. In winter, though, I concentrate on the nourishing peasant type—not an elegant start to a meal, to be drunk out of small cups, but a meal in itself, to be consumed from large bowls, and needing little to follow, perhaps a raw vegetable salad, or a platter of cheese and celery. These soups are warming and restoring. They are nourishing but not too time-consuming or expensive to make. They improve on reheating, so they can be prepared in advance and in large quantities, and thus can feed an unexpected number of people, when such an occasion arises.

All too often soup is considered a way of using up remains, rather than as a dish in its own right, or it is added to a meal as an afterthought, to give a warming element, or to stretch the amount of food. I, on the other hand, tend to think of the soup first, and plan a meal round it, or even a succession of meals. At the weekend I often buy a large chicken and poach it; I make a chicken and barley soup from the stock, and on the following day I make a dish from the bird itself: chicken pie, a noodle dish or a chicken salad. The carcass is then used to make a second supply of slightly weaker stock, which makes another soup, perhaps a vichyssoise or an *avgolemono*. During winter I often buy a casserole grouse and make a game pâté from the flesh of the bird and an excellent lentil soup from the stock. A splendid bortsch can be made for a family dinner by using a duck for the basis of the stock; *pirozhkis* can be served with it to make an almost complete meal, and then the duck itself eaten cold the following day, with a dish of cold rice with pine kernels and raisins and an orange and watercress salad.

I have experimented with the idea of adding a piquant taste to the soup at the last moment, as one adds the *pistou* to a soup of the same name, or a *rouille* to a bouillabaisse. I find that a minestrone is enormously improved by a last minute addition of a paste similar to a *pistou*, but made with winter alternatives. A few spoonfuls of onions and garlic gently fried in olive oil can with advantage be added to a soup of dried vegetables —peas, lentils or beans. It is common practice in parts of France to add something of this sort— called *la fricassée* or *le hachis*—to soups; sometimes a spoonful of the vegetables from the soup is chopped and fried in goose or bacon fat, or bacon, onion and garlic cooked in oil.

The method is similar to one I have come across in Middle Eastern recipes and in some Indian dishes, in which a measure of freshly cooked onions is often added to a dish that has been cooked for a long time, thus adding texture and freshness. In some curries, the chopped onions are divided into two parts, the one forming the basis of the curry, and the other fried in clarified butter and added at the very end, by which time the first lot have cooked away to a completely indistinguishable purée.

It is only when made with care and thought that soups are as good as they should be, but on the whole I find them very rewarding. They respond well to accompaniments such as carefully chosen bread—a saffron bread with a fish soup, garlic bread with minestrone, or black rye bread for cabbage soup. A bowl of sea salt, a peppermill filled with black peppercorns and some unsalted butter should always be on the table, while a bowl of chopped parsley or one of freshly grated Parmesan cheese is indicated in many cases. A large tureen and pretty bowls make soup eating more enjoyable.

1 *Portuguese cabbage soup*
2 *Green cabbage*
3 *Red kidney beans*
4 *Kabanos (Polish sausage)*
5 *Parsley*
6 *Rice*
7 *Watercress*
8 *Salt*
9 *Sausage and vegetable ingredients for the soup*

Smoked fish

An ancient method of preserving made unnecessary by technology, the smoking of fish continues to create myriad subtle flavours for the discriminating palate

1 Kipper
2 Smoked mackerel
3 Smoked eel
4 Smoked cod's roe
5 Smoked trout
6 Smoked mackerel fillet
7 Smoked sprats

Smoked fish has for many years been one of our most famous delicacies. No other country can produce anything better than Scotch smoked salmon, or Loch Fine kippers, and nowadays more unusual fish are being smoked too. One of the best smoked fish I have ever eaten was conger eel.

Another fish which I like very much is smoked halibut, and almost my favourite is the Arbroath smokie; this is a small haddock smoked whole, and quite unlike the more familiar smoked haddock with yellow flesh, which needs to be cooked. I find smoked mackerel a bit oily to eat plain, but it is one of the best-flavoured fish for making into pâtés and mousses. Smoked eel is delicious, but almost as expensive as smoked salmon, while smoked sturgeon is not, in my opinion, worth its high price. A small and inexpensive smoked fish which I now rarely see is buckling; its disappearance is probably due to the shortage of herrings. Another inexpensive smoked fish is the sprat; this is very good.

Smoking was originally a method of preserving food, usually pork or fish, during the winter months. Over the past thirty years, however, the process has changed radically. For one thing, the traditional smokery was a home-based operation, which did not lend itself to expansion, and, for another, the problem of finding suitable fuel became acute. The smokeries grew up side by side with the ship-building yards and carpentry shops, which kept them supplied with oak sawdust, the ideal fuel for smoking food. With mechanization the sawdusts became mixed and were no longer so suitable. Then it was discovered that the three effects which smoke imposed upon food could be achieved more simply by other means: the preservation was more easily effected by refrigeration, the colouring by dyes, and the flavour by brief periods of curing and smoking, or in some cases by merely painting the food with liquid "smoke flavour", a concentrate of distilled smoke. The resulting product was inevitably a different article, for it was smoke-flavoured rather than smoke-cured.

I once spent a most fascinating day with a man who has made a prolonged study of smoking, and has worked out his own way of producing traditional results. Mr Pinney is in his late sixties and has lived near Woodbridge in Suffolk for the past thirty years. He gradually built up a smoking business and other enterprises over the years.

Now, with the help of his wife, Mathilde, and his son, he runs an oyster hatchery, two fishing boats and a smokehouse. He is an extremely interesting person with enormous enterprise and imagination. Some twenty years ago, faced with the difficulty of finding an adequate supply of oak sawdust, he took the nearest possible alternative in the form of oak logs, and set about inventing a stove which would burn them in such a way as to produce smoke without much heat. On holiday once in Portugal, finding himself with nothing to do, he built a portable smokebox with which he smoked the local seafood and sold it to the nearest hotel.

Smoking by traditional methods is a fairly primitive process, except for the smoke production, which must be very precise. When wood is heated, a succession of different vapours are released, each at a different temperature. The most suitable are those released at a low heat, as they get progressively more acid. While the first smoke is sweet, and hazy blue in colour, the smoke which is produced at higher temperatures is acrid, rank and yellowish grey.

The main virtue of sawdust as a fuel is that it will not burn naturally at a high temperature, because the minute particles restrict the oxygen intake. Most modern smoking equipment subjects the sawdust to a forced draught, thus raising the temperature. In some cases moisture is added, introducing steam, which formerly had no place in the smoking process. Mr Pinney, doubtful about both these refinements, proceeded to develop his own stove, which by a degree of oxygen control allowed him to retain carbon dioxide around the unburnt logs, causing them to smoke without allowing them to burn. In this way the wood is converted into charcoal, which he then uses for the second process.

There are two stages in smoking: cold-smoking and hot-smoking. Both these terms are misnomers, for there is some heat in cold-smoking, while hot-smoking is virtually a cooking process involving no smoke at all. Most fish undergo both processes, except salmon and kippers which are cold-smoked only (kippers are, of course, heated before eating). Mr Pinney smokes Irish salmon, herrings, sprats, mackerel, trout, eels, pollan (a member of the salmon family) and cod's roe. All this is done in a smokehouse not much larger than two sentry boxes back to back.

Shellfish - naturally

Though they are exclusive and highly prized, shellfish are amongst our most natural and primitive forms of food, still retaining their freshness and individuality

I find I become more and more attached to the few foods that still retain their own individual character and cannot be tampered with. Shellfish are among the most primitive of foods—not only do they taste and smell of the sea, even their appearance is redolent of natural things. There is a curious feeling about handling food that is still actually living; while we were photographing what appeared to be a *nature morte*, the mussels suddenly started making the strangest kissing noises, opening and closing in protest, I imagine, at the heat of the lamps. Although I am very squeamish about having to actually kill something in order to cook it, at the same time I cannot help appreciating the inevitable freshness that is the result. Shellfish are certainly the least plastic of foods, and in an age when more and more foods are losing their own individual flavour, this is a valuable characteristic.

It was only recently that I started cooking shellfish again. Apart from seaside holidays, I had grown lazy and had managed to convince myself that they were either too expensive—like lobster —or too much trouble to prepare—like mussels and crab. Now I have overcome this resistance and am totally won over. Lobsters are certainly expensive all over the world; even on remote Greek islands they now fetch a startling price, but there are other shellfish just as delicious. Mussels, for instance, are one of the cheapest of foods, especially in relation to their goodness and the valuable amounts of iron and calcium they contain. They are a certain amount of trouble to clean, and I would not think of preparing *moules marinières* for more than four people, but there are other ways of treating them, using smaller quantities. They make a good risotto, or a rice salad, or they can be made into an unusual first course by steaming them open, dipping the mussels in egg and breadcrumbs and deep frying. Or they can be threaded on skewers and grilled. Mussels make a delicious soup, and can be gratinéed: fill each half-shell (after cooking) with a mixture of browned breadcrumbs, finely minced shallot, garlic and parsley, dot with butter and brown under the grill.

Scallops are another beautiful food, and full of flavour. They can be cooked in a variety of ways, and their shells make pretty dishes to serve them in. I usually poach them in a mixture of white wine and water, then chop them into pieces and mix with minced shallots in a sauce made from the cooking liquid blended with cream. They are then piled back into their concave shells, sprinkled with parsley and breadcrumbs, and browned under the grill. Other ways to serve them, not in their shells, are in a mild curry-flavoured sauce or as a part of a mixed fish salad. They also make an excellent *seviche*, marinated in fresh lime or lemon juice, and dressed with oil and herbs. Frozen scallops are quite good but expensive. It is worth keeping a few shells for serving the frozen ones in, when fresh ones are unobtainable; they are pretty and practical.

Clams are for me an important part of memories of childhood holidays in Maine. In London I buy large clams, not unlike the New England *quahog*; though full of flavour they are quite tough and not suitable for steaming. They are excellent, however, for chowders, or dishes using minced clams, and they are not expensive, as two or three per person is ample.

Dressing a crab at home is a good two hours' work, so I think the answer is to buy it already dressed from the fishmonger and add the final touches oneself. I do not care much for the brown meat, so I only use a little of this, or omit it altogether. I add other things, like chopped hard-boiled eggs, spring onions, capers and herbs; then I moisten it with oil and lemon juice and pile it back in the shell. Alternatively, finely chopped avocado can be mixed with the flaked white meat, then flavoured with plenty of lemon juice and freshly ground black pepper.

Prawns come in varying sizes, ranging from the crayfish and giant prawns down to the minuscule shrimp. The larger ones are very handsome, and should be served simply in their shells, with bowls of home-made mayonnaise. The smaller ones can be made into a fresh-tasting summery pâté, tart, with plenty of lemon juice—or rolled in thin rashers of streaky bacon, threaded on skewers and grilled. They can be served as a first course, with sauce remoulade or quarters of lemon or on a bed of rice as a main course. But when really fresh, prawns are best eaten simply with quarters of lemon and thinly sliced brown bread and butter.

1 *Saffron shellfish salad*
2 *Lobster, clam, mussels, Dublin Bay prawns*
3 *Oysters*
4 *Dressed crab*
5 *Stuffed clam*
6 *Moules gratinées*
7 *Skewered prawns in bacon*
8 *Prawn pâté*
9 *Coquilles St. Jacques*
10 *Avocado relish*
11 *Tomato vinaigrette*

dressed crab p75
stuffed clams p76
moules gratinées p76
mussels in saffron
  sauce p76
seviche of scallops p77
saffron shellfish salad p77
prawn pâté p80

The best of beef

Festive roasts and noble sirloins, tender steaks, and hearty stews, with all the traditional accompaniments, will sustain you through the long, dark months

1 Roast rib of beef
2 Stewed beef
3 Boiled salt beef
4 Steak tartare
5 Beef olives
6 Horseradish sauce
7 Boiled beef with dumplings
8 Sirloin steak

roast beef with Yorkshire
  pudding p85
sea pie p85
steak with coriander p87
beef olives p86
stewed beef p86
marrow and herb
  dumplings p88
horseradish and apple
  sauce p103

"Beef is the soul of cookery." Carême once said, and I am totally in agreement. The bull is a noble animal, and it is not for nothing that roast beef has been a symbol of England for centuries. (The fact that the best beef comes from Scotland, and has done so for hundreds of years, is another matter.) English beef cookery has a strength and character all of its own, and owes nothing to foreign influence. A standing wing rib, like the one in the picture, or a sirloin complete with undercut, is both a marvellous sight and one of the few gastronomic delights that does not seem to have deteriorated in recent years. Even the traditional English accompaniments—Yorkshire pudding, English mustard, horseradish sauce and clear unthickened gravy—cannot be improved upon. They are perfect.

When I lived in Scotland as a child, our Sunday joint was invariably a roast sirloin, for it was my father's favourite food. We loved it even more when it was cold and once before going unwillingly on holiday, one of my sisters was heard moaning plaintively, "I just don't know how I'll manage without cold roast beef."

In those days, the sirloin always came with its undercut intact, nestling up against the bone, basted with its marrow and protected by the flap of rib ends folded over it, and deliciously moist. Nowadays there is such an insatiable demand for whole fillets and fillet steaks that most butchers tend to remove the undercut and sell the sirloin on its own, which makes a much less splendid joint, unfortunately.

I far preferred the older fashion, for a slice of undercut served with a thinner slice of the rarer sirloin made a most delicious combination. A whole roast fillet always seems rather an effete joint; it is too soft somehow, and lacking in character. Possibly because it is often treated in a rather decadent way, smeared with *pâté de foie gras* and wrapped in pastry, it has come to symbolize the food of the ultra-rich. Even fillet steaks do not appeal to me; I far prefer a sirloin steak, which comes halfway between the rump and fillet in price, and is to me more desirable than either, in flavour, texture and appearance.

My first choice of a joint for roasting on a less lavish scale than sirloin or standing ribs would be a rolled joint from either of these two prime cuts. A particularly nice-looking joint is the French *contre filet*, or *faux filet*. This is the same cut of meat as our rolled sirloin, but is trimmed and tied differently to give a neat compact shape, ideal for carving. Whenever possible meat should be cooked on the bone, which contributes both fat and flavour. In the case of beef, however, this is only possible on a very large scale, as a rib roast consisting of two bones would make a thin dry joint. An American friend of mine compromises by getting the butcher to bone and roll the meat, then to tie it back on the bone. In this way he feels that he retains some of the benefits, yet has at the end a compact joint, easy to carve.

Many of the old English beef dishes are rarely seen nowadays, and some of them are well worth reviving. Beef olives is one: thin slices of tender beef beaten out even thinner with a mallet, then rolled round small handfuls of bread and onion stuffing, flavoured with herbs. They are neatly tied with string, then braised with sliced carrots and onions in a meat gravy, and served on a bed of mashed potatoes. Steak and kidney pudding is good on a cold winter's day; a lighter version is the lesser known and strangely named sea pie, which consists of stewed beef with onions and carrots topped with a lid of suet pastry. A popular dish in men's clubs used to be marrow bones; the cut ends were sealed with puff pastry, and the bones boiled standing upright and served wrapped in a napkin. The marrow was extracted by each diner armed with a narrow silver spoon and eaten with toast. Beef marrow was also served as a savoury, either cooked in the above fashion then spooned on to rounds of toast, or extracted from the bones before cooking and poached, then sliced and served on toast.

Most butchers now have so little demand for marrow, the bones can often be had free for the asking. This is an amazing giveaway of precious material, for beef marrow is the richest and most easily digested of all fats, perfect for feeding invalids and children. It adds succulence to a risotto, or can be made into delicate dumplings mixed with chopped herbs. Alternatively, it can be used as dripping, for frying onions, bread, meat stews, and a variety of other uses.

In terms of food values, beef is by far the most valuable of meats. It is richer in protein and minerals than mutton, the only comparable mature meat, very much richer in iron, calcium and vitamin B than lamb or veal, and richer than pork in calcium and iron.

 The bountiful pig

The pig provides us with a wider range of food than any other animal—spicy sausages, pâtés, smoked hams and salamis, succulent roasts and much more besides

The pig is without doubt the most versatile animal from the cook's point of view. Almost every part of it can be eaten, from the nose to the tail, although I would rather not have to put that to the test. Its snout, cheeks, ears, heart, intestines, liver, tongue, brains, kidneys, feet, tail and even its testicles are all highly prized by some people, while it also gives excellent fat and a particularly tasty skin.

Apart from these side-products, the best cuts of the pig are also highly adaptable and can be prepared in a number of ways according to regional tastes. These include salting, or pickling in brine; smoking; salting and smoking; preserving as in *confit de porc*; and cooking fresh. Thus it gives an enormous range of sausages, both smoked and fresh; bacon, smoked, green (unsmoked) and sweet-cured; and many different hams ranging from the raw smoked hams of northern Italy to the mild cooked York ham. Pork fat is useful in different forms: the solid back fat that one buys from the butcher for adding to pâtés; and melted fat or lard, and speck, which can be bought smoked or plain in foreign delicatessens, and is invaluable for starting off thick soups like chowders or bean soups. It gives a good flavoured fat for frying the other ingredients, and leaves a residue of tasty crisp pieces to add texture to the finished dish. Each country has different priorities: in Italy the first preference is towards raw smoked delicacies, such as Parma ham and salamis. The French have a vast range of *charcuterie*, many different sausages, both smoked and fresh, and countless pâtés. In England, we have our own wide choice of first-rate hams, gammons, bacon and sausages. We are also the only country I know lucky enough to get crackling with our roast pork. In France, they pare away most of the fat, leaving only enough to enclose the joint, and the *bardes* of fat are sold separately, as is the skin.

Pigs' feet are fairly easy to come by and I find them invaluable. With their highly gelatinous quality, together with knuckle of veal, they provide the best way of making a good natural jelly, at the same time adding flavour and nourishment to other dishes. They can also be eaten either cold, in a vinaigrette, or hot: boiled, coated with breadcrumbs, grilled, and served with a mustard sauce. A fillet of pork is a useful small joint; it is extremely tender and can be cut in slices and cooked like *scallopini* of veal (at half the price). Spareribs are one of my favourite treats, but they are not easy to buy in this country for we cut up our animal so that they are usually incorporated in another joint. It is best to ask for American spareribs or spareribs for barbecuing; as a main course one should allow a full pound per person. They are not too expensive, but troublesome to cook in large quantities, unless on a barbecue. Pork figures highly in Chinese cooking, and its bland flesh goes exceptionally well with sweet and sour combinations, and with spicy flavours as well.

Some butchers sell ready minced pork, and I find this useful for stuffings, meatballs and for making stuffed cabbage dishes. A whole sucking pig is something I have yet to experience. Much as I love all forms of ham, bacon, salami and sausage, I am too squeamish a cook to relish making things like brawn or head cheese—the very words make me blanch. So for these and other dishes of this sort I rely on good *charcuteries*, with their appetizing arrays of *crepinettes, andouillettes, boudins noirs et blancs, museau de tête, pieds de porc vinaigrette*, as well as a wide range of sausages, both smoked and fresh, and excellent pure pork pâtés.

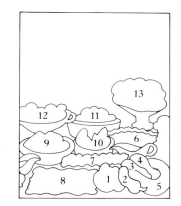

1 *Pure pork chipolatas*
2 *Boudin blanc*
3 *Saucisse de Toulouse*
4 *Boudin noir*
5 *Saucisson sec*
6 *Pork fillets in cider sauce*
7 *Sausage roll*
8 *Bacon*
9 *Pork chops in juniper berries*
10 *Breaded pigs' trotters*
11 *Pork pie*
12 *Spareribs in barbecue sauce*
13 *Gammon*

The surprising sausage

From the spicy, smoked salamis of Eastern Europe to the ubiquitous frankfurter, the sausage, whatever the size or shape, is a favourite item in every cuisine

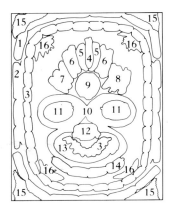

1 *Beef sausages*
2 *Pork chipolatas*
3 *Pork cocktail sausages*
4 *Algerian merguez*
5 *Auvergne fumées*
6 *Toulouse sausages*
7 *Saucisson Mont Belliard*
8 *Italian salamelles*
9 *English black pudding*
10 *French boudin noir*
11 *Boudin blanc and parsley*
12 *Scottish haggis*
13 *German bockwurst*
14 *German knackwurst*
15 *Parsley*
16 *Sage and thyme*

Sausages are an ancient form of food: they were much prized by the Romans, for whom pork was a favourite meat. Their sausages were probably heavily cured by smoking or salting; for them the sausage was a means of preserving those parts of the pig which were not suitable for roasting. The art of smoking sausages is one that the Italians have excelled at ever since.

Apart from the salamis, which have been so lengthily cured that they are then eaten uncooked, the majority of Italian sausages have been lightly salted or smoked, which adds to their flavour and acts as a slight preservative. Some of the best come from the Romagna area around Bologna. In Modena they make the *cotechino*, a large sausage of pure pork, lightly salted, weighing from one to two pounds. Cooked by long simmering, it is one of the traditional ingredients of *bollito misto*. The *zampone*, also made in Modena, consists of the same filling encased in the skin of a pig's trotter. The fresh sausages of this region, called *salciccia* to distinguish them from the smoked *salamelle*, are also very good, similar to French *saucisses de Toulouse*, coarsely cut and highly seasoned.

In France there is an even greater number of lightly smoked or salted sausages, quite apart from the *saucissons secs*, which can, indeed must, be kept for five or six months before eating raw, like the *saucisson à l'ail*. The semi-cured varieties vary greatly according to the region; some, like the little *saucisson d'Arles*, can be eaten raw or cooked. Others, like the more heavily smoked *saucisses de Francfort*, need only to be reheated, while the fresh *saucisses de Toulouse* need thorough cooking on account of the coarsely cut meat and high fat content. A coarse garlic-flavoured poaching sausage of about three-quarters of a pound is ideal for adding to a cassoulet, or for serving with hot potato salad, haricot beans, chick-peas or lentils. These make hearty meals, perfect for cold weather, but are not to be recommended for those who suffer from weak digestions.

In Spain a coarse sausage of the *chorizo* type, highly seasoned with garlic and hot peppers, is often cooked in stews or added to soups. In Germany and other central European countries the sausages have a different character; they tend to be smoother in consistency, firm and quite highly smoked. These, the many different types

of *wurst*, go exceptionally well with dishes of sauerkraut, and red and white cabbage. Another I particularly like is the Polish *kabanos*; a small spicy sausage, it can be eaten raw with salads, heated and served with lentils, or thinly sliced and added to pizzas.

The traditional English sausage is a very different thing; it is always cooked fresh and its texture is finer and less highly seasoned. From the Second World War until quite recently, English sausages were rather unsatisfactory; the choice lay between the bland commercial product, with a too-high proportion of cereal, and the individual butcher's own blends, which were usually too highly seasoned with dried herbs for my taste. Now the situation has changed and many shops are making their own excellent blends, for the most part influenced by continental sausages. I have had excellent pork sausages (called link sausages) in the United States, where they are often eaten for breakfast, with scrambled eggs or griddle cakes.

For those who have the time, I recommend making one's own sausages. This is neither difficult nor complicated, so long as one has the necessary aids. Some mixers have a sausage-making attachment, and casings are now also available. Originally made from the intestines of the pigs—on average each pig has from fifty to sixty feet of small intestine—these are now made from sheeps' stomachs. A food processor is useful for making the filling, since it allows one to vary the texture according to taste, but good sausages can be made perfectly well with a mincer. I have made seven different fillings and they have all been good. Probably the best was a pork sausage, quite coarsely cut, and highly seasoned with garlic, juniper berries, sea salt and very coarsely ground black pepper. In the summer, I add fresh basil and parsley; in winter, a little fresh sage and parsley. I have also used mixtures of beef and pork, venison, veal and rabbit; whatever mixture of meat one uses, the proportions should be roughly two parts lean meat to one of fat. The best fat is the hard back fat of the pig, but few butchers sell it in this country: instead use a fairly fat cut like belly of pork and mix with an equal quantity of lean meat. The freshly made sausages are a beautiful sight, with a marble-like mosaic of pink, green and white shining through their translucent skins.

New World cuisine

Shaking off the strictures of the Old World, the New England settlers evolved a cooking style of their own based on native resources and epitomized by the Thanksgiving dinner

Although the turkey is often eaten at Christmas time throughout the United States, as in this country, its true place in American cuisine is at Thanksgiving. Held on the fourth Thursday in November, the feast commemorates the landing of the Pilgrim Fathers in 1620, and the foods that are chosen for it are those same foods that they found already in existence in the New World. The turkey itself, corn, sweet potato, squash, cranberry and pumpkin are all representative of native American foods, while the holiday also serves as a version of our own harvest festival. The wild turkey was a native of Central and North America, and the Indians had already started to domesticate it by the time of the landing of the *Mayflower*. Wild turkeys still exist in parts of the USA and are supposed to be superior in flavour to the domestic birds. Corn was the basic food of the Indians, but the variety they grew was probably closer to maize than the sweet-corn we know today. The Indians discovered it growing wild as a grass in the Mexican highlands, and started to cultivate it. They made it into corn bread, hominy and succotash—a true Indian word. Corn may make its appearance along with the turkey on the Thanksgiving table, in chowder as a first course, or as fritters, or in bread or stuffings.

Squash is another indigenous food closely related to our vegetable marrow. There are literally dozens of different varieties in America, from the soft-skinned summer squash, which must be eaten soon after harvesting, to the hard-skinned winter squash, which can be stored for months. The pumpkin, another native food, is almost invariably made into a sweet pie and served as a dessert. Yams and sweet potatoes were another of the Indians' basic foods. They still form a central part of the Thanksgiving dinner, usually candied.

The settlers also found a rich variety of wild game, birds and fish; also beans, peas, melons, sunflower seeds, groundnuts and waterlily roots. But the first colonists were ill-equipped to find food; and for the first few years four out of five died of starvation. By the mid 1620s things began to improve; they stopped receiving irrelevant instructions from England and began to rely on their own common sense.

Gradually the New England cuisine began to evolve, and for 200 years it changed little. By the nineteenth century, the Americans' food had become more refined without losing its basic

simplicity. A typical supper might consist of fried ham, baked beans in chilli sauce and johnny cake, with sour cream pie and Dutch cheese to follow. A more elaborate dinner, on Sundays, would be fricassée of chicken with hot biscuits and gravy, mashed potatoes and boiled onions. In the summer, communal meals were sometimes eaten outdoors; a whole ham would be simmered in cider with a handful of raisins, then covered in a crust of brown sugar and mustard, and baked until golden brown. Huge pots of beans were cooked with salt pork; platters of cold chicken and hard-boiled eggs were accompanied by pickled beets, home-made chilli sauce, and freshly baked bread. For dessert, there would be an array of frosted layer cakes oozing cream. Another of these open air meals was the corn roast, somewhat like an inland version of a clambake. Great numbers of corn cobs and potatoes were roasted in a pit, buried in smouldering ashes, and eaten with fried chicken and watermelon to follow. When I think of American food, this is the sort of cooking that comes to mind; simple and delicious dishes cooked in ways that evolved naturally from the variety of local resources.

In some respects American food has stayed closer to the English Elizabethan table than our own. (That is, the food of the northeastern seaboard which was settled by the English, for of course other immigrants to other parts of the country brought specialities with them, all of which have influenced the cuisine of the nation as a whole.) If you compare a list of classic American dishes with an English cookery book of the sixteenth century, you cannot fail to be struck by the similarities. The cheesecake is a very close relative of the "loaves of cheese curds" so often found in books of the Stuart period; pumpkin pie is very like the many sweet vegetable tarts that were common at that time; cinnamon toast was an old English treat that has since been forgotten in this country, as was hot spiced wine, still served at American hunt breakfasts. Mincemeat in America is still made in the old English way, to include a proportion of beefsteak—a custom which has not been practised in Great Britain for hundreds of years. Indeed, up until 1878 the English and American pint were the same size; it was the English measure that changed, so that the American measures are in fact truer to those of early English recipes than ours are.

1 *Roast turkey*
2 *Pumpkin*
3 *Varied squash*
4 *Corn on the cob*
5 *Corn fritters*
6 *Hot rolls*
7 *Wild rice with onions and almonds*
8 *Pumpkin purée*
9 *Blueberries*
10 *Corn chowder, crackers*
11 *Cranberry sauce*
12 *Candied sweet potatoes*

roast turkey p81
candied sweet
  potatoes p95
cranberry sauce p104
corn bread stuffing p106
celery and breadcrumb
  stuffing p106
cheesecake p114
pumpkin pie p115
corn bread p120

Goose and duck

Dark, succulent and crisply browned, this brace of birds, served hot or cold with a feast of different vegetables and special sauces, will grace any festive table

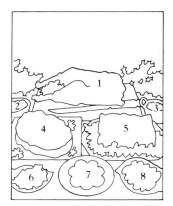

1 Roast goose
2 Cranberry sauce
3 Apple sauce
4 Cold duck and chicken in jelly
5 Duck pâté
6 Bacon rolls
7 Forcemeat balls
8 Pork chipolata sausages

duck pâté p79
roast goose p82
stuffed goose neck p82
pork sausages p94
horseradish and apple
  sauce p103
cranberry sauce p104
cherry sauce p104
plum sauce p104

Although in its culinary aspect the goose is firmly rooted in France and its cuisine, in its live form I connect it vividly with the English rural scene: the village green with geese waddling and honking round the pond, or the farmyard where geese and ducks scrabble together for grain. I have never thought of it as a culinary creature, but more as something figuring in myths or fairy tales. I suppose I have, over a period of years, eaten goose in various forms, but until recently I had never actually cooked one.

The English goose is a very different creature from the French one, which has been artificially fattened to such a degree that a bird can yield as much as two and a half pounds of fat, while its liver may weigh anything up to two pounds or more, perhaps a quarter the weight of the whole bird. One must adapt French recipes accordingly: *confit d'oie*, for example, can only be made outside France by adding a large proportion of pork fat to the goose's own fat; and a goose liver pâté is out of the question, although its liver can, with advantage, be added to a regular liver pâté mixture. In France a goose was not usually killed for one special meal, but rather as a stand-by during winter (in its way it resembles the pig in the English domestic scene). A *confit d'oie* was never eaten straight away, or all at once, but used gradually during the lean winter months between Christmas and Easter, hot or cold, in soups or stews, as an improvement to other dishes rather than a dish in itself. Some of the fat would be stored and used instead of pork fat, beef dripping, butter or olive oil. This delicate fat, the best of all in my opinion, gives the cooking of certain regions of France a very special character.

In England in times past, a goose would be killed for a special occasion like a wedding or a family reunion; the bird would be eaten at one meal, and the residue of fat carefully stored and kept for many uses, few of them related to the kitchen. (Goose grease was used in poultices, for the softening of stiffened leather, oiling of dairy churns, and polishing of horses' hooves before a show, among other things.) A goose is still killed and eaten occasionally in rural England, usually at Michaelmas or at Christmas, but in most places the turkey has usurped its popularity.

The first goose I ever cooked was so delicious, particularly when we ate some of it cold, that I would highly recommend it for any festive occasion, served cold with a choice of sauces and salads. I feel instinctively that goose is better not stuffed, for this allows more fat to escape. But many people would prefer it hot, and would consider stuffing an essential, which has the advantage of making the bird go further. Perhaps a very plain one is the answer: cored and quartered apples for instance, or boiled chestnuts, or sliced onions, or a celery and breadcumb mixture, or an excellent one based on mashed potatoes. A large amount is needed, for the goose, like the duck, is a hollow bird with a shallow breast and there is no point in making two stuffings for there is only one cavity. The traditional English accompaniment would be apple sauce, onion sauce or bread sauce, but I prefer a sauce of horseradish and apples, or a cranberry sauce, which goes so well with all poultry and game. Both are equally good with a hot or cold bird. With the hot goose I would serve roast potatoes; although rich, they are so delicious when cooked in the goose fat that they are irresistible. A green vegetable might be the usual choice, but I would make red cabbage the day before and reheat it. For a meal at any other time than Christmas, when a certain degree of conventionality seems inevitable, I would serve *kasha*, or buckwheat, and just a green salad. *Kasha* is the old Russian accompaniment for goose and is excellent either as a side dish or as a stuffing. With a cold roast goose I would serve a hot purée of potatoes or two salads; one of beetroot, chicory and watercress, the other of cos lettuce, green pepper, avocado and orange.

Duck is similar to goose, with its crisp brown skin and dark tasty flesh, but it is considerably smaller. With a good rice stuffing, an apple sauce flavoured with orange juice, a creamy dish of mashed potatoes and a green vegetable, and with a watercress and orange salad on the side, it will make a festive meal for two. A fruit sauce served with it makes it more unusual: Cumberland sauce, or one made from cherries or plums.

Duck also gives a valuable amount of first-rate fat, plus liver for adding to a pâté, and excellent stock for really good onion soup. A useful dish for post-Christmas meals is a cold duck in jelly, or it can be made, as in the picture, with duck and chicken in alternate layers.

Game birds

The traditional roasting and serving of game birds with all the last-minute chores is a daunting task; braising is a simpler and more flexible alternative

I have felt for some time that there are two distinctly opposed forms of cooking—in English cooking, at least, if not in every cuisine. One is that practised by good restaurants, with chefs and sous-chefs, numerous helpers, and batteries of saucepans keeping hot in *bains-marie*; while the other is more appropriate to home cooks. There might almost be a third sub-division for the few families who still employ a cook, for on the whole it is the limitation placed on the home cook who must both prepare the food and eat it which separates the amateurs from the professionals. There are a few occasions when I prepare a meal for a friend, when I can indulge in dishes such as fritters, which are eaten as they come from the pan; but even then I resent not being able to give my whole attention to either the friend or the food, and both inevitably suffer.

This belief holds particularly true when applied to game cookery. Few things are more delicious than a perfectly roasted bird, hung to the right degree and roasted to the minute, served with game chips, gravy, bread sauce and fried breadcrumbs. But for a home cook to attempt this is over-ambitious, and I have given up trying. Instead I have evolved a new system of cooking game which I find almost as delicious and half as much work. It is quite simply to braise rather than roast. In the past, I have been put off braised game because only old birds were considered suitable for this treatment. But I find that young birds respond excellently to braising, and this way you can also avoid the danger of dryness, which occasionally results from roasting a bird, especially pheasant. A further advantage is that timing is not so vital as in roasting; the dish can be kept hot for an extra half-hour without any fear of spoiling it.

My recipe for braised game can be used for any bird; I have used it with pheasant, grouse, partridge, pigeon, and even guinea fowl, all with excellent results. The accompaniments to braised game are quite different from the usual ones for roast game, and far less time-consuming and worrying. Instead of gravy and bread sauce, a simple sauce made from the cooking liquor enriched with sour cream is quickly made. Celery or red cabbage, which are my two favourite accompaniments for game, can be braised in the oven at the same time as the birds. All the other autumn vegetables—leeks, onions, fennel,

white cabbage—are very good with braised game, too. Root vegetables have a special affinity with game, and a mixture of carrots, parsnips and turnips or swedes, softened in game fat and then gently stewed in its stock, cannot be improved upon as a vegetable dish to accompany game. It can also be puréed as a soup.

Chestnuts are another particularly appropriate accompaniment, but I would only embark on these if I had the time and energy to spare for the shelling, for tinned chestnuts are just not the same thing. A thin purée of potatoes, or pieces of bread fried golden in dripping, can complete the main course. Another point in favour of braising is that the remains make a wonderful soup, combining the flavours of the bird with those of the braised vegetables, and you can add any remaining sauce to the soup as well.

I think lentils and game a most excellent combination, and I frequently make a soup using these two together. A game stock is the best of all for flavouring vegetable soups, transforming them from light summer dishes to warming and sustaining cold weather foods. Even quite ordinary soups such as onion, bean or beetroot (bortsch) have a whole new potential when made with game stock. A strained game stock, that is well reduced and highly seasoned, makes a first-rate consommé.

Old game birds are rarely seen nowadays in the shops, but when I do come across one I buy it and make pâtés with the best meat, and a soup with the remainder. The braising recipe can, if desired, be adapted for old birds by extending the cooking time, but I prefer to use them in other ways. I find my pressure cooker is an extremely good way of cooking tough old birds; they respond well to being cooked under pressure, and in this way much precious time and fuel is saved.

Now that it has become such an expensive luxury, I usually only cook game two or three times a year. For this reason my game recipes have been limited, for when I have found one that I like I am happy to vary it by using different birds, substituting partridge for the more usual pheasant, and so on. The soup, of course, also varies with the choice of bird and vegetables, and the character of the pâtés alters completely depending on the variety of bird, and which wine and seasonings are used.

1 Cold game pie
2 Game pâté with chestnuts
3 Game soup with lentils
4 Game pie
5 Buckwheat with vegetables
6 Small game pies
7 Cumberland sauce
8 Whole grain mustard

*H*andsome pies

Rediscover the great pleasures of baking day and make a batch of delicious and sustaining pies to share with friends or freeze for future unexpected occasions

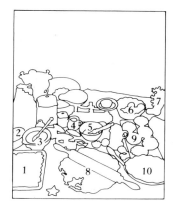

1 *Poached chicken, pre-cooked vegetables for chicken pie*
2 *Butter*
3 *White sauce with parsley*
4 *Cream*
5 *Egg yolk*
6 *Eggs*
7 *Parsley*
8 *Pastry dough*
9 *Small meat pies*
10 *Rabbit pie*

tomato and mustard
  quiches p73
small game pies p84

Recently, I find that my cooking has become much simpler. The general shortage of money has contributed to this, but in a surprisingly constructive way. I find I work best within limitations, and whether these are imposed by lack of cash or of materials does not matter. It is in times of comparative affluence that I start to panic, when I feel people's standards have become too high, and we have been spoilt by restaurant meals, too many dinner invitations, and so on. I remember hearing a fellow guest complain at a dinner party that he could not face another salmon trout, and hearing someone else recommend *filet de boeuf en croûte* as ideal picnic food. In this sort of atmosphere I quickly become defeatist; when anything is within the bounds of possibility, nothing seems good enough to serve guests.

Until recently I think many of us were still trying to live according to a pattern laid down by our grandparents in an era of prosperity, living in large houses without the servants that were an integral consideration in the original plans for the house, giving dinner parties that would in previous times have kept a staff of two or three fully occupied for a couple of days; in short, we were trying to keep jobs, bring up children, run houses, maintain gardens, and entertain in a way that was far too demanding for most of us to accomplish without a degree of strain. I find it a relief that the economic realities of recent times have forced us to abandon all this, and to find a simpler way of living, more within our reach.

In my house, at any rate, the planning of large dinner parties has become a thing of the past; so long past, in fact, that it has almost faded into myth. With the obvious handicaps such as lack of time, money, help and inclination, I hesitate to commit myself to any great culinary effort more than a couple of days in advance. Rather than organizing dinner parties one simply asks friends in for a meal. This informality means a much less rigorous menu; one hot dish is really all that is needed, although more can of course be added, as you feel inclined. I like meat pies for this sort of meal, as they are a good example of a dish that can stand alone. A large pie is a handsome thing, and quite delicious and sustaining enough to form the basis of a meal. These pies are also adaptable, will feed an elastic number of people, and can be filled with a wide range of food according to one's pocket, from quails stuffed with pâté to the humble rabbit.

However busy I am, I am determined not to give up cooking for pleasure; one must not lose sight of the fact that both cooking and eating are enjoyable activities. I try to keep an afternoon free, once a fortnight at least, just for cooking; not in the old hectic rush of preparing for one special meal, but in a quieter, calmer way, making a series of related dishes for future use. The old-fashioned system of having a special "day" for baking, for instance, was a sound idea that still makes sense, economically and practically. With two or three pounds of pastry one can make a series of pies, tarts and linings for quiches. One can be eaten the same day and the others frozen for future meals. I made the pies in the photograph in an afternoon, and it was immensely satisfying to see how much I had accomplished at the end of three hours. Particularly with a modern freezer at hand, it is a lovely feeling to have more food than one actually needs at any given time, and a perfect incentive to telephone friends and invite them over. Viewed in this way, cooking becomes enjoyable again; the pleasure of doing things for fun rather than necessity is regained.

One-pot cooking

A range of different ingredients cooked together makes for a wonderful mingling of flavours and is a highly practical, economical and energy-saving way to entertain

My idea of a perfect meal has changed. It used to be a selection of different foods—meat or fish, vegetables and sauces—all cooked separately and meeting for the first time on my plate. I still think this can be delicious, but I realize how wasteful it is in terms of pots and pans, fuel and labour. As far as home cooking is concerned, I have now swung to the opposite extreme, which is both more practical and more economical. In this system, a group of different foods is cooked together, either in the same pot or above it, each adding its flavour to the others and various separate ingredients merging into a whole.

Almost every country has its own version of a "one-pot" meal: the New England boiled dinner, the Scottish cock-a-leekie, the French *pot-au-feu*, the Italian *bollito misto*, the Moroccan couscous, and the Chinese steamed dinners, where little wicker containers, each holding a different food, are piled on top of each other over a wok. Some of these dishes require special equipment, but in most cases one can devise one's own version with a little ingenuity. The only ones that are difficult to improvise are the Chinese steamers, and these can be bought cheaply in shops specializing in oriental goods.

Before the days of kitchen ranges, when cooking was still done over the open fire, whole meals were cooked in one huge pot, or cauldron. I used to think that this contained one vast watery stew, or a large joint boiling in gallons of water, but I was wrong. Apparently as many as six or seven different foods were often cooked at one time, by an ingenious method of co-ordination. Inside the giant pot, a flat plank of wood was wedged near the bottom, and under this a joint of meat—probably bacon or salt beef—was boiled, while on top of the board stood two or three earthenware jars, tightly sealed. Inside these might be found meat combined with root vegetables for soups and stews, eggs in the shell, and cut-up chickens. In a muslin bag hanging from the handle simmered either some dried vegetables or a boiled pudding. By careful timing, all these foods could be combined to provide quite elaborate meals.

A similar method was used by the bargees, who used to cook their dinner in an iron bucket over a fire on the tow-path. Inside the bucket, on a platform of sticks or flat stones, stood a large earthenware jar, probably filled with a mixture of meat, vegetables and suet dumplings, tightly sealed with a flour and water paste. Also cooking in the bucket might be a pudding in a bag, or simply a bottle of tea keeping hot. In modern times, with our efficient electric and gas ovens with pre-set timers, one-pot meals are more apt to be in the form of baked casseroles than pots of boiled food. The word casserole originally meant the pot in which the food was cooked; now it has come to mean the food itself. Casseroles range from traditional meat stews—*daubes* of beef, *navarins* of lamb, cassoulet, moussaka, Lancashire hotpot—to combinations of vegetables. Filling and delicious dishes can be made by using layers of different foods: at the bottom goes a layer of cooked rice, buckwheat or couscous, then various uncooked vegetables, usually moistened with a sauce. Over it all goes a covering of dried bread, grated cheese, or breadcrumbs. Alternatively, all three layers can be of vegetables, the top layer a purée of potatoes, celeriac, parsnips or turnips.

These inexpensive and heartening dishes are eminently suitable for life today; the work of preparing them can be done in advance, and the final cooking done in the oven, possibly pre-set, or even over the fire. Many of us these days have friends who are vegetarian, and it is not always easy for non-vegetarians to think of a filling meal without using meat. These sort of dishes need only a green salad and some crusty bread as accompaniment, and they can be kept hot for as long as you like.

1 The "bargee's" meat and vegetables
2 Steamed pudding

Cooking round the hearth

Gather the family around an open fire to enjoy the crackling, sizzling and bubbling and the delicious aroma of food cooking to perfection in the roaring flames

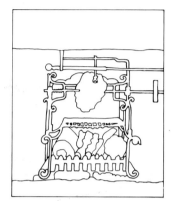

A baron of beef on a spit over an open fire

fish cooked over an open
  fire p74
chicken over an open
  fire p81

I once read the fascinating fact that until 1850 all the cooking for the White House was done in two huge open fireplaces. The old cook was said to be hostile towards the new range installed in that year—perhaps understandably since he had been in the habit of cooking dinners for up to thirty-six people without it.

Open fire cookery, both out of doors and inside, has always appealed to Americans, who have a gift for simple living combined with a degree of comfort (something the more puritan English have never understood). In 1939, when King George VI and Queen Elizabeth visited the United States, President Roosevelt threw a huge informal picnic in their honour at his Hyde Park estate outside New York, at which much of the food was cooked over an open fire.

Many Americans are also ardent devotees of open fire cooking in their kitchens, and in Richard Olney's *The French Menu Cookbook* (Collins 1970), there are detailed drawings of the fireplace in his house in the south of France, built expressly for cooking. Here he roasts and grills meats, bakes vegetables in the ashes, and smokes foods in the chimney.

I once visited a family who were living in a tiny cottage on the side of a mountain in County Kerry. For three years the wife had been doing all the cooking for her husband and two small children—and all the heating of water—in the fireplace. She had been lucky enough to find the cottage still equipped with its original fireplace crane in good working order, and by scouring junk shops and markets far and wide she had acquired a complete set of original pots and pans, plus the hooks from which they hang. A friendly blacksmith had made her a trivet by welding together three horseshoes and attaching legs to them. This would support flat pans like skillets directly over the fire. Thus equipped, there was literally no cooking she could not manage. An excellent and inventive cook, she made soups and stews and cooked fresh and dried vegetables and grains; pot-roasted rabbits, hares, chickens, deer and even kid; made flat bread like *chapatis* on a griddle, and baked yeast bread and cakes in a bastable, a sort of Dutch oven.

The day I visited them was a typically Irish day of the worst sort: grey and drizzling. The small living room was both lit and warmed by the fire in its huge chimney breast, seemingly out of all proportion to the size of the room, but with reason. For it was the hub of all activity; a stew was cooking for lunch, bread was slowly rising at the edge of the fire, damp clothes were hung over the end of the crane, a kettle was permanently on the verge of boiling, and the cat was asleep on the hearth.

Despite the inconveniences, and they are many, there is something very appealing to me in this sort of life, although I am sure I would not have the stamina to endure it, day in and day out. The main disadvantage is the black greasy skin the flames produce on the outside of the cooking pots; even with plenty of hot water they are very hard to clean. The main benefit is that it brings cooking back into the heart of family life. Rather than the mother working alone in the kitchen, other members of the family are drawn in, and can help in positive ways. Even quite young children, who might be confused or misled by many modern refinements like pressure cookers and microwave ovens, understand and respect the heat of an open fire.

The age-old device of the crane, the iron bar hanging within the chimney breast high over the fire, on a swivel so that it can be swung from the fire when desired, combined with the varying lengths of the different hooks, gives a surprising degree of heat control. As well as the pots which hang from the crane, which include a cauldron for heating large amounts of water, a kettle and different sized lidded pots, there are a number of flat pans like skillets and griddles for standing on trivets, and the bastable. This, the traditional baking pot of Wales and Ireland, is shaped like a modern French casserole with the addition of three short legs for standing among the hot ashes, and a flat lid. On this lid are piled red-hot peats, which create the even heat of an oven.

The only modern invention I can think of which adds to the possibilities of open fire cookery is aluminium foil. This, especially when used in double strength, can be used in countless ways: pieces of meat, poultry, or fish can be wrapped alone or with garnishes of vegetables and baked in the ashes or over the fire on a grill; whole vegetables can be wrapped and baked in the ashes; foil-wrapped eggs can be baked in the shell and shellfish can be wrapped and steamed.

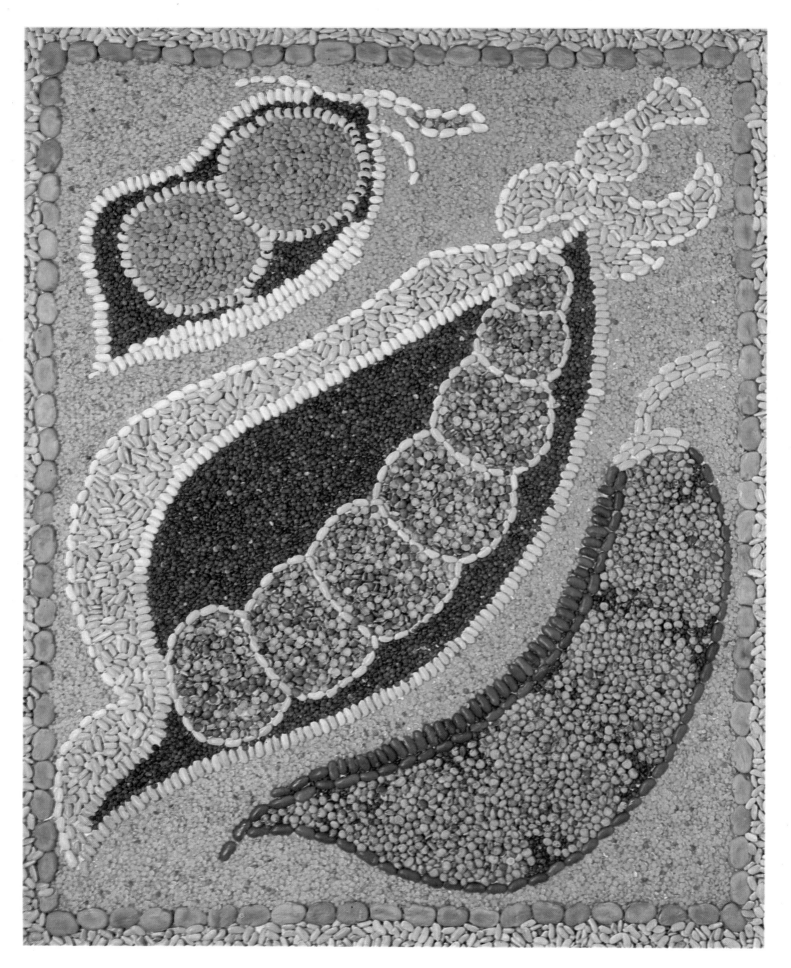

36

Dried peas and beans

From Mexico to Morocco, almost every country has a national dish based on dried peas or beans that is restoring, comforting and packed with real goodness

In winter months when one reaches home cold and tired at the end of the day, one yearns for food as an antidote to chills and fatigue. The French rarely eat cold food, especially in the evening, avoiding what they call *froid à l'estomac.* At this time what one needs is warming food, not merely served hot, but food with a comforting quality. Lentils rate high on my list for there is something essentially restoring about them. Hot, semi-liquid, easily digestible, full of iron and vitamins, they are a perfect example of good, wholesome winter food.

My favourite dish of this sort is a Middle Eastern stew of lentils and rice, supposedly the very potage which induced Esau to sell his birthright. Lentil soup is also a good restorer, as is split-pea soup. Dried beans in general provide a wide range of sustaining and nourishing dishes for cold weather, while in the summer months they can be made into delicious vinaigrettes and salads, or smooth pastes to eat with hot bread.

I believe that all dried vegetables should have a measure of fat or oil added at some stage, to counteract their very dryness. Animal fats are particularly good used in this way; a piece of beef marrow stirred into freshly boiled haricot beans will make the beans into a rich and luxurious dish. In summer, if they are to be eaten at room temperature— they should never be eaten chilled—they should be well moistened with the best olive oil, cut with a little white wine vinegar or lemon juice. Apart from split peas, all my favourite varieties of dried vegetables come from abroad. I don't particularly like the tiny English haricot, much smaller than its French or Italian equivalent, nor do I prize the vast butter bean, while the English lentil disintegrates into a mush before you can say *dhal.* I like the French *soisson,* a medium-sized white kidney-shaped bean, and the Italian *cannellini,* which is very similar. I also love the pale green *flageolets,* and the dark red kidney bean. These three can be mixed in a well flavoured vinaigrette to make a pretty tri-coloured dish. I like the so-called brown lentil from the Continent (actually dull olive green) and the rare green lentil, generally prized above all others. There are many beautiful varieties of dried peas and beans, ranging from warm chestnut browns to mottled red.

Almost every race has a national dish based on some form of dried bean or pea. The English have pease pudding and pea soup; the Americans have Boston baked beans; the Mexicans have black beans; in India it is *dhal,* in Egypt *ful medames,* the Arabs eat *hummus,* and the Spaniards have many dishes of *garbanzos* (chick-peas). It seems, moreover, that some day we will all come to rely at least in part on soya beans, as these most nutritious and easily grown of foods contain vast amounts of minerals and vitamins. They can be bought in health food stores, both in their natural state and made up into imitation meat granules. I prefer to eat them in their original form; they are quite acceptable if well seasoned. They can be treated in exactly the same way as haricot beans, soaked and cooked slowly, with plenty of fat and salt and pepper added, and served hot; or they can be served cool in a vinaigrette made of lots of good olive oil, chopped raw onion, fresh parsley and garlic, salt and pepper.

Chick-peas can also be bought in health food shops, as can *adzuki* beans, which grow in China and Japan. Although tiny, these take as long to cook as other larger beans. The chick-pea, familiar in Spain, is also part of the staple diet throughout the Middle East, in Morocco and in parts of France and Italy. They are an acquired taste; but once one has grown to like them, they can become a real passion. I like them best made into *hummus,* mixed to a smooth paste with *tahini,* lemon juice and garlic. They also make good soups, and are one of the essential ingredients of a genuine couscous.

1 *Dried broad beans*
2 *Red lentils*
3 *Brown lentils bordered by black-eyed peas*
4 *Black lentils*
5 *Haricots blancs*
6 *Green flageolets*
7 *Split peas*
8 *Red kidney beans*
9 *Haricots roses, black lentils*

chick-pea soup p68
three bean salad p99
haricot beans with garlic butter p100
curried lentils p100
hummus p102

Root vegetables

An obstinate refusal to submit graciously to canning or freezing, and an apparent determination to remain unfashionable, endears root vegetables to lovers of fresh food

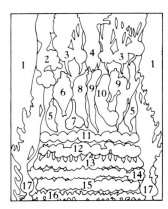

For some years now I have been growing steadily more attached to root vegetables—I mean the old favourites, turnips and swedes, beetroot and horseradish, parsnips and carrots, and Jerusalem artichokes. They seem determined to remain unfashionable which is one reason I love them. Totally resistant to modern times, they cannot be frozen or tinned successfully, and the best way to store them is still to dig a pit underground, as our ancestors used to do.

The more unusual root vegetables—salsify, scorzonera, celeriac, kohlrabi and fennel—seem scarcely more popular. It takes imagination, certainly, to visualize these ugly swollen tubers as smooth soups and elegant purées. Perhaps the trouble is that root vegetables are rarely sold young enough to be at their best. Those people lucky enough to have their own gardens soon discover the virtues of picking them while still quite small, for it is then that they are at their most versatile. Many are delicious eaten raw like radishes. Turnips, swedes, celeriac and kohlrabi are all unusually good, cut in slices and chilled, as part of a platter of *crudités*. When picked at this stage, their leaves can be cooked separately as a green vegetable. Turnips can also be left in the ground all winter to yield a crop of green leaves to use in early spring.

It has become fashionable in France recently to serve a selection of two or three vegetable purées with a meat dish, and root vegetables are ideal for this purpose. A purée of Jerusalem artichokes makes a delicious accompaniment to steaks, and celeriac purée is excellent with game or poultry. A purée of turnips or swedes is good with lamb; a mixture of carrots and turnips goes well with veal or pork. When serving two or three purées at the same time, they should not all be made of root vegetables, obviously, for this would be quite monotonous. A purée of beans, either broad, runner or French beans, would be delicious together with one of parsnips and another of mushrooms, served with ham. A green pea purée would be good with one of celeriac and a third of broccoli, to accompany roast capon. The purées should be well seasoned and very smooth, almost like thick sauces.

One of the reasons root vegetables are not more popular in Great Britain may be due to our insistence on eating potatoes with every dish, for they do not go well with potatoes, themselves a root crop. A proportion of potato, however, can with advantage be mixed with the other root vegetable for this helps give a firm, dry purée; one made in this way of parsnips, for example, makes a delicious accompaniment for grilled steaks, with the juices poured over it. A purée of celeriac and potato can be used as a bed for poached eggs, sprinkled with grated cheese and browned under the grill, while a covering for shepherd's pie can be made with a combination of potatoes and swedes.

These same purées, thinned with stock or milk, constitute excellent soups. The vegetables provide all that a soup requires in terms of flavour, nourishment, texture and colour, so nothing need be added beyond perhaps a sprinkling of parsley. In combining them I particularly like beetroot with fennel, turnip with carrot and parsnip, carrot with celeriac. They are best of all when made with a good game or beef stock, for they have a special affinity with strong meaty flavours. For the same reason they should be sautéed whenever possible in animal fat; beef dripping, goose or duck fat are ideal for the purpose. Remember that they are highly absorbent, and must not be allowed to retain water; for this reason, after boiling, they should be well dried in a warm oven and then allowed to absorb plenty of butter.

40

A feast of potatoes

The humble potato, whether transformed into pancakes, soufflés, gnocchi, bread, scones or cakes, or simply boiled in its skin is the perfect foil for meat, poultry and fish

Anyone who has not visited Britain cannot know just how good potatoes can be. Of all the basic starchy foods—bread, rice, pasta and potatoes— I think potatoes are my favourite. Irish potatoes have always seemed best of all to me, although those grown in Wales are also very delicious. Not only do they grow well in our temperate climate, they also seem ideally suited to eating on damp winter days, being warming and sustaining, and valuable in vitamins as well so long as they are cooked correctly. The vitamin content lies largely in the skin, or just below it, so that, whenever possible, potatoes should be eaten in their skins; or if peeled, this should be done after cooking. Remember, however, that their vitamin content diminishes progressively in relation to the time they are out of the ground. Growing them in my own garden, I find it very rewarding to cook them straight from the soil when they are still in perfect condition—with smooth pale skins, free of blemishes.

They are the most adaptable of vegetables: they can be baked, boiled, steamed, or fried. Grated, they may be made into pancakes from the Jewish *latkes* to the Swiss *rösti*; they can be mashed and mixed with flour to make gnocchi, scones, little cakes, or even bread. Puréed, they can form the base for a soufflé or be made into sweet cake with apples. They can be used as a covering for a savoury pie or mixed with other puréed root vegetables: celeriac, turnips, parsnips or swedes. They made a good creamy soup in combination with leeks or onions, and parsley. They can even be used as a garnish: a plain boiled potato in a plate of steaming hot, deep red bortsch makes an exquisite combination.

When I was living in Paris just after leaving school, my first choice on being taken to a restaurant was a grilled pork chop on a potato purée, and nothing has ever seemed better. I have been repeating it ever since. I make the purée by pushing the boiled potatoes through a vegetable mill and returning them to a clean pan to dry out. In another pan I heat a generous amount of butter with some milk, adding plenty of sea salt and freshly ground black pepper. This I beat into the potatoes until they are light and almost liquid. If it is not to be served at once, I pour a film of melted butter and hot milk over the surface to prevent a skin forming, and only beat it in at the last moment. This is surely the best of all accompaniments to grilled and roast meat, poultry and fish.

Potatoes make the perfect foil for other food with their bland flavour and smooth consistency. They need never be wasted, for they can be reheated in a number of ways. They can be mixed with chopped cabbage or kale, as in "bubble and squeak" or colcannon, or made into cakes and fried in bacon fat for breakfast. A flat cake of mashed potato mixed with fried onion and browned in a frying pan makes one of my favourite supper dishes, served with bacon and eggs and fried tomatoes.

As school children in the north of Scotland we sometimes used to spend Saturdays picking potatoes in the fields. We were paid a shilling an hour. It was gruelling work, involving continual stooping for six or seven hours. In the evening, when it had grown too dark to see the potatoes clearly, we used to make a bonfire and roast some of the day's harvest in the ashes, before riding home on the tractor. The smell of roasting potatoes always brings back the exhilarating feeling of relief at having managed to get through the long day, for the other children were much tougher than I was.

Those Scottish potatoes were good but not as delicious as those I was to eat later in Ireland. There they are almost always cooked to perfection. Boiled in their skins, they are then drained and left to steam under a folded cloth for some minutes, when they are dished up and sent to the table with their brown skins splitting here and there and the floury white flesh bursting its way through.

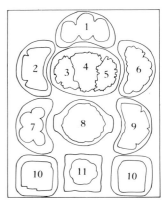

1 Baked potatoes
2 Rösti
3 Chips
4 Waffle-cut potatoes
5 Shoestring potatoes
6 Potato gnocchi
7 Potato pot potatoes
8 Gratin dauphinois
9 Potato scones
10 Potato bread
11 Pommes Anna

Pasta galore

Delicious, so easy to cook and supremely versatile, pasta comes in all shapes and sizes and can be simply glistened with oil or dressed up for dinner with an exotic sauce

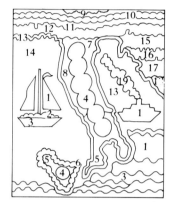

1 Lasagne
2 Tomato paste
3 Lasagne verdi
4 Capelli d'angelo
5 Rotelle
6 Anelli
7 Gramigna
8 Ditalini
9 Pagliaccio
10 Tortellini
11 Riccioli
12 Farfalle
13 Chifferi
14 Linguine
15 Margherite
16 Rigatoni
17 Stelline
18 Conchigliette
19 Taglierini verdi

Pasta takes myriad forms: stars, shells, wheels, letters of the alphabet, strips and tubes of countless different thicknesses and lengths. Admittedly almost all are made from the same basic mixture, but a new look can be given to a dish by using one of the more uncommon shapes.

There are three main varieties of pasta: first, the majority, like spaghetti, made from white semolina flour; second, the same pasta enriched with eggs, usually for noodles; third, the basic paste coloured green by the addition of spinach and made into lasagne and noodles of varying widths and lengths.

Spaghetti is probably most people's idea of a cheap and easy meal, and it is indeed one of the most inexpensive and convenient of foods. Easy to cook, capable of being stored for reasonable periods of time, it can be served with different sauces and is popular with almost everyone, including children and vegetarians, when covered with one of a wide variety of sauces.

When eating in certain Italian restaurants in London I am always seduced by the sight of that day's freshly made pasta—usually noodles in green and white—lying in soft nests on the trolleys alongside the hors d'oeuvre. These are a far cry from the dried pasta we buy in packets from the grocer. In Soho, one can buy green and white noodles, freshly made each day, or choose from a vast selection of pasta shapes, which are stored in a huge chest of drawers.

Pale brown pasta, made from wholewheat or buckwheat flour is something I cannot recommend too highly, especially a very thin buckwheat spaghetti, which I served topped with a garnish of thinly sliced vegetables—leeks, carrots and onions—gently stewed in oil and eaten in the Japanese manner, while still slightly crisp, and flavoured with soy sauce or sesame salt. I would not serve it with meat sauce, for the nutty buckwheat flavour has a special affinity with vegetables, but with a delicious carbonara sauce it is a revelation.

Wholewheat spaghettis and macaronis are also good, although less delicate in flavour. I always use a wholewheat macaroni in minestrone; the pale brown colour blends well with the other ingredients, and the taste and slightly firmer texture seem an added advantage. When I was in Vermont recently, a friend recommended a spaghetti made from Jerusalem artichokes. It was rather like our buckwheat spaghetti, and quite delicious, but I have yet to find it on sale in any English shop.

As a dish on its own I usually serve spaghetti, spaghettini, or noodles with one of my favourite sauces. I may use one or another vegetable mixture, or a sauce of clams, mussels or other shellfish, or a nut sauce. I rarely make meat sauces, but I like a chicken and vegetable sauce very much. Seafood sauces are surprisingly good although rarely seen in England; a quick last-minute dish can be made from canned minced clams. The other shapes I am more apt to use simply dressed with butter or oil as an accompaniment to other dishes—a meat stew for instance, or cooked vegetable dishes.

In summer, spaghetti can also be eaten cold. In this case it must be well moistened with plenty of olive oil—four tablespoons to a pound of spaghetti would be about right—and dressed with a suitably oily sauce. A good uncooked sauce for hot or cold spaghetti can be made by simply putting a tin of Italian peeled tomatoes in the food processor, then pouring over the hot spaghetti; additions in the way of chopped salami, flaked tunny fish, or chopped black olives complete the dish without further cooking.

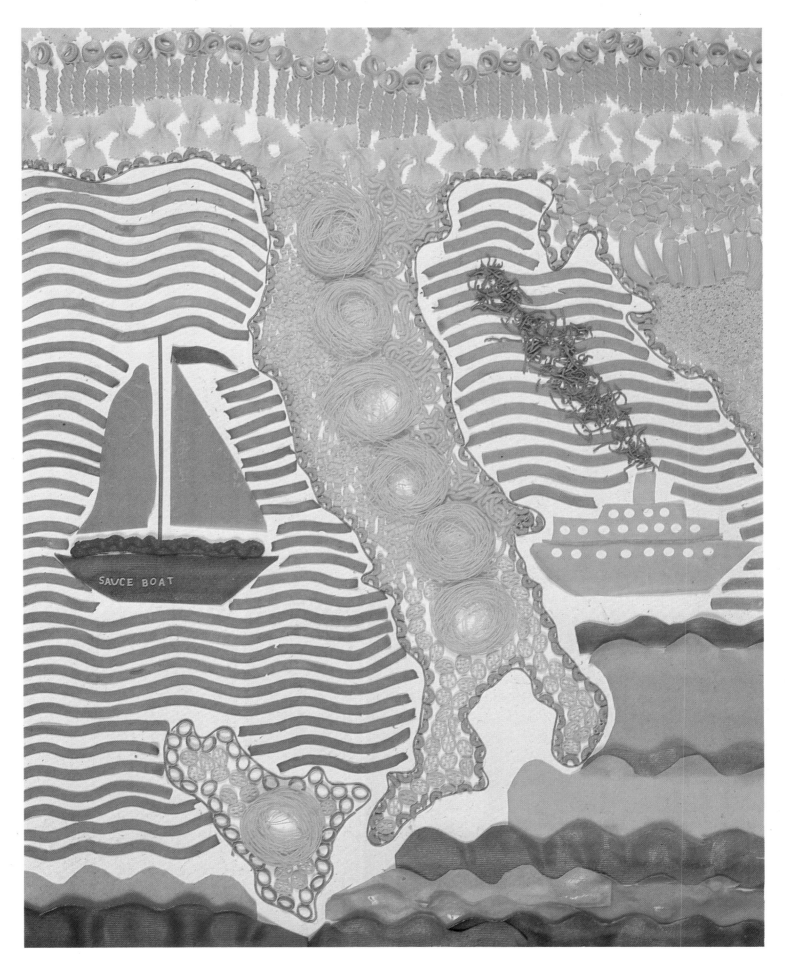

43

The goodness of grains

Grains in their less well-known varieties are staple foods in many countries, but their excitingly different flavours are too often overlooked by unadventurous cooks

Although grains are the staple food for a great part of the world, they have been sadly neglected in England. The only large-scale use the English have made of grain is wheat in its most refined form, as the basis of white bread and flour. In Scotland, however, oatmeal has been a basic source of nourishment since time immemorial, in soups (such as cullen skink), in haggis and porridge and delicious oatcakes. As potatoes have proved themselves an unreliable crop it would seem sensible for us to explore other possibilities of basic nourishment. Since the spreading popularity of health food shops in recent years, it has become possible to buy most of the different grains that form the main diet of large parts of the rest of the world.

Rice and spaghetti have been adopted into our national cuisine, but beyond that none but health food freaks have ventured. I find this sad, for we have chosen to ignore a rich and interesting family of foods, as anyone who has travelled at all in Eastern Europe and the Middle East will realize. Perhaps because I grew up in Scotland, where we ate porridge every day of our lives, I have a deep affection for these sustaining and warming foods, and look immediately for the foreign equivalents whenever I travel.

At the top of my list of favourite grains is *kasha*, the buckwheat that was the staple food of the Russian peasants. In a more refined form it made blinis for the rich. The whole buckwheat groats can be bought roasted or plain. The roasted variety is better but more expensive; one can achieve the same result by stirring the unroasted buckwheat carefully in a heavy pan over low heat for four or five minutes, then leaving it to cool before cooking. I cook a fairly large amount of buckwheat and keep it in the refrigerator, reheating it with various fried vegetables as needed. It is good just with fried onions, but it needs some addition of this sort. I always have a bowl of sesame salt on the table as seasoning. This can be bought in health food stores, or be made at home by pounding seven parts of sesame seeds with one part of sea salt. Keep the mixture tightly bottled and do not store it for too long for it soon loses its flavour.

Another of my favourites is cracked wheat, known as *bulgur* in Turkey and *burghul* in the Middle East. It is extremely nourishing, in either hot or cold dishes, and is inexpensive, but hard to find in shops here.

Couscous is the staple food of Morocco which, as a result of the French occupation, became very popular in France after the French refined and vastly improved what was originally a rough peasant food. It can be bought in a precooked form that is excellent and quick to cook. In Paris restaurants on the Left Bank devote themselves entirely to different dishes of couscous.

The first time I ate couscous, in a small restaurant built up against the walls of Taroudant, in central Morocco, I found it perfectly disgusting. It was only years later, after eating it in a restaurant in the rue des Saint-Pères in Paris, that I realized its delicious possibilities.

White polished rice is less nutritious than unpolished brown rice, which can be made into tasty dishes, yet I continue to use white rice to accompany meat dishes, because the brown variety adds a heavy quality that is not always desirable. Wild rice, aptly named in relation to its price, is a real luxury, and part of its appeal lies in its rarity; thus it is delicious eaten occasionally in small quantities. It does make an excellent stuffing for quail or other small game birds. There is a commercial package containing a mixture of plain and wild rice, which gives one an idea of its taste without crippling one financially.

A rather ersatz sort of grain is wheat germ, but I find it delicious none the less. An unsweetened form, rather like bran, can be sprinkled on salads and vegetable dishes. A crunchy, sweetened variety, which is perfectly delicious and not really sweet in taste, is considered best of all in my house. We eat it in plain yoghourt as a dessert. I find it also makes a good and unusual ice-cream, on the lines of an old-fashioned English brown bread ice.

For hundreds of years rice and semolina were only used in a sweet form, as a pudding. A much better savoury way of eating semolina is as gnocchi, flavoured with Parmesan cheese. Another grain worth mentioning is *polenta*, which I like occasionally as an accompaniment to game. Or it can be made into little cakes and fried; in this way it is served with cocktails at Harry's Bar in Venice.

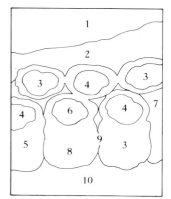

| 1 Oatmeal |
| 2 Brown rice |
| 3 Millet |
| 4 Wheat germ |
| 5 Polenta |
| 6 Buckwheat |
| 7 Semolina |
| 8 Pourgouri (Cypriot cracked wheat) |
| 9 Cracked wheat |
| 10 Wild rice |

buckwheat kasha with
 egg p110
cracked wheat risotto p110
cracked wheat salad p110
couscous with
 vegetables p110
rice and yoghourt
 salad p111
vegetables with brown
 rice p111
polenta p111
wheatgerm ice-cream p118

The delights of bread-making

Soft chapatis, Irish soda bread, saffron loaves and Russian pirog — just a sampling of the many delicious varieties of the simplest and most satisfying of foods

1 *Finnish rye bread with green cabbage filling*

2 *Saffron bread*

3 *Onion bread*

4 *Russian pirog with mushroom filling*

5 *Onion rolls*

Making bread has always seemed to me one of the most creative forms of cookery, whereby, with the addition of water and yeast, plain flour is transformed into a hot and fragrant loaf. It is at the same time the simplest and the most mysterious of processes; anyone who has worked with live yeast will know the strange feeling of handling the growing organism, and watching it double in volume continues to amaze me.

Like all really pure and basic processes, it is virtually impossible to spoil. I don't think I have ever seen a loaf of bread that was not visually pleasing, for decoration beyond a certain degree is not really practical. Those who enjoy decorating their food at length will prefer cake-making—something that has never attracted me.

One of the most appealing aspects of bread is its history, for it is one of the most ancient of foods, and has changed little over the centuries. It is rich in symbolism, and figures in religious ceremonies, and traditional codes of friendship and hospitality in many different cultures. There are few countries where bread does not form part of the staple diet. It is often the poorest countries that have the most delicious and interesting breads. Irish soda bread, for example, or the breads of India: the soft *chapati*, which takes the place of rice in Northern India and is used as a vehicle for the spicy dishes of that region, and the delicious *nan*, cooked in a matter of moments in the fierce tandoori ovens, stuck against the walls of the oven like pieces of chewing gum. In parts of China they make a steamed bread which I have always longed to try, while in the Middle Eastern countries they make a flat bread, round or oval in shape, with a hollow pouch in the middle. This can be bought at Greek or Cypriot shops, and it is marketed commercially in the United States under several names such as

Syrian bread. I have tried to make it many times, but with no success. I even had a friend bring me back a bag of flour from the Lebanon, with instructions from a local baker, but my attempts were to no avail.

It is a strange anomaly that such an ancient food should respond so well to modern technological developments, for not only does bread freeze remarkably well—it can be frozen either before baking, or even half-way through the rising—but the refrigerator can also be used to slow down the actual rising time.

Bread-making is a simple but lengthy process; it is not particularly economical, for the cost of good flour is almost the same as that of bread, but it is very rewarding. I would suggest, however, that if you are going to the trouble of making your own bread you try one more interesting than the ordinary loaf, after mastering the basics. Saffron bread for instance, adapted from an early English recipe, makes an unexpected accompaniment to a *soupe au pistou*, a fish soup, or a ratatouille. It is also good toasted, or made into croûtons to serve with bouillabaisse. Onion bread is also delicious, and can turn an ordinary *pâté de campagne* into a memorable meal; it is good too with fish pâtés, or vegetable hors d'oeuvre. The Russian *pirog* is fairly tricky to make, and not recommended for a first attempt at bread-making. It is similar to a brioche dough, and the high fat content makes it sticky to handle. It is extremely good, however, and makes a substantial and delicious meal when served with two or three hot vegetable dishes. The Finnish rye bread can be made with a vegetable filling, but it is also good unfilled; it is a firm dark bread with a good flavour. I also include a recipe for a plain white loaf; for anyone who has not made bread before, this is a good recipe to start with.

A hoard of nuts

Among the most nutritious of foods, nuts are a highly concentrated source of energy — and, in some unexpected ways, the source of fine flavours in many exciting dishes

The gathering of nuts has been part of the English rural scene for hundreds of years, but strangely, cooking with nuts is rare. While nuts and raisins are sometimes eaten at the end of a meal, apart from the stuffing for the Christmas turkey, nuts figure little in contemporary English cookery. Even in baking, there is only the occasional walnut cake, or macaroon. In France on the other hand, there are many delicious cakes and pastries based on nuts. When I lived in Paris as a young girl, one of my favourites was a sort of biscuit made of a meringue mixture of hazelnuts and egg whites, sandwiched together with coffee cream. In the United States, nuts appeal to the Americans' sweet tooth, and are included in many sweet dishes. Pecans, like a more delicate walnut, are often added to cake mixtures, and scattered over innumerable ice-cream sundaes and banana splits; and pecan pie is a favourite regional dish of the southern states.

Since my own sweet tooth is almost non-existent I prefer the way nuts are used in Middle Eastern countries. In Syria and Lebanon, pine kernels are scattered over rice dishes or mixed with stuffings for green peppers. In Turkey, walnuts are combined with breadcrumbs in a delicate sauce for chicken; ground almonds are used as a thickening for sauces in Egypt, and walnuts complement the local sour plums in many dishes in the Armenian/Georgian region of Russia. Farther east, in Burma and Malaysia, peanuts are ground into delicious oily sauces for serving with *satay*, tiny skewers of grilled meat, and in parts of central Africa they are blended with vegetables to make soups and sauces.

Nuts are indeed among the most nutritious of foods, and have been used in many cultures as a substitute for meat, since they contain many of the same properties. Almonds and Brazil nuts are particularly rich in iron and calcium, while peanuts are a valuable source of protein and phosphorus. All nuts are a highly concentrated source of energy; a handful of nuts and raisins makes a quick and sustaining snack. All nuts, however, are high in fat, so are not really suitable for those on diets.

One of my favourite nuts, little seen in England and sadly expensive, is the pine kernel. This is the nut of a special pine tree, widely grown in Lebanon, Greece and Italy. The only nut much grown in this country is the Kentish cob, or filbert. These are delicious eaten fresh, in the autumn, as are green walnuts before they have dried. A fairly recent development in nuts is the discovery of the macadamia nut in Australia by Dr Macadam, at the end of the nineteenth century. They were later introduced into Hawaii, where they are now widely grown, and in Malawi. They have such hard shells that they cannot be cracked by hand and must be shelled by machinery, which makes them very expensive. They do not have the oily quality of most nuts and have an unusual subtle, dry taste. They are best eaten with cocktails, chopped in salads, or scattered over sweet dishes.

In medieval times, nuts were much more evident in English cookery than today. "Almond milk", used both as a thickening agent and as a flavouring, appears again and again in recipes from the fourteenth century onwards, particularly in soups, dishes of fish or chicken, and in sweet dishes. It was used in a dish of lobsters and rice at Henry IV's coronation feast. It was also found in early versions of cold dishes of chicken, aspics of calves' feet and meat loaves; and a recipe for salmon and eels called for cooking them in a combination of almond milk and verjuice, a slightly fermented juice of crab apples also much in use in early English cookery. (This last dish illustrates an early form of sweet/sour cooking.)

During the seventeenth and eighteenth centuries, the use of almond milk declined. Its place was probably taken by the use of spices, whose popularity spread with the growth of trade with the East. In the nineteenth century, an essence of bitter almonds called ratafia was much used in making cakes and biscuits, but by that time the use of nuts in all forms was sadly declining as the bland and uninspiring dishes preferred by Queen Victoria and her household became fashionable, bringing their depressing effect on our national cuisine.

1 Cob nuts
2 Hazelnuts

A touch of spice

Evoke faraway places with the fragrant aromas of spices. Pungent or subtle, they give even the very simplest of food an interesting touch of individuality

1 *Paprika, mustard powder, cumin, cardamom seeds, mixed spices*
2 *Cloves*
3 *Black mustard seed, sea salt*
4 *Ground fenugreek, whole fenugreek, dried red pepper*
5 *Dried marigold petals*
6 *Mustard powder, whole fenugreek, dried yellow pepper*
7 *Dried rosebuds*
8 *Mixed pickling spices*
9 *Turmeric*
10 *Grey poppy seeds*
11 *Peppercorns*
12 *White poppy seeds, juniper berries, star anise*
13 *Sesame seeds, star anise*
14 *Cristalo, juniper berries, star anise*
15 *Mustard seed*
16 *Juniper berries, red chilli peppers*
17 *Lemon grass*
18 *Licorice root*
19 *Mustard powder*
20 *Red chilli peppers*
21 *Cinnamon sticks*

Spices are among the most aromatically evocative of all ingredients. Their mere smell calls to mind foreign places and each combination of spices has its own special character. A mixture of cumin and coriander, for instance, evokes memories of India and the Middle East; with the addition of chilli and cinnamon a Moroccan flavour emerges.

Spices have become as important to me in winter as fresh herbs are in summer. They fill similar roles, enlivening basically simple food and adding an individual touch to one's cooking. Many of our winter foods are bland and lend themselves to the addition of certain spices. One thing I like to have on hand is the French blend known as *quatre-épices*, but one can make this easily enough by adding a pinch of nutmeg, cloves and cinnamon to a teaspoon of ground black pepper.

After years of making unsatisfactory curries with prepared curry powder, I ventured out and bought a selection of relevant spices in an Indian spice shop. Since then I have stuck to my own mixtures, although I sometimes use a light American blend for adding a slight curry flavour to certain dishes. I make only mild curries of fish, chicken, vegetables or eggs, although I love to eat fiery mutton *dhansak* in an Indian restaurant. After experimenting with different proportions, I settled on a rough formula of equal parts ground cumin, coriander and turmeric with half a part of ground chilli. For dishes other than curries, too, coriander and cumin are useful. I use them interchangeably, or mixed in equal parts, particularly in dishes of cabbage, mushrooms or courgettes. One teaspoon each of ground coriander, ground cumin and celery salt makes a delicious seasoning for hard-boiled eggs.

Turmeric gives a warm spicy taste to rice, onions or fish, while juniper berries are incredibly good with sauerkraut and all cabbage dishes,

game and pork. Allspice is very subtle, tasting curiously like a blend of cloves, nutmeg and cinnamon, although it is in fact the berry of one tree. It can be used alone for sweet dishes, or combined with plenty of black pepper for savoury ones. My favourite spice of all is saffron, and this is too special and too expensive to mix with any other. I once ate a risotto in a restaurant in Vicenza at two in the morning, after seeing *Manon Lescaut* in the open-air opera house; although the risotto consisted of nothing more extraordinary than rice, onions, butter, chicken stock and saffron, it was one of the best dishes I have ever eaten.

Although the use of spices is ancient, there has been a new development in the past few years in the harvesting of peppercorns. First the soft green peppercorn appeared and this has since been followed by the dried green peppercorn; now there is a pink peppercorn bottled in vinegar. The soft green peppercorns are available in tins from most good food shops. I add a small tin of them to a duck pâté; they add a delicious sharp juicy taste to the usual "hot" pepper flavour. A few dried green peppercorns make an excellent addition to a mixture of spices, or can be used alone for coating a steak au poivre, while the pink peppercorn has a flavour all its own.

The delicate spices we use in sweet dishes—cinnamon, vanilla, ginger and nutmeg—are no less delicious than the more robust spices. The genuine vanilla pod gives off a subtle and delicate taste which never fails to delight me each time I make a *sauce à la vanille*, or any of the exquisite puddings based on it, such as floating island or *oeufs en niege*. Both apple Charlotte and apple crumble benefit from the addition of cinnamon. From Cumberland comes a delicious spiced fruit bread which I enjoy making and like better than any cake I know.

51

52

Fresh flavours from dried fruit

Bring a taste of sunshine to warming winter dishes with the goodness that is stored in dried apricots, figs and apples, pears, grapes, peaches and plums

Drying has a curious effect on fruit; it alters its character completely, turning it into something intrinsically different. Who could guess that a raisin was once a grape, or a prune originally a plum? Not only does the process of dehydration change the consistency, flavour and colour of the fruit, it also increases its vitamin content. Both dried apricots and prunes are higher in food value than in their original state, while raisins are much more nutritious than grapes.

Hundreds of years ago, dried fruits were enormously popular in England. In the thirteenth century they were imported from Portugal and the Levant, while by Elizabethan times every household of any size had a larder well stocked with dried figs, dates and raisins. At that time, dishes of mixed sweet and savoury foods were very much the vogue in England, as they have continued to be in some Middle Eastern countries. In a fifteenth-century English cookery book we find capon with dried figs, and huge pies combining beef, game and poultry, beef marrow and suet, with prunes, dates and raisins, saffron, mace and cinnamon. In a seventeenth-century book are instructions for cooking salt cod with raisins and currants, hard-boiled eggs, spinach, parsley and candied orange and lemon peel. These intricate dishes are amazingly like many of those in a thirteenth-century Persian manuscript. Here are numerous descriptions of dishes combining meat or chicken with dried apricots, quinces, prunes, apples and currants—very similar to certain dishes still found in North Africa today. In these, also, the combining of such diverse ingredients is helped by additions of saffron, spices and nuts.

In the twentieth century dried fruit has enjoyed little popularity in this country, at least until the advent of health food shops. Too many of us were put off prunes at school; my daughter says she is unable to think of prunes without automatically thinking of custard. In the United States prune juice is enormously popular and prunes are also eaten stewed, for breakfast, or made into elegant desserts for luncheon and dinner parties. American cookery books contain endless recipes for prune soufflés, mousses, whips and jellies which are both delicious and pretty, for the subtle colour of the prune contrasts admirably with the whipped cream that so often accompanies it.

Even if the prune never regains its popularity in this country, there is a selection of other dried fruits available. Some are so lightly dried that they do not need soaking; indeed, they are often plump and soft enough to eat straight from the packet. My favourite is dried peaches, very lightly cooked so that they are only just soft and still quite chewy. They are delicious served still warm, with lightly whipped cream mixed with yoghourt. Dried pears are also extremely good, while the more familiar apple rings, apricots, figs and raisins can be used in countless different ways. Mixed dried fruit makes a good winter fruit salad, scattered with chopped nuts and eaten with whipped cream. The same mixture, chopped and fried in butter with a chopped onion, makes an unusual stuffing for a roast chicken, duck, guinea-fowl or game bird. For adventurous cooks, there are many interesting dishes of stewed lamb, veal or chicken with dried fruit in the sauce. The inevitable sweetness that results from the addition of the fruit can be counteracted by adding lemon juice.

In Eastern shops, a paste made from dried apricots can be bought wrapped in orange cellophane and decorated with brightly coloured labels; it is called (phonetically) *Kamar-el-deen*, and is very good indeed. The paste dissolves when soaked overnight in water; it needs no cooking, and can be made immediately into mousses, ice-creams or whips. It also makes a delicious summer drink when put in the blender (after soaking) with buttermilk or yoghourt. Or it can be eaten straight from the packet, as a sort of sticky, chewy sweet.

The large Californian prunes are also good eaten raw, as are dried peaches and pears. For some of us, however, the prune can never recover from its dreary image, however undeserved. I remember making a prune mousse some years ago, based on one I had eaten in the Ritz in Paris, for an old lady who could no longer cook for herself. She surveyed it gloomily, and as she ate it I heard her say to herself, "I would never have given my husband prunes."

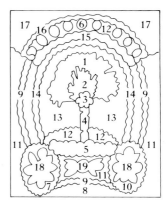

1 Citron, dried apricots
2 Angelica
3 Glacéed cherries
4 Dried bananas
5 Figs
6 Dried peaches
7 Currants
8 Sultanas
9 Prunes
10 Raisins
11 Dried apple
12 Chopped mixed peel
13 Dried coconut
14 Dates
15 Dried pears, apricots
16 Prunes, dried apricots
17 Kamar-el-deen
18 Dried pears, peaches, candied
    pineapple, orange peel
19 Dried peaches, candied
    pineapple, orange peel

chicken stuffed with dried
  fruit p81
veal with apricots p90
Moroccan lamb with
  pears p91
dried fruit salad p115
prune mousse p116

Exotic fruits

Sadly neglected in their fresh form in all but their homelands, tropical fruits are fragrant and irresistible in their mouthwatering shades of pink, orange and green

1 *Sugar cane*
2 *Lychees*
3 *Kumquats*
4 *Papaya*
5 *Mango*
6 *Green Jamaican orange*
7 *Pomegranate*
8 *Passion fruit*
9 *Chinese gooseberry (Kiwi fruit)*

a tropical fruit salad p116
mango fool p116
passion fruit sorbet p119
pineapple sorbet p119
Monaco p125

Tropical fruit has an exotic appeal, both visual and symbolic, that acts strongly on those of us living in temperate countries, especially during the gloomy mid-winter months. These strange and intriguing fruits come as a welcome contrast to our own more familiar varieties. Yet, apart from the pineapple and the avocado pear (which we treat as a vegetable), they have not been widely adopted by Anglo-Saxons in general. Although we are happy to eat tinned lychees and mango chutney in Chinese and Indian restaurants, we seem wary of buying them fresh.

Almost their strongest appeal is that of sight and smell for they are, almost without exception, in mouth-watering shades of pink, orange and green, often in contrast to their exterior skins, and most of them have a strong fragrance. To be honest, I often find their taste comes as something of a disappointment; they nearly all share a curious, bland texture, not unlike that of the avocado, and a sweet, rich flavour. Others are so richly endowed with seeds as to be almost unmanageable, like the passion fruit. Yet their qualities should not be overlooked, for they can be made into ravishingly pretty dishes, ideal for serving in small quantities to end a dinner.

Probably the best known tropical fruit is the mango, which is a curiously difficult fruit to eat. It must first be skinned and then the flesh has to be cut from the stone, even when ripe, which results in a lot of messy pulp and juice. It is the best-loved fruit in India, where some two million acres are devoted to growing mangoes, producing about five million tons a year. They can be made into dessert dishes, but I prefer them cooked when still green to make the best of all chutneys. More delicious, I think, is the pawpaw, or papaya. This can be mixed with other fruits, but is best simply skinned and cut in cubes, sprinkled generously with lime juice and chilled for two or three hours before eating. The guava is a strange fruit, rich in vitamin C, very sweet, and with a strong fragrant aroma. It can be included in a mixture of tropical fruits but I like it best made into guava jelly, which is so delicious when eaten with cream cheese and water biscuits. Passion fruit, with a funny wrinkled skin, has a more appealing fresh tart flavour, but its disadvantage is the multitude of tiny seeds that are almost impossible to separate from the flesh. Luckily I do not mind them, just as I do not mind the pips in raspberry jam, but for others more fussy than I am the only answer is to sieve them. This will give you only a small amount of pulpy juice but it is good for adding to a fruit salad or sorbet. Chinese gooseberries (or Kiwi fruit as they are called in New Zealand) are, on the other hand, simplicity itself to eat and are extremely pretty when cut in slices, with a few black seeds nestling in the pale green flesh. They can be sliced and added to salads, eaten with yoghourt, or simply cut in half and eaten with a teaspoon. I like to use them in a dish of mixed pale green and yellow fruit: honeydew melon, pineapple and lime juice. Almost prettiest of all the tropical fruits is the little lychee, with its hard, red rind opening to reveal a pearly-white fruit with a luscious sheen, shaped like a small bird's egg. These are excellent, either for adding to mixed fruit salads or simply served alone, in a thin syrup flavoured tartly with fresh lime juice. Many of the exotic fruits make exquisite sorbets, rather than ice-creams, for they are too rich for mixing with cream and egg yolks. Alternatively they can be cut in small pieces and mixed with scoops of other tart fruit sorbets, such as raspberry, lemon and lime.

The pomegranate is an exceptionally sweet fruit but the original wild pomegranate, like the Seville orange, was bitter; years of cross-breeding have resulted in the familiar sweet pomegranate which is the only one we find in our shops. I like to use it simply as decoration, for it is a remarkably pretty fruit and can be kept for weeks without losing any of its beauty; the dark pink skin simply hardens slightly into a shell-like exterior. I encountered the bitter pomegranate for the first time recently in southern Spain. It is sad that we cannot buy these outside Spain, for they give one of the best fruit juices I have ever tasted, which is a beautiful dark crimson colour. The juice of the sweet pomegranate is used commercially to make grenadine—a sweet, red syrup much loved in France. Those with a very sweet tooth may like it poured over ice-cream, but I much prefer it in cocktails.

Old-fashioned puddings

Forget the fashion for fresh fruit and yoghourt and finish off a light meal with a hearty English pudding sticky with syrup and jam or adorned with fruit

Some of our best-loved dishes, just as popular with foreign visitors as with ourselves, are our hot puddings. (It is surely indicative that the word "pudding" is the only true English word to describe this course, for "dessert" is an American contribution, "sweet" a horribly refined addition to our vocabulary, and "afters" is clearly derived from the menus of second-rate restaurants.) The dishes I have in mind are indeed true puddings, in that they are composed of flour, butter and eggs, with additions such as fruit or jam as flavourings. These are the same ingredients that go into the making of a cake, but the pudding mixture is usually moister, and is often steamed instead of baked.

Many of the best old English puddings have been forgotten, though a few still remain popular. While rice pudding, bread and butter pudding and jam pancakes can still be found on the menus of some old-fashioned hotels and restaurants, others are practically never seen except occasionally in private houses. This may be due in part to the modern avoidance of fattening food, and to the fact that many of us have taken to ending our meals with fruit and cheese or yoghourt. However, in midwinter, when yoghourt seems a trifle chilly and fruit expensive, a hot pudding can make the perfect end to a light meal; there is something very heartening about it, particularly on weekends and holidays.

Among my favourites as a child were "castle puddings", which reminded me of sand castles, in the shape of tiny inverted buckets. These were always served, like many other puddings of this sort, with a delicious sauce made from golden syrup heated with a little lemon juice.

England is the only country I know that grows apples expressly for cooking, and these apples combine so well with the bland tastes of sponge, bread and cream. It is not surprising that there is such a wide range of apple puddings to choose from. Eve's pudding is one of the best: simply a dish half-filled with stewed apples under a topping of soft sponge, served hot with cream. Almost every pudding I can think of is improved by cream, except those containing citrus fruits.

Some of the hot jam puddings are also very good: queen of puddings in particular, with layers of soft breadcrumbs, jam and meringue. Treacle tart is almost too sweet for me, though many people love it; there is another very popular toffee pudding made with fingers of bread soaked first in milk and then in a hot toffee sauce. Many of the best puddings are based on bread; the mixture of crisply fried bread with juicy apples is one of the best imaginable.

Most widely known of all English puddings is of course the plum pudding, or Christmas pudding. There must be literally thousands of different recipes, and they vary hugely. The one I like best is a comparatively light mixture, with lots of brandy and fruit but neither flour nor sugar. It is not quite so rich and dark as some, but is more to my taste. It recalls one often served in Scotland when I was a child, although that version had less fruit and no brandy. It was called seven cup pudding, and was simplicity itself to make. Although very similar to a plum pudding, this was made and eaten on the same day. I cannot help feeling that the inordinately lengthy steaming, for two sessions, that is traditional for Christmas puddings is not really essential, as our one-day version, though lighter in colour, was always delicious.

I wish I enjoyed Christmas pudding more on the actual day. I feel sure that it is because it follows the turkey with its rich stuffing that I invariably feel so awful afterwards. I think one year I shall change the plan and serve both dishes, but at separate meals: perhaps have the turkey at lunchtime, followed by a citrus fruit salad to counteract the richness of the stuffing, and in the evening, serve some Brandenham ham on the bone with a salad, followed by the pudding in all its glory.

1 *Brandy butter*
2 *Buttered apples*
3 *Golden syrup sauce*
4 *Grapes and peaches*
5 *Rice pudding*
6 *Christmas pudding*
7 *Queen of puddings*
8 *Castle puddings*
9 *Jam tarts*
10 *Turkish delight and sugared almonds*
11 *Mince pies*

The essence of coffee

The history of coffee is as colourful as its popularity is constant. It has a strong, almost compulsive appeal, both as a drink and as a flavouring in cakes, ice-creams and desserts

1 Black coffee
2 Macaroon
3 Amaretti
4 Candied melon
5 Figs
6 Chocolates
7 Glacéed fruit
8 Crystallized fruits
9 Cherries in brandy
10 Chocolate mints
11 Nuts, dates
12 Nuts
13 Grapes
14 Pineapple
15 Oranges

When the price of coffee rises sharply, I, like other coffee addicts, find myself unable either to find a substitute or to go without. In fact, the realization that I am actually prepared to pay inflated prices makes me appreciate it the more.

Apart from the joys of coffee drinking, I have long been fond of it as a flavouring for sweet dishes, for ice-creams, mousses and custards. I find it delicious combined with chocolate, with nuts and cream. When used as a flavouring, only very small amounts are needed, so the price becomes of less importance. There is an Italian instant coffee available in individual foil packets which I find extremely useful for making small quantities, and when wanted it can also be made in double or triple strength.

The history of the coffee bean makes a fascinating story. The plant, *Caffea arabica*, originated in Abyssinia, where it still grows wild. It was discovered by Arabs, who took it back with them to Aden and the Yemen, where there are records of coffee drinking as early as the ninth century. Its anti-soporific properties made it much prized by devout Muslims, who used it to keep awake during long nocturnal prayers. It was not known in Western Europe until the mid-seventeenth century, when it was brought back from the East by travellers for their own use. It reached Venice in 1615, Marseilles in 1644 and Paris in 1647. It did not become generally known in France until 1669, when the Turkish ambassador started serving it to his guests, as he was accustomed to do at home. It quickly became the fashion in Paris.

The first coffee house in London was opened in 1652 by an Englishman called Edwards. He had recently returned from Smyrna, where he had been British Consul. Encouraged by his friends' enthusiasm, he set up his servant in a small coffee house off Cornhill. Soon coffee houses were springing up like mushrooms, becoming the accepted meeting places for seeing one's friends.

The coffee bean reached Vienna in a most romantic way. When the Turks were defeated in their third attempt to conquer the city in 1683, they were forced to withdraw, leaving behind a vast encampment of more than 500,000 tents with all their provisions. These included sacks of coffee beans, which were at first thought to be camel food. However the hungry Viennese soon realized their mistake, and learnt to roast and brew their first coffee. They proceeded to strain it, which the Turks and Arabs never did, and to drink it mixed with milk and honey.

The love of coffee houses spread quickly among the Viennese and has never left them. They have a gift for making coffee houses welcoming and comfortable, like a home from home, with newspapers and magazines, chess and draughts boards. Vienna is still full of these delightful places, where as many as 27 different sorts of coffee are sometimes served, as well as chocolate, ices, cakes and pastries. There is a charming custom among the Viennese of having a meal in a restaurant then removing to a coffee house for the dessert and coffee.

The world-wide spread of coffee was greatly influenced by the East Indian coffee trade, started by the Dutch in 1690, when they began to grow coffee in Java.

In the reign of Louis XIV, the French introduced the plant to Martinique, where it flourished, and later to French Guiana, from where it spread to Brazil and Central America. Two-thirds of the world's coffee now grows in Brazil and is almost all exported to the United States. Opinions vary about the best quality, but general opinion seems to favour coffee grown in the Blue Mountains of Jamaica, and in some of the Central American countries such as Costa Rica and Colombia. Arabian coffee, particularly from the Yemen, is supposed to be excellent but it is almost all used for home consumption.

Arabian or Turkish coffee, like that of the Greeks, is made in a totally different way from ours, which makes it hard to compare the two. First, the beans are roasted over charcoal until almost charred, then pounded in a mortar. Both these operations are usually performed in the home, just before brewing. The pounded coffee is then put with water and sugar in a small pot with a narrow neck and a very long handle. Sometimes a few cardamom seeds are added. It is brought to the boil twice, with time to settle briefly in between. The ritual is central to Arab hospitality, and a guest will be served coffee as soon as possible after his arrival. The nature of the occasion determines the degree of sugar to be added—after a wedding the coffee will be very sweet, while after a funeral it will invariably be bitter—but usually the guest will be asked how sweet he likes it and it will be made accordingly.

The food of childhood

The adult's yearning in adulthood for the simple dishes so beloved in childhood has led to a naïve but satisfying style of English cooking, a sort of "haute nursery"

As a concept, nursery food is peculiarly English; it just does not exist in any other language, and is virtually untranslatable. What it means, to me at any rate, is the sort of very simple English food which children used to eat in the nursery, and to which many Englishmen formed a lasting addiction. An Englishman of this type, unimpressed by the complexities of French or "gourmet" cooking, will go on eating "nursery food" whenever he can get it, if not at home, then at his club, hotel, or favourite restaurant. At White's, one of the most distinguished of the London clubs, this need is understood, and hardly a day goes by without some acceptable dish of this sort on the menu, be it sausages and mash, Irish stew, or liver and bacon, while rice pudding or an apple pie of sorts can almost always be found among the puddings. At Wilton's, one of the best and most expensive restaurants in London, liver and onions and sausages and mash figure frequently, and what is more they are served by waitresses with a distinct aura of the nanny about them. Even the Connaught, filled as it is with foreign visitors, makes a point of offering one such dish each day for their old-fashioned English clientele at lunch time.

I cannot help feeling that this sort of food may soon cease to exist, for the next generation will have had no experience of the proper English nursery, or of its food. The modern child presumably eats the same food as its parents, and probably suffers from the passing trends, learning to adapt first to ratatouille and then to brown rice without having any firm culinary background to return to in later nostalgic years.

In the pre-war English houses the nursery was a world of its own; it had its own timetable, heirarchy and diet. Since traditional English food is basically simple, it is ideally suited to the feeding of young children. Such dishes as Lancashire hotpot, fish pie and Scotch broth make ideal fare for children, while the vast range of English puddings, both hot and cold, seem tailor-made for the nursery.

It is not surprising that these dishes remain so popular with many Englishmen, decades after they have outgrown the nursery. For it seems to me that it is in such simple dishes that the English have always excelled. The grander food

served in old-fashioned English houses at dinner, (after the children are all in bed) seemed much less appealing. A sort of watered-down version of French cooking, it was likely to follow a monotonous pattern: a clear soup with some indiscriminate garnish floating in it, whitings served with their tails in their mouths, a meat dish often in a wine-based sauce, followed by a dessert or savoury. To me certainly, as a small child growing up before the Second World War, this sort of food fared poorly in comparison with the cosy dishes we had in the nursery: creamy mashed potato with boiled beef and carrots, minced "collops" of beef served with little triangles of toast, crisp macaroni cheese, mushrooms on toast. There was little doubt in my mind who had the better deal.

One of my favourite cookery books, Alexis Soyer's *The Modern Housewife*, published in 1856, recommends as a proper day's diet for children: "bread and milk for breakfast at eight; the dinner at one, composed as follows throughout the week: roast mutton and apple pudding, roast beef and currant pudding, baked apples, boiled mutton with turnips, after which rice or vermicelli pudding; occasionally a little salt beef, with suet dumplings . . . or pease pudding . . . and at five o'clock, their bread and milk again, previous to going to bed."

For my part, bread and milk was a dish I never experienced. Perhaps it was not eaten in Scotland, or maybe it had gone out of fashion by my day. Soyer's version of it sounds quite delicious: thin slices of white bread broken in pieces in a large cup, with slightly sweetened boiling milk poured over it. (It was also much given to invalids in Victorian times, and in a slightly more sophisticated version, he suggests replacing the bread with crusts, and adding a little butter, cinnamon and nutmeg.)

It must be admitted that when he returns to nursery food later in life, the particular Englishman is served with slightly superior versions, a sort of "haute nursery". The Irish stew for instance would be made with best end of neck trimmed in neat cutlets, while the cod in the fish pie would be replaced with halibut, but the dishes themselves, and their manner of cooking, remain unchanged.

1 *Lancashire hotpot*
2 *Bread and butter pudding*
3 *Toad-in-the-hole*
4 *Cauliflower cheese*
5 *Eggs*
6 *Boiled egg with brown bread and butter*
7 *Liver and bacon with onions and tomatoes*
8 *Milk*

Christmas presents

Avoid the seasonal battle in the shops and conjure up Christmas gifts in the calm of your own kitchen. Pickles and pâtés, candies and jams are fun to make and delightful to receive

I have always loved the idea of making things to eat for presents. Not only does it save time and money, it also avoids a rush in the shops. One of the nice things about being given presents to eat is that they can neatly incorporate two presents into one: once the contents have been eaten one is left with a container which may well be useful or pretty in its own right.

Another point in their favour is that, much as I enjoy making pickles and preserves, for some obscure reason once they are made, I never actually want to open and eat them. Presents I receive are different; I love being given things to eat and consume them immediately. Curiosity about other people's cooking makes it appeal to me more than my own. Eating one's own food inevitably brings a sense of déjà vu.

Bearing in mind the inevitable cold turkey and ham of the post-Christmas days, it is a good idea to give preserves that will complement this sort of cold food. Cumberland sauce, for instance, is one of the nicest accompaniments to almost all cold meat. Spiced melon is delicious with cold ham, as is a sweet mustard pickle. A good chutney would go well with curried turkey, or devilled turkey legs, but I have not yet succeeded in making one I like as much as the ones I can buy. A pâté makes a very acceptable present (particularly for a single person who would find it impractical to make pâté on a small scale) and even better when accompanied by a small jar of Cumberland sauce to eat with it. When made in pretty dishes and decorated with bay leaves and cranberries under a thin film of aspic, pâtés can be enchanting to look at. These should go into the refrigerator and be eaten within a week. If the pâté is sealed with a layer of melted lard, it can be kept for several weeks in a cool place; in this case it can still be decorated, but in the bottom of the dish, before piling in the pâté mixture. It is then turned out before eating.

Rum or brandy butter keeps well, and makes a welcome present if the recipients have not already bought or made their own supply. The same applies to home-made mincemeat. A large glass jar of whole peaches in brandy (actually a brandy-flavoured syrup) makes a handsome present; the peaches keep for weeks, and can be eaten as a dessert or as an accompaniment to a hot baked ham. Dried apricots soaked in a sweet white wine, such as Sauternes, are easily made in small jars, and make a delicious accompaniment to after-dinner coffee; prunes can be treated in

the same way. Spiced Christmas cookies made in seasonal shapes make good small presents, and can also be used for decorating the tree. Little packets of salted almonds are useful for last-minute presents; they should really be given, and eaten, the same day they are made. Home-made fudge and coconut ice wrapped in little bags of cellophane and tied with coloured ribbon make nice presents for visiting children. The frosted grapes in the picture are not suitable for giving, as they are too fragile to wrap, but they are fun to prepare, and make pretty decorations for the Christmas table. Home-made drinks are also ideal Christmas presents; sloe gin should have been made and bottled in October, but flavoured vodkas can be made right up until the middle of December. My favourite is lemon vodka, but it can also be flavoured with hot chilli peppers or fresh tarragon, both of which are good.

One shopping expedition will be necessary to buy containers. For any foods that need vacuum sealing, I would suggest the French preserving jars with spring-type lids rather than the more familiar Kilner jars; they make a useful possession after the contents have been eaten. Small earthenware dishes are the ideal containers for pâtés. Look out for biscuit cutters and small cake tins in pretty shapes—stars, hearts or fishes.

Most of the preserves for which I give recipes do not need vacuum sealing due to their high content of vinegar, sugar or alcohol; however they still need to be kept in air-tight jars or the liquid will evaporate, leaving the contents to dry up. The rum or brandy butter can be packed into a jar without a lid, and simply covered with a piece of greaseproof paper and a square of brightly coloured material tied round the rim. A roll of cellophane paper and some coloured ribbon is all that is needed for the cookies, fudge, and coconut ice, while aluminium foil and coloured sticky tape will make an air-tight wrapping for the salted almonds. For spirits, pretty bottles can be found in markets.

Even if you have neither the time nor the inclination to make your own presents, food still need not be discounted. There are many unusual delicacies around that make delightful presents; at good-quality delicatessens and grocers you can find a most tempting range of pickles, preserves and chutneys, many of which I would love to try. I think these sorts of things make ideal presents, for they are just too expensive to warrant buying for oneself, yet still make inexpensive presents.

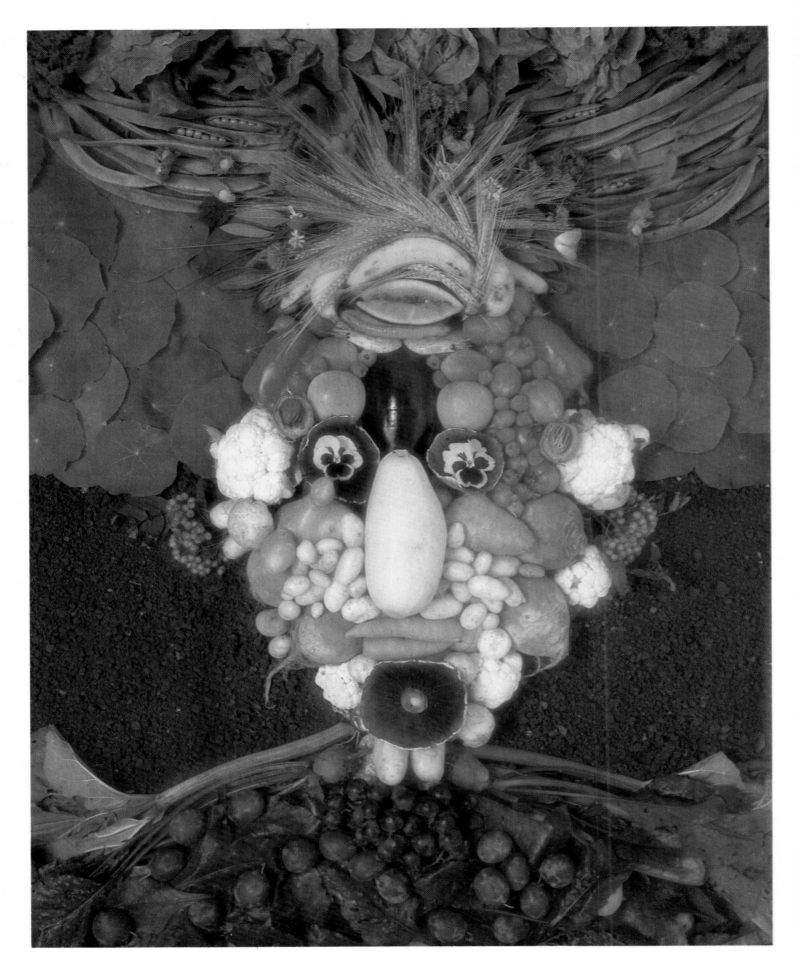

Winter recipes

In this book all metric equivalents are approximate (weights have been rounded up and volume measures have been rounded down, for convenience). Tablespoons and teaspoons are standard measure; amounts given are for level spoonfuls. Oven temperature conversions are those recommended by the Metrication Board.
The number of people each recipe serves is indicated wherever appropriate.
In all recipes requiring salt, sea salt is recommended, but only specified when necessary.

Soups/beans and vegetables

ribollita

This soup is traditionally made with the remains of yesterday's minestrone, the name ribollita meaning literally re-boiled. I find it so good, however, that I make it for its own sake, even going so far as baking the bread

¼ lb/120g	*cannellini beans*
½ lb/240g	*tomatoes*
1	*large onion*
2	*large carrots*
3	*stalks celery*
1	*head fennel*
½ lb/240g	*courgettes*
4½	*tablespoons olive oil*
2	*cloves garlic, crushed or minced*
2 pints/1	*litre stock*
6–8	*thick slices bread (preferably home-made)*
1	*small cabbage*
	salt and black pepper

SERVES 6–8

The day before: put the beans in a pressure cooker, cover with cold water, and bring to the boil. Turn off the heat, cover the pan, and leave for 1 hour. Peel the tomatoes and cut in small pieces, discarding the seeds. Coarsely chop the onion, carrots, celery, fennel and courgettes. Heat 4 tablespoons of the oil in a heavy frying pan and cook all the vegetables gently for 8–10 minutes, stirring occasionally. Towards the end, add the garlic. Drain the beans, return them to the pressure cooker and add the vegetables with their juices. Add the stock to the pan, cover, bring to the boil and cook under pressure for 20 minutes. Reduce the pressure and test the beans. If they are still hard, cook under pressure for an additional 5 minutes. When they are soft, add salt and pepper to taste and cool. Cover and refrigerate overnight. The next day, put the soup over low heat to reheat slowly. Meanwhile cook the cabbage, cut in quarters, in 1 pint/6dl of boiling salted water until just tender; drain and chop coarsely. Warm as many large soup bowls as there are people, and lay a slice of bread in each one. Pile the chopped cabbage on top of each piece of bread. Ladle the hot soup over the cabbage quarters in each bowl, and sprinkle a little olive oil over the top of each.

Tuscan bean soup

¾ lb/360g	*cannellini beans*
3	*tablespoons olive oil*
2	*cloves garlic*
4	*tablespoons chopped parsley*
	salt and pepper

SERVES 3–4

Soak the beans for 3–4 hours, or overnight. Drain, put in a pressure cooker and cover with 2 pints/1 litre cold water. Bring slowly to the boil, cover the pan and cook for 20 minutes under pressure. Reduce the pressure and test the beans; if not yet soft, cook for another 5 minutes under pressure. (Alternatively you can cook the beans without a pressure cooker: use a heavy pan and allow 1 hour's cooking time before testing the beans.) Add salt. Lift out about half of the beans with a slotted spoon and reserve. Put the remaining beans with their cooking liquid into a liquidizer and blend. Put the resulting purée into a clean pan and add salt and pepper to taste. Stir in the whole beans. Heat gently, stirring often. Chop the garlic finely and fry very gently in the olive oil in a small frying pan, being careful not to let it burn. When lightly coloured, add the parsley and stir for a moment or two longer, then stir the mixture into the hot soup. Remove from the heat and stand, covered, in a warm place for 5–10 minutes before serving.

la potée

2 oz/60g *smoked fatty bacon or pickled pork*
1 *large onion*
2 *leeks*
3 *cloves garlic*
2 oz/60g *bacon*
¼ *chicken*
1 *small turnip*
1 *medium potato*
1 *small green cabbage heart*
2½ *pints/1.25 litres light chicken stock*
2 *tablespoons chopped parsley*
salt and pepper
1 lb/0.5 kg *green peas or broad beans, weighed in the pod (optional)*
2–3 *Toulouse-style pure pork sausages (optional)*

SERVES 6–8

Cut the fatty bacon in small dice and fry gently in a pressure cooker, or heavy pan. Cook slowly about 10 minutes, until it has rendered all its fat. Remove with a slotted spoon and reserve. Chop the onion and put into the pan. Cook slowly until lightly coloured, adding a little extra fat if there is not enough from the bacon. Finely slice the leeks. Mince or crush the garlic and add these. Cook for another 4–5 minutes. Cut up the streaky bacon and add. Put the chicken into the pan and brown on all sides. Finely slice the turnip, potato and cabbage and add. Heat the stock and pour on, adding salt and pepper. Cover the pan, bring to the boil and cook for 40 minutes under pressure (or simmer for 2 hours). Take out the chicken and remove the meat from the bones; cut in small pieces and put back into the soup. Add more salt and pepper to taste, if needed. Pour the soup into a heated tureen. Sprinkle with chopped parsley and serve. If you wish to add peas, beans, and/or sausages, these should be cooked separately and added at the end.

pasta e fagioli

½ lb/240g *dried haricot beans*
¼ lb/120g *onion*
2 oz/60g *carrot*
1 oz/30g *celery*
3 *cloves garlic*
3 *tablespoons olive oil*
½ lb/240g *raw gammon or bacon, in one piece*
2 oz/60g *spaghetti, broken in 1 inch/2.5 cm pieces*
grated Parmesan cheese
salt and black pepper

SERVES 5–6

Put the dried beans into a pan with plenty of cold water to cover them, bring to the boil, turn off the heat and leave to stand, covered, for 1 hour. Chop the onion, carrot, celery and garlic until reduced to a coarse hash. Heat the oil in the bottom of a pressure cooker and cook the hash gently for 6–8 minutes, stirring often. Drain the beans and keep the water. Add the beans to the pan, and make up the water to 3 pints/1.5 litres. Pour into the pressure cooker and put in the gammon or bacon and some black pepper. Add salt later if required. Bring to the boil and cook for 30 minutes under pressure, then reduce the pressure and test the beans to see if they are almost tender. If so, remove the gammon and spoon roughly half the beans into a food processor or food mill. Add the spaghetti to the cooker and boil gently for 12–15 minutes, not under pressure, until the pasta is tender. Chop the gammon in small cubes and stir into the soup, then add salt as needed. Stir in the puréed beans and simmer all the ingredients together for 2–3 minutes, then pour into a tureen and serve with grated Parmesan cheese. This soup can be made in an ordinary saucepan instead of a pressure cooker, in which case allow 1½ hours simmering.

chick-pea soup

6 oz/180g *chick-peas*
2 *onions*
3 *carrots*
3 *leeks*
3 *stalks celery*
4 *tablespoons olive oil*
½ lb/240g *tomatoes*
4 *tablespoons chopped parsley*
salt and black pepper
SERVES 6

Cover the chick-peas with cold water and soak for about 6 hours, or bring them to the boil, turn off the heat and leave covered for 1 hour. Drain and cover with fresh cold water. Cut 1 onion, 1 carrot, 1 leek and 1 stalk of celery in pieces and add. Bring to the boil, then reduce the heat and simmer until the chick-peas are soft; this may take as long as 2 hours. Drain, reserving the liquid. Chop the remaining onion, carrots, leeks and celery, keeping them separate. Heat the oil in a heavy pan and add the chopped onion. Cook gently until pale golden, then add the chopped carrots, a few minutes later the leeks, and finally the celery. Peel the tomatoes and chop them, discarding the seeds. Add to the pan and stir in; cook gently for a few more minutes. Heat the reserved stock and add to the pan. Bring to the boil, reduce the heat, cover and simmer for about 20 minutes. Add the chick-peas and bring back to the boil. Simmer for 5 minutes, then press everything through a coarse sieve. Reheat, adjust the seasoning to taste, sprinkle with chopped parsley and serve.

chicken barley soup

An excellent soup, filling and with an unusual fresh taste
2 oz/60g *pearl barley*
4 *leeks*
2 oz/60g *butter*
2½ pints/1.25 *litres hot chicken stock*
½ pint/3 dl *buttermilk or yoghourt*
juice of ½ *lemon*
4 *tablespoons chopped parsley*
salt and black pepper
SERVES 6–8

Soak the barley for 2–3 hours. Chop the leeks. Melt the butter in a large, heavy pan, and sauté the chopped leeks for a few minutes, without letting them brown. Drain the barley and add. Pour on the heated stock. Add salt and pepper. Bring to the boil, reduce the heat, cover and simmer for 1 hour. Beat the buttermilk or yoghourt until smooth. If using yoghourt, it can be mixed with a little cream for added richness. Add a ladleful of the hot soup, mix well, then add the mixture to the pan. Reheat gently, keeping below a simmer. Add the lemon juice to sharpen the flavour, more salt and pepper if needed, and the parsley just before serving.

lentil and pasta soup

6 oz/180g *brown lentils*
2 *cloves garlic*
¼ lb/120g *cooked ham*
1 *large onion*
1 *carrot*
1 *stick celery*
3 *tablespoons olive oil*
2 oz/60g *spaghetti broken into 1-inch/2.5 cm pieces*
½ *teaspoon paprika*
salt and pepper
SERVES 4–5

Soak the lentils for 3–4 hours. Chop the garlic, ham, onion, carrot and celery finely. Heat the oil in a large, heavy pan or pressure cooker and add the vegetables and ham. Cook gently, stirring often, for 8 minutes. Drain the lentils and add; stir until well coated with oil. Heat 3 pints/1.5 litres water (or light stock if available); add to the pan. Bring to the boil, reduce heat, cover and cook for 1 hour, or 20 minutes under pressure. Add the spaghetti, and cook a further 12–15 minutes (not under pressure), until the spaghetti is just tender. Add salt and pepper to taste and serve.

game soup with lentils

carcass of 1 pheasant or other game bird	
½ lb/240g brown lentils	
2 onions	
2 carrots	
2 leeks	
2 stalks celery	
1 bay leaf	
3 tablespoons olive oil	
salt and black pepper	

SERVES 6–8

Put the carcass in a large heavy pan. Cut in half 1 onion, 1 carrot, 1 leek and 1 stalk of celery and add with the bay leaf and plenty of salt and pepper. Cover with cold water. Bring slowly to the boil, reduce the heat, cover and simmer gently for 2–3 hours, or alternatively cook for 1 hour in a pressure cooker. Strain and cool; remove the fat from the top after it solidifies. Measure the liquid and add water if necessary to give 3 pints/1.5 litres. Chop the remaining onion, carrot, leek and celery. Heat the oil in a heavy pan and stew the chopped vegetables gently for 10 minutes, stirring now and then. Wash the lentils and add. Stir until they are well mixed with the vegetables and

coated with oil. Heat the strained stock and add. Bring to the boil, reduce the heat and simmer for 45 minutes. Add salt and pepper to taste. This soup is also delicious when made with a whole pheasant. In this case, simmer the bird with the vegetables for 45 minutes only, then remove and cut from the bones all the white meat and return the bones to the stock and simmer for another 2 hours. Proceed as above, and finally chop the white meat and add to the soup a few minutes before serving.

game soup with parsley

1 large onion	
2 large carrots	
1 medium turnip	
1 large potato	
2 oz/60g beef dripping	
1¾ pints/1 litre hot game stock	
juice of ½ lemon	
4 tablespoons chopped parsley	
salt and black pepper	

SERVES 5–6

Slice the onion, carrots and turnip very thinly indeed. Heat the fat in a large heavy pan; add the vegetables and stew them gently for 8–10 minutes. Thinly slice the potato and cook for another 3 minutes. Add the stock, and salt and pepper to taste. Bring to the boil, reduce the heat, cover and simmer for 35 minutes, leave to cool slightly; then put, in at least 3 batches, into a liquidizer and blend briefly. Reheat, adding the lemon juice and extra salt and pepper if needed. Add the parsley just before serving.

peanut soup

¼ lb/120g shelled peanuts
2½ pints/1.25 litres chicken stock
1 medium onion
1 large leek
1 small green cabbage
½ lb/240g tomatoes
salt and black pepper

SERVES 6

Chop the nuts coarsely and put into a heavy pan with ½ pint/3 dl of the chicken stock. Bring to the boil and simmer gently for 10 minutes. Slice the onion and leek and quarter and slice the cabbage heart, putting the outer leaves aside for another use. Add to the pan with the remaining chicken stock and add salt and pepper to taste. Simmer for 20 minutes. Meanwhile peel and chop the tomatoes, discarding the seeds. Add, and bring back to the boil; simmer for 10 minutes.

almond soup

2 oz/60g coarsely chopped almonds
1½ pints/9 dl chicken stock
1 small onion
1 leek
1 stalk celery
2 oz/60g butter
1 tablespoon rice flour or potato flour
¼ pint/1.5 dl single cream
pinch of mace
salt and black pepper

SERVES 4–5

Put the chopped almonds in a heavy pan with the stock. Bring to the boil and simmer for 10 minutes. Slice the onion, leek and celery. Melt the butter and sauté the sliced vegetables gently for 5 minutes, then add to the stock. Add salt and pepper to taste and simmer for 25 minutes. Put the flour into a small bowl, add 4 tablespoons of the hot soup; mix to a paste. Add to the pan and simmer, stirring, until smooth. Stir in the cream and add a tiny pinch of mace.

lettuce and almond soup

2 Cos lettuces
4 shallots or 1 bunch spring onions
2 oz/60g butter
1½ pints/9 dl chicken stock
4 tablespoons single cream
2 oz/60g coarsely chopped almonds
salt and black pepper

SERVES 4–5

Wash the lettuces and shake dry. Cut them across in thin strips. Chop the shallots or spring onions; if spring onions use the best green leaves as well as the bulb. Melt the butter in a heavy pan and sauté the chopped shallots or spring onions for a minute or two. Add the shredded lettuce and continue to cook gently in the butter for 3–4 minutes. Add the stock and bring to the boil. Reduce the heat, cover the pan and simmer gently for 20 minutes. Blend briefly, or press through a medium-mesh sieve; return to the pan and reheat, adding salt and pepper to taste. When very hot, stir in the cream. Pour into a tureen and sprinkle the chopped nuts over the soup.

potato and onion soup

1½ lb/0.75 kg potatoes
1 large Spanish onion
2 oz/60g butter
1½ pints/9 dl chicken stock
½ pint/3 dl milk and cream, mixed
2 tablespoons chopped parsley
salt and black pepper

SERVES 5–6

Slice the onion thinly. Heat the butter in a large, heavy pan and sauté the onion slowly until soft but not browned. Peel and slice the potatoes and add to the pan. Pour on the stock and add salt and pepper. Bring to the boil, lower the heat, cover and simmer gently for about 25 minutes, stirring occasionally until the vegetables are quite soft. Heat the milk and cream almost to boiling point and stir into the soup. Adjust seasonings and remove from the heat. Leave for 5–10 minutes to allow the flavour to develop. (At this point the soup can be put in the liquidizer and blended, but I like it better as it is.) Reheat gently and scatter the chopped parsley on top of the soup just before serving.

root vegetable soup

½ lb/240g turnips
½ lb/240g parsnips
1 medium onion
½ lb/240g carrots
2 oz/60g beef dripping or butter
1¾ pints/1 litre game stock
3 tablespoons sour cream
salt and black pepper

SERVES 4–6

Peel and slice the vegetables. Sauté them gently in the fat in a heavy pan for about 5 minutes. Add the stock and bring to the boil; add salt and pepper. Reduce the heat, cover and simmer for about 30 minutes. Pour into a liquidizer and blend, then reheat in a clean pan. Add more salt and pepper if needed, and just before serving stir in the sour cream; heat through, but do not allow to boil.

celeriac soup

1 lb/0.5 kg celeriac
½ lb/240g potatoes
2 oz/60g beef dripping or butter
1½ pints/9 dl hot game stock
4 tablespoons sour cream
2 tablespoons chopped parsley
salt and black pepper

SERVES 4–5

Peel the celeriac and cut in pieces. Peel the potatoes and slice thinly. Heat the fat in a large heavy pan and cook the celeriac gently in it for 5 minutes. Add the potatoes and cook for another 2–3 minutes, stirring around to coat everything evenly with the fat. Pour on the heated stock, and add salt and pepper. Bring to the boil, reduce the heat, and simmer for 30 minutes. Blend briefly in a liquidizer, in batches. Reheat, gently, adding the sour cream and more salt and pepper if necessary. Sprinkle on the chopped parsley and serve.

consommé

stock from cooking pigs' feet
1 lb/0.5 kg skirt or shin of beef
½ lb/240g tomatoes
3 stalks celery

SERVES 4

Remove all fat from the cold stock. Cut the beef in cubes and add; bring slowly to the boil. Simmer very gently for 1½–2 hours, then remove the beef and reserve for another dish. Cut the unpeeled tomatoes and the celery in pieces, put them into the pan and bring back to the boil. Simmer for another half-hour, then strain. For a delicate golden broth, serve this hot, or chill and serve as a firm jelly.

gratin of eggs and onions

6 *hard-boiled eggs*
2 *Spanish onions*
1½ *oz/45g butter*
2 *tablespoons flour*
¾ *pint/4.5 dl chicken stock*
¼ *pint/1.5 dl single cream*
2 *oz/60g grated Gruyère cheese*
pinch of mace or nutmeg
salt and black pepper

SERVES 4–5

Slice the onions quite thickly. Sauté them gently in the butter until soft, about 10 minutes. Add the flour and cook for another minute, stirring. Heat the stock and the cream and add; stir until blended, then simmer for about 15 minutes. Add the grated cheese, stirring until it melts; then add the salt and pepper, and mace or nutmeg. Preheat the grill. Cut the eggs in quarters and stir them into the onion mixture gently. Reheat, then pour into a shallow dish and brown.

poached eggs on celeriac purée

4–5 *eggs*
1 *medium celeriac*
¾ *lb/360g potatoes*
2 *oz/60g butter*
4 *tablespoons cream*
3 *tablespoons grated Gruyère cheese*
salt and black pepper

SERVES 4–5

Peel the celeriac and cut in pieces. Cover with cold water, add salt, bring to the boil and cook until just tender. Drain well and dry out over gentle heat. Boil the potatoes, drain and dry out also. Press both vegetables through a medium-mesh sieve into a clean saucepan. Add butter and a little cream and stir over low heat, adding salt and pepper to taste. When smooth and well mixed, pour into a shallow ovenproof dish. Poach the eggs and lay them on top of the purée. Cover with the grated cheese and brown under the grill.

curried eggs

8 *hard-boiled eggs*
1 *medium onion*
2 *oz/60g butter*
1 *tablespoon light curry powder*
1 *tablespoon flour*
¾ *pint/4.5 dl hot chicken stock*
¼ *pint/1.5 dl single cream*
1½ *tablespoons lemon juice*
1½ *tablespoons orange juice*
2 *tablespoons chopped almonds*

SERVES 4

Chop the onion and sauté in the butter until golden. Add the curry powder and the flour and cook gently for 2–3 minutes, then gradually add the stock. Stir as it thickens; when smooth and blended lower the heat and barely simmer for 10–12 minutes. Stir in the cream and the fruit juices. Add the nuts and stir until all is well mixed. Taste and add salt and pepper if needed. Cut the eggs in quarters; add them carefully to the sauce over low heat. Serve as soon as the eggs are hot.

smoked haddock soufflé

1 *smoked haddock or other smoked fish*
(*about 9 oz/270g*)
½ *pint/3 dl milk*
1 *oz/30g butter*
2 *tablespoons flour*
2 *tablespoons grated Parmesan cheese*
4 *eggs*
black pepper

SERVES 4

Cut the fish in pieces and put into a pan. Add the milk and enough water almost to cover. Bring to the boil, reduce the heat, cover and simmer gently for 12 minutes. Lift out the fish and strain the liquid. Flake the fish, discarding all skin and bone. Weigh 6oz/180g, discarding any extra. Melt the butter, stir in the flour and cook, stirring, until well blended. Add ⅓ pint/2dl of the strained fish stock, gradually stirring as it thickens. When smooth, add pepper to taste. Stir in the grated Parmesan and the flaked fish. Pour the mixture into a liquidizer. Separate the eggs and beat the egg yolks. Add to the mixture and blend. Pour into a bowl. Preheat oven to 350°F (180°C, Gas Mark 4). Beat the egg whites until stiff. Fold into the mixture in the bowl and transfer to a buttered soufflé dish. Bake for 25 minutes.

tomato and mustard quiches

¾lb/350g pastry (see recipe, page 126)
2 eggs + 1 yolk
¾lb/360g tomatoes
¼ pint/1.5dl double cream
2oz/60g grated Gruyère cheese
2 tablespoons Dijon mustard
salt and black pepper
SERVES 6

Preheat oven to 400°F (200°C, Gas Mark 6). Make the pastry and roll out on a floured surface. Line 6 small tins (3–4 inch/8–10cm diameter). Beat 1 egg yolk. Prick the pastry with a fork and brush with the beaten egg yolk. Put into the oven and bake for 5 minutes. Cool. Reduce the oven heat to 325°F (170°C, Gas Mark 3). Peel the tomatoes, discard the seeds and chop coarsely. If very juicy drain away the liquid. Beat two eggs in a mixing bowl with the cream and add

salt and pepper to taste. Stir in the cheese and the chopped tomatoes, reserving a little cheese. Brush a layer of mustard over the bottom and sides of each pastry shell. Pour the mixture into the pastry shells and scatter over the remaining cheese. Bake for 15 minutes.

artichoke soufflé

¾lb/360g Jerusalem artichokes
2oz/60g butter
3 tablespoons flour
¼ pint/1.5dl milk
2 tablespoons finely chopped parsley
4 eggs
salt and black pepper
SERVES 4–5

Scrub the Jerusalem artichokes, cover with lightly salted cold water and bring to the boil. Cook until just tender and drain, reserving a scant ¼ pint/1.5dl of the cooking water. As soon as they are cool enough to handle, peel the Jerusalem artichokes and make a purée by pressing them through a medium-mesh or coarse-mesh sieve. Dry out the purée as much as possible by stirring in a pan over gentle heat. In another pan, melt the butter, stir in the flour, and cook, stirring, for a minute or two. Heat the milk and the reserved cooking water together and add, gradually, to the butter and flour mixture. Stir until smooth; bring to boiling point, lower the heat and cook gently for a few minutes. Preheat the oven to 400°F (200°C, Gas Mark 6). Stir in the puréed Jerusalem artichokes and the chopped parsley and add plenty of salt and pepper. Separate the eggs and beat the yolks. With the pan off the heat, stir in the yolks. Then beat the whites until stiff and fold in. Spoon into a buttered soufflé dish and bake for 20 minutes.

Fish/seafish and shellfish

fish pie

1½ lb/0.75 kg fillet of haddock or similar fish
1½ lb/0.75 kg potatoes
3½ oz/105 g butter
1 pint/6 dl milk
2 tablespoons flour
2 tablespoons single cream (optional)
2 hard boiled eggs
2 tablespoons chopped parsley
salt and black pepper

SERVES 4–5

Peel and cook the potatoes in plenty of salted water until tender; drain. Mash to a purée, adding 2 oz/60 g of the butter and ¼ pint/1.5 dl of the milk, and salt and pepper to taste. Keep warm. Put the fish into a large, heavy pan and add the rest of the milk. Add enough water to almost cover the fish, and some salt. Bring to the boil and simmer until the fish flakes easily, about 10 minutes. Lift out the fish and strain the cooking liquid. Measure ½ pint/3 dl and reserve this; keep the rest for a soup. When cool enough to handle, flake the fish, discarding all skin and bones. Melt 1½ oz/45 g butter, stir in the flour and cook for 1 minute. Add the measured fish stock and stir until blended. Simmer for 3–4 minutes, adding salt and pepper to taste, and the cream, if used. Chop the hard-boiled eggs and stir in these with the flaked fish and reheat gently. Stir in the chopped parsley and pour into a buttered soufflé dish. Spoon the creamy potato purée over the fish and serve with broccoli, spinach, or a green salad. If made in advance, reheat very gently or the sauce will boil up and merge with the purée.

fish cooked over an open fire

8 small (6–8 oz/180–240 g) rainbow trout, red mullet or mackerel
2–3 tablespoons light oil
1 oz/30 g melted butter
1 lemon

SERVES 4

Make two or three diagonal cuts on both sides of each fish with a sharp knife, and rub them all over with the oil. If you have a hinged sandwich-type grill (much the easiest way to handle small fish) it will need to be rubbed with oil too, to prevent sticking. Put the fish into it, and lay it on the flat grill in the fireplace. Allow 3–4 minutes for each side over a good fire. Turn on to hot plates and pour a little melted butter over each fish. Serve with lemon wedges. You will find the skin of the fish, charred by the heat of the fire, one of the most delicious things imaginable.

grilled fish on skewers

Serve as a first course or double the quantity and serve, on a bed of rice, as a main course

1½ lb/0.75 kg firm white fish such as halibut, monkfish, or conger eel
3 tablespoons olive oil
2 tablespoons lemon juice
1 small onion
1 tablespoon chopped parsley
2 lemons

SERVES 4

Cut the fish in small pieces and put into a bowl. Sprinkle over 2 tablespoons olive oil and 1 tablespoon lemon juice. Finely slice the onion and stir in with the chopped parsley. Leave for 3–4 hours. Thread the fish on to small skewers and grill carefully, turning often and basting with the remaining oil and lemon juice. Serve with quartered lemons.

gratin of mixed haddock

1 *smoked haddock*
¾ *lb/360g fresh haddock, filleted*
½ *pint/3 dl milk*
1½ *oz/45g butter*
3 *tablespoons flour*
¼ *pint/1.5 dl single cream*
2 *oz/60g grated Gruyère cheese*
salt and black pepper

SERVES 4–5

Cut the smoked haddock in four pieces and put into a pan with the milk and enough water almost to cover it. Bring to the boil; lower the heat, cover the pan and simmer gently for 12 minutes. Lift out the smoked haddock and put the fresh haddock into the pan. Bring back to the boil, and simmer for about 8 minutes, or until the fish flakes easily. Lift out and strain the cooking liquid. Measure ¾ pint/4.5 dl of it. When cool enough to handle, flake all the fish, discarding the skin and bones. Put them into a bowl and mix together. Melt the butter, stir in the flour and cook, stirring, for 1 minute. Add the measured fish stock and stir until blended, then add the cream. Cook very gently for 3–4 minutes, adding salt and pepper to taste. Stir in the cheese, reserving a little to scatter over the top. Add the flaked fish and reheat. Pour into a gratin dish and brown under the grill.

baked smoked haddock

2 *lb/1 kg smoked haddock*
4 *large tomatoes*
2 *oz/60g butter*
¼ *pint/1.5 dl milk*
¼ *pint/1.5 dl single cream*
2 *tablespoons chopped parsley*
black pepper

SERVES 4

Preheat oven to 350°F (180°C, Gas Mark 4). Cut the haddock in large pieces (either whole fish or fillets can be used). Lay in a shallow ovenproof dish. Peel the tomatoes and chop them coarsely. Melt the butter in a sauté pan, add the tomatoes and cook briefly, stirring, over medium heat. Pour with their juices over the fish. Heat the milk and cream together in a saucepan, then pour over the fish and tomatoes. Sprinkle with plenty of black pepper and bake for 20 minutes. Serve sprinkled with the chopped parsley and accompany with rice and a tossed green salad.

dressed crab

1 *crab, dressed*
2 *hard-boiled eggs*
½ *bunch spring onions*
¼ *green pepper*
1 *tablespoon capers*
2 *tablespoons lemon juice*
2 *tablespoons chopped parsley*
salt and black pepper

SERVES 3–4

Order a dressed crab large enough for three or four people the day before. Remove all the meat and mix the white meat with a little of the brown in a bowl. Chop the whites of the hard-boiled eggs, finely slice the bulbs of the spring onions and finely chop the green pepper. Add these to the crabmeat together with the capers. Add lemon juice to taste and salt and pepper. Spoon the mixture back into the shell. Sieve the yolks of the hard-boiled eggs and sprinkle with the parsley over the top of the crabmeat mixture. Serve with thin sandwiches of brown bread and butter or fill them with watercress.

Fish/shellfish

stuffed clams

10–12	*large clams*
4–5	*shallots*
3 oz/90 g	*butter*
½ pint/3 dl	*fresh breadcrumbs*
½ pint/3 dl	*chopped parsley*
1	*tablespoon flour*
¼ pint/1.5 dl	*creamy milk*
4	*tablespoons browned breadcrumbs*
	salt and pepper

SERVES 4–5

Clean the clams thoroughly with a very stiff brush and several changes of cold water. Simmer ¼ pint/1.5 dl water or wine and water mixed, and put the clams in to steam open— this should take 8–10 minutes. Remove the clams and set aside, reserving the stock. Mince the shallots. Melt 2 oz/60 g butter in a heavy pan and sauté the shallots. When pale golden, remove the pan from the heat and stir in the soft breadcrumbs. Remove the clams from their shells and chop them finely. Add them and the chopped parsley to the pan. Season with salt and pepper to taste. Melt the remaining butter and stir in the flour. Stir in ¼ pint/1.5 dl of the clam stock with the creamy milk. Simmer a little to reduce, then add to the clam mixture and mix well. Pile into half of the clam shells and press down to make neat mounds. Cover with the browned breadcrumbs, dot with a little extra butter and brown under the grill.

moules gratinées

These may be served as a first course and eaten with a teaspoon

1 quart/1 litre	*mussels*
2	*shallots*
2 oz/60 g	*butter*
1	*clove garlic, crushed (optional)*
½ pint/3 dl	*dry breadcrumbs*
4	*tablespoons chopped parsley*
	salt and black pepper

SERVES 3

Clean the mussels thoroughly with a very stiff brush and several changes of cold water. Drop into ¼ pint/1.5 dl water, or wine and water mixed, simmer and cover for 4–5 minutes. When all have opened remove them and cool slightly. Remove the empty half from each, and keep the mussels warm. Finely chop the shallots. Melt the butter and sauté the shallots until pale golden, adding the garlic (if used), halfway through. Add the crumbs and stir until all are lightly browned. Remove from the heat and stir in the chopped parsley. Moisten with 2 tablespoons of the cooking liquid and add seasoning to taste. Spoon a little of this mixture over each mussel, enough to cover the mollusc and to fill the shell. Place the filled shells in a gratin dish, dot with butter and put under a hot grill until nicely browned all over.

mussels in saffron sauce

2 quarts/2 litres	*mussels*
	pinch of saffron + 1 shallot
2	*stalks parsley*
1	*stalk celery*
1 oz/30 g	*butter*
½ pint/3 dl	*dry white wine*
½ pint/3 dl	*single cream*

SERVES 3–4

Clean the mussels thoroughly with a very stiff brush and several changes of water. Chop the shallot, the parsley and the celery, including the leaves. Melt the butter in a broad heavy pan and sauté the chopped shallot, celery and parsley for 2–3 minutes, stirring. Add the mussels in their shells, then add the wine and cover the pan. Cook gently over very low heat for 5–6 minutes, until the mussels have opened. As they open, lift them out and discard the empty shells leaving the mussels in their half-shells. Put them into a large tureen in a warm oven. When all the mussels are out, strain the stock into a clean pan and boil it up to reduce slightly. Heat the cream, add the saffron to it, and stir. Add to the stock and season to taste. Pour three-quarters of the sauce over the mussels and serve the rest in a separate sauceboat. Serve with rice.

seviche of scallops

Serve as a first course

8 *scallops*
¼ *pint*/1.5 *dl fresh lime or lemon juice*
1 *tablespoon finely chopped shallot or mild Spanish onion*
1 *tablespoon finely chopped parsley*
1 *tablespoon olive oil*

SERVES 4

Wash the scallops and, putting aside the red parts, cut in slices about ½ inch/1 cm thick. Put into a bowl and cover with the lime or lemon juice. Refrigerate for 24 hours. Just before serving, drain off all the juices and mix in the shallot (or onion) and parsley. Add enough olive oil just to moisten. To serve, spoon into scallop shells.

saffron shellfish salad

1 *quart*/1 *litre mussels*
1 *lb*/0.5 *kg cooked prawns*
½ *lb*/240 *g rice*
pinch saffron
4 *tablespoons olive oil*
4 *tablespoons lemon juice*
¼ *lb*/20 *g shelled peas*
salt and black pepper

SERVES 4

Cook the rice in plenty of boiling salted water until tender and drain well. Bring 4 level tablespoons water to the boil in a small pan; add the saffron and turn off the heat. Let stand for 3–4 minutes, then pour it over the cooked rice in a bowl. Mix well, then drain again. Dress while still warm with half the olive oil and lemon juice, adding some salt and pepper to taste. Clean the mussels thoroughly with a stiff brush and several changes of cold water. Put them in a pan with 4 tablespoons water. Cover and steam over medium heat for 4–5 minutes. When all the shells are open, remove them from the pan and take them from their shells. Mix with the rice. Shell the prawns, and soak them for 10 minutes in a bowl of salted water. Drain and add to the rice. Cook the peas briefly in a little salted water. Drain and add to the salad. Add the remaining oil and lemon juice, and salt and pepper to taste, stirring all together. Serve as soon as possible.

Pâtés/game and fish

game pâté with chestnuts

1 *old pheasant*

1½ *lb/0.75 kg belly of pork*

¼ *lb/120g fat green bacon*

2 *cloves garlic*

10 *juniper berries*

½ *lb/240g chestnuts*

¼ *pint/1.5 dl stock*

2 *tablespoons brandy*

6 *fl oz/180 ml red or white wine*

1 *tablespoon sea salt*

15 *black peppercorns*

SERVES 10–12

Preheat oven to 400°F (200°C, Gas Mark 6) and roast the bird for 15 minutes, then let it cool. Strip the meat from the bones, leaving some scraps on the carcass for making game soup. Chop the meat finely by hand. Cut a few thin strips of fat from the bacon, and reserve. Cut the belly of pork and the rest of the bacon in pieces and put through a meat grinder or food processor. Mix with the chopped pheasant. Put the garlic, salt, peppercorns and juniper berries all together in a mortar, and pound until well crushed. Add to the meat mixture. Shell the chestnuts and parboil them for 8 minutes in the stock. Drain, and chop them coarsely by hand or in a food processor and add to the mixture. Mix very thoroughly, then add the brandy and the wine. At this stage the mixture should be left for a few hours, or overnight, to allow the flavours to develop. Then test for seasoning by frying a tiny ball, and tasting it. The pâté should be quite highly seasoned. Preheat oven to 300°F (160°C, Gas Mark 2). Lay the reserved strips of bacon fat diagonally across the bottom of two fireproof dishes, or one large one. Pile in the mixture and place the dishes, uncovered, in a roasting tin half-full of hot water. Put in the oven and leave for

1¼–1½ hours. (For one large pâté allow 1¾ hours.) Take out and cool for a couple of hours; then lay a piece of aluminium foil on top of each pâté with a 2lb/1kg weight on it, and refrigerate. This pâté tastes best if it is left for 2–3 days before eating. It will keep for a week in the refrigerator. If it is to be kept longer, seal by covering completely with a thin layer of melted lard; it will keep this way for as long as two months.

potted game

¼ *lb/120g cooked game, preferably pheasant, grouse or partridge, white and brown meat mixed*

2 *oz/60g butter*

2 *tablespoons double cream*

pinch of cayenne pepper

1 *sprig of parsley*

salt and black pepper

SERVES 2–3

Chop the meat finely and then pound in a mortar until reduced to a paste. Add the butter, cut in small pieces, and pound until smoothly blended in. Add the cream, salt, pepper and cayenne, and mix together well. Pack into a small dish and refrigerate. Garnish with a sprig of parsley and serve like a pâté with hot toast and butter.

pâté de campagne

1 *lb/0.5 kg fat pork (belly or throat)*

1 *lb/0.5 kg pie veal*

½ *lb/240g pig's liver*

3 *oz/90g fat mild bacon*

3 *cloves garlic*

16 *juniper berries*

½ *teaspoon mustard seed*

½ *teaspoon mace*

4 *tablespoons brandy*

4 tablespoons wine, white or red
1 tablespoon sea salt
16 black peppercorns

SERVES 10–12

Preheat the oven to 300°F (160°C, Gas Mark 2). Put the pork, veal and liver through a meat grinder or food processor. Chop the bacon by hand. Mince the garlic. Put the peppercorns, juniper berries, salt, mustard seed, mace and garlic into a mortar and pound. Put the ground meats and the bacon into a large bowl, and add the garlic and spices. Mix well. Add the brandy and the wine and mix again. Fry a tiny ball and taste for seasoning; it should be quite spicy. Pile into small ovenproof dishes. Half-fill a roasting tin with hot water and set the dishes in it, uncovered. Put the roasting tin into the oven and bake for about 1 hour and 20 minutes. Cool; then put a piece of foil over each pâté and place a 2lb/1kg weight on top. When cool, remove the weights and refrigerate overnight. Next day you could decorate the pâtés with bay leaves.

duck pâté

1 duck
¾ lb/360g fat pork
¾ lb/360g pie veal
¾ lb/360g slab bacon
1½ tablespoons soft green peppercorns
2 cloves garlic
½ teaspoon mace
⅓ pint/2dl dry white wine
3 tablespoons brandy
a few strips bacon fat or 3 small bay leaves and a few cranberries or juniper berries
1 tablespoon sea salt

SERVES 8–10

Preheat oven to 400°F (200°C, Gas Mark 6). Put the duck into a roasting tin and roast for 25 minutes. Let it cool. Put the pork, veal and bacon through a mincer or into a food processor, together with the liver of the duck. Cut the meat off the duck and chop by hand in neat dice. Stir all together well and add the soft peppercorns, whole, and the garlic, crushed. Add the salt and mace, the wine and brandy. Mix well. Leave for an hour or two. Preheat oven to 300°F (160°C, Gas Mark 2). Line the pâté dish with a few strips of bacon fat, placing them diagonally across the dish, or with red berries and bay leaves. Pile in the pâté mixture and place the dish in a roasting tin half-full of hot water. Put in the oven for 1¾ hours. Cool, then place a 2lb/1kg weight on top of the pâté over a piece of foil, and set in a cool place overnight. The next day, remove the weight and refrigerate the pâté. Turn out to serve.

smoked salmon pâté

¼ lb/120g smoked salmon trimmings
2oz/60g Philadelphia cheese
2oz/60g butter
1–2 tablespoons lemon juice
2 tablespoons sour cream
salt and black pepper

SERVES 3–4

Chop the salmon and then pound in a mortar, or use a food processor. Beat in the cheese, a little at a time, and then the butter cut in small pieces. Continue to beat or process, add the sour cream, then the lemon juice and salt and pepper to taste. Put into a small bowl and chill for several hours before garnishing with parsley. Serve with toast.

Pâtés/fish

smoked mackerel pâté

This pâté can either be served on its own, with toast, or rolled up inside slices of smoked salmon, accompanied by lemon quarters

2 fillets smoked mackerel
2 oz/60 g Philadelphia cheese
1 tablespoon sour cream
1 tablespoon lemon juice
black pepper
SERVES 3–4

Remove the skin from the fillets and weigh the flesh—you should have 4–5 oz/120–150 g. Chop it finely and pound in a mortar or push through a sieve or food mill. Alternatively put all the ingredients into a food processor. Add the cream cheese, a little at a time, and then the sour cream, beating with a wooden spoon, or processing, until all is incorporated smoothly. Add lemon juice and some freshly ground black pepper to taste.

smokie pâté

1 large smokie
2 oz/60 g medium fat cream cheese
1 tablespoon sour cream
1 tablespoon lemon juice
salt and black pepper
SERVES 3–4

Weigh 3½–4 oz/105–120 g of the smokie's flesh. Chop it finely and pound in a mortar or push through a sieve or food mill. Or you can use a food processor. Beat in the cheese, a little at a time. Continue to beat, or process, adding the sour cream, lemon juice and a little salt if needed. Add plenty of black pepper. Chill in a small dish until quite firm. Garnish with parsley and serve with slices of brown toast and butter.

kipper pâté

1 plump kipper
2 oz/60 g Philadelphia cheese
2 oz/60 g butter
1 tablespoon lemon juice
black pepper
SERVES 3–4

Cook the kipper by covering it with boiling water and leaving it for ten minutes. Scrape all the flesh away from the skin and bones and weigh 4–5 oz/120–150 g. Chop this finely, then pound in a mortar, or push through a sieve or food mill. Alternatively, put all the ingredients together in a food processor. Beat in the cream cheese and butter cut in small pieces and add lemon juice and pepper to taste. Spoon into a small dish and chill in the refrigerator until quite firm. Serve very cold, with wholemeal toast and quartered lemons.

prawn pâté

This pâté can also be made with frozen prawns

½ lb/240 g prawns, shelled
2–3 tablespoons lemon juice
2 oz/60 g butter
salt and black pepper
SERVES 3–4

Chop or mince prawns finely, preserving one for garnish, then pound them in a mortar. Alternatively use a food processor. Add lemon juice and the softened butter cut in small pieces. Continue to pound or process until it is a smooth paste, adding salt and pepper to taste. Pile into a small dish and refrigerate for a few hours, with the one whole prawn on top. Serve with brown toast.

Poultry/chicken and turkey

chicken over an open fire

For this you will need to arrange a grill in your fireplace. I do not advise trying to cook more than one chicken at a time over a normal fireplace

one small chicken, 2½–3 lb/1.25–1.5 kg, halved

Dijon mustard

olive oil

lemon juice

SERVES 4

About 1 hour before cooking, brush the chicken on the skin side with mustard. Pour over a little olive oil and lemon juice. When ready to cook, lay over a good fire, skin side upwards. Cook steadily for 15 minutes, then turn over. Allow another 15 minutes for the smaller side, and an extra 5 minutes for the half incorporating the backbone. The outside will look charred but tastes delicious.

chicken stuffed with dried fruit

one 3½–4 lb/1.75–2 kg chicken

1 medium onion

3 oz/90 g butter

½ lb/240 g mixed dried fruit: apples, apricots, prunes, peaches, pears, raisins

1 oz/30 g chopped almonds

salt and black pepper

SERVES 4–5

Soak the dried fruit and remove the stones. Have the chicken untrussed, ready for stuffing. Chop the onion and cook in 1 oz/30 g butter until pale golden. Chop the dried fruit and add. Stir around for 2–3 minutes, then add the chopped nuts and salt and pepper to taste. Leave to cool. Stuff the chicken and tie up, leaving any extra stuffing in the frying pan. Melt the remaining butter in a casserole and brown the chicken on all sides. Sprinkle with salt and pepper, leave the chicken on its side and cover the pan. Cook for 1½ hours at 300°F (160°C, Gas Mark 2) turning over once or twice. Reheat the extra stuffing and lay round the chicken on its dish. Serve with rice.

roast turkey

one 10–20 lbs/5–10 kg turkey

stuffing (see recipes, page 106)

1½ oz/45 g butter

1 carrot, chopped

1 onion, chopped

1 stalk celery, chopped

salt and black pepper

SERVES 10–20

Stuff the turkey. Weigh the turkey after stuffing it, to allow the correct roasting time: 12 minutes a pound/0.5 kg for a large bird (around 20 lb/10 kg), 15 minutes a pound/0.5 kg for a medium bird (around 15 lb/7.5 kg) and 18–20 minutes for a small bird (around 10 lb/5 kg). Preheat oven to 450°F (230°C, Gas Mark 8). Arrange the bird, rubbed all over with butter and sprinkled with salt and pepper, sitting upright in a large piece of aluminium foil within a roasting tin. Fold the foil back to expose the breast. Put in the oven, and immediately turn the heat down to 350°F (180°C, Gas Mark 4). Baste once or twice during the first 15 minutes, then wrap the foil completely around the bird until the last 15 minutes, when it can be removed to complete the browning. Baste again during this last period. Meanwhile make the giblet gravy: chop the carrot, onion and celery and put with the giblets in water to cover; bring to the boil, reduce the heat, cover and simmer for 45–60 minutes. Strain and reserve. When done, put the bird on a dish. Strain the juices into the giblet gravy; reheat, then serve with the carved turkey.

roast goose

one 8–10lb/4–5kg young goose
1 onion
1 carrot
1 stalk celery
½ bay leaf
salt and pepper
SERVES 8–10

Only young goose should be roasted, so your bird should not weigh more than 8–10lb/ 4–5kg when ready for the oven. (The stuffing will add a further 1½lb/0.75kg to the weight.) Preheat oven to 375°F (190°C, Gas Mark 5). Put the goose upside down on an oven rack in a fairly deep roasting pan. Prick the skin here and there with a skewer to allow as much fat to escape as possible. Put in the oven and allow 2½–3 hours roasting time for an unstuffed bird, 3–3½ hours for a stuffed one; or 20 minutes a pound/0.5kg weighed after stuffing. Baste occasionally and, about halfway through the roasting time, reduce the oven heat to 350°F (180°C, Gas Mark 4), and pour off the fat from the roasting tin. Meanwhile, cut up the onion, carrot and celery, and put into a saucepan with the giblets (excluding the liver), the half bay leaf and about ¾ pint/4.5dl of water. Bring to the boil, reduce the heat, add salt and pepper, and simmer until reduced to a strong stock, about ⅓ pint/2dl. Strain this and reserve. During the last hour of roasting time, baste the goose so as to brown the breast nicely. When the roasting time is up, remove the goose to a carving dish and pour off most of the fat from the pan leaving only a residue. Put the fat in a cool place and put the roasting tin over low heat, stirring as you add the stock to the residue. Scrape all the juices and residue together, season with salt and pepper, and serve in a heated sauceboat. The fat should be refrigerated until solid, then the bottom scraped free of all solid particles. The fat should then be reheated gently and poured through a strainer into jars, cooled, then covered and refrigerated, for another use.

stuffed goose neck

This dish is best made either after you have roasted a goose, or at the same time

1 goose neck
½lb/240g pure pork sausage meat
2oz/60g streaky bacon rashers
2–3oz/60–90g scraps from roast goose
1 clove garlic
¼ teaspoon mace or nutmeg
1 egg
salt and black pepper
SERVES 4

Pull the skin off the neck, like taking off a light glove, so that it ends up inside out. Roll right way out, and sew up the narrower end with a needle and coarse thread. Finely chop the bacon and mix the sausage meat with the bacon and scraps of goose. (If you are making this before cooking the goose, some of the liver or some of the giblets could be substituted.) Crush the garlic and add, with plenty of salt and pepper, and the mace or nutmeg. Stir together. When well mixed, beat the egg and add; mix again. Push the mixture into the bag of skin. When fully stuffed, sew up the second end. Cook either in the roasting pan with the goose – in which case, add it about 1 hour before the end of the roasting time – or it can be cooked alone over medium heat, completely submerged in goose fat or lard, for 45 minutes. As an alternative, it can be added to a garbure or a cassoulet, cooked and served at the same time. To be served cold, it can be cut in slices.

duck in aspic

2 ducks
1 large onion
2 carrots
2 stalks of celery
4 stalks parsley
1 bay leaf
½ bottle white wine
½ oz/15g gelatine
1 small orange
1 lemon
salt and a few black peppercorns
SERVES 8–10

Cut up the onion, carrots and celery in large chunks. Put the two ducks into a casserole that just fits them nicely, and strew with the vegetables, herbs and seasoning. Pour in the wine and enough water to half-cover the ducks, about 1½–2 pints/9dl–1 litre. Bring slowly to simmering point, removing any scum that rises to the surface. Cover closely and poach gently for about 35 minutes. Turn the ducks over and continue cooking for another 35 minutes. Remove them and let cool. Strain the stock, measure about 1½ pints/9dl and let cool. Add a little orange juice and taste for seasoning. Dissolve the gelatine in a little of the stock, then pour the mixture back into the stock. Strain again. Carve the ducks; cut the meat in neat strips, removing the skin. Pour a layer of the stock into a round or oval dish. Cut the orange and the lemon in very thin slices. Lay these slices in the jelly while it is still liquid. Put the dish in the refrigerator. When set, put a layer of duck pieces on top of the jelly and cover with more stock. Refrigerate to set this layer. Build up the whole dish in this way; or if you haven't the time, simply fill up the dish with the sliced duck and pour the jelly over it. Refrigerate overnight. Serve on a flat dish.

braised game birds

1 pheasant, or 2–3 grouse, partridge, etc.
1 carrot
1 onion
1 leek
1 stalk celery
1½ oz/45g beef dripping, bacon fat or butter
½ pint/3dl stock
¼ pint/1.5dl red wine
1 teaspoon flour
¼ pint/1.5dl sour cream
salt and black pepper
SERVES 3–4

Preheat oven to 300°F (160°C, Gas Mark 2). Chop the carrot, onion, leek and celery. Heat the fat in a heavy casserole and add the chopped vegetables; cook them gently, stirring, for 2–3 minutes. Push to the sides of the pan and put in the pheasant (or other birds) and brown on all sides. Heat the stock with the wine and pour on to the birds. Add salt and pepper, cover the casserole and put into the oven. For well-done game, pheasant will take 1 hour, grouse 45 minutes, and partridge 35–40 minutes. Baste and turn the birds from one side to the other now and then. When done, remove from the oven and carve. Lift out the vegetables with a slotted spoon and put into a serving dish; lay the carved birds over them. Keep warm while you make the sauce: mix the flour into the sour cream in a saucepan. Measure ¼ pint/1.5dl of the cooking liquor and strain into the saucepan. Stir over gentle heat until slightly thickened and smooth. Serve in a sauceboat, with the game, or pour it over if you prefer.

Game/pheasant and pies

small game pies

It is best to use a pressure cooker for this recipe, but alternatively the birds can be roasted for 35 minutes in a moderate oven

1 *brace pheasants, or 2 grouse and* 1 *pigeon, or* 1 *pheasant and* 1 *grouse, covered with bacon by the butcher*

3 *oz/90 g butter*

2 *tablespoons brandy*

1 *stalk celery*

3 *sprigs parsley*

1 *bay leaf*

3 *oz/90 g salt pork or bacon*

12 *pearl onions*

12 *tiny carrots*

4 *small leeks*

1½ *tablespoons flour*

¾ *lb/360 g short pastry (see recipe, page* 126)

1 *egg yolk*

salt and pepper

SERVES 6–8

Put ½ oz/15 g butter inside each bird, and melt the remaining butter in the pressure cooker. Brown the birds, then flambé them with the brandy. Cut up the celery, and add with the parsley and bay leaf to the pan. Cover and cook for 15 minutes under pressure. Lift out the birds and put them on a platter. Discard the flavouring vegetables, strain the juices into a bowl, and allow the stock to settle before removing the fat. Take the meat from the bones and cut in neat pieces. Put the carcasses back into the pressure cooker, cover with water and bring to the boil; add salt and cook under pressure for one hour. Reduce the pressure, remove the lid and boil until the stock is reduced and well flavoured. Cut the salt pork or bacon in strips, peel the onions but leave them whole, cut the carrots in chunks, and thickly slice the leeks. Melt the remaining 1 oz/30 g butter in a heavy

casserole and brown the salt pork, bacon and vegetables. Add the flour, and blend. Gradually add ½ pint/3 dl strained stock and juices from the braised birds, mixed. Simmer until smooth then add the cubed meat. Let it cool while you make the pastry. Preheat oven to 375°F (190°C, Gas Mark 5). Line 6–8 small tins, such as muffin tins, with the pastry and fill with the meat and vegetable mixture, moistened with the sauce. Cover with more pastry. Beat the egg yolk and brush the pastry with it. Bake for 25 minutes.

pressure-cooked pheasant with cabbage

1 *roasting pheasant, about* 2½ *lb/1.5 kg*

1 *small white cabbage*

3 *oz/90 g butter*

salt and black pepper

SERVES 3–4

Shred the cabbage and put into boiling salted water to parboil for 5 minutes. Drain. Put 1 oz/30 g butter inside the bird and the rest of the butter into the pressure cooker, over a low heat. When the butter is melted, brown the bird on all sides. When lightly coloured all over, sprinkle with salt and pepper and cover with the shredded cabbage, adding more salt and pepper. Cover the pressure cooker and cook for 20 minutes under pressure. To serve, carve the bird and lay on a dish surrounded by the cabbage.

84

Meat/beef

sea pie

2 lb/1 kg best stewing beef	
1 large onion	
2 carrots	
2 tablespoons chopped parsley	
6 oz/180 g self-raising flour	
3 oz/90 g shredded suet	
salt and black pepper	
SERVES 4–5.	

Cut the beef in thin rectangular pieces and put into a casserole. Add salt and pepper. Thinly slice the onion and carrots and add. Cover with hot water and bring to the boil. Reduce heat, skim and simmer, covered, over low heat for 1 hour. Meanwhile make the suet paste: mix the suet into the flour with the blade of a knife, adding a pinch of salt and enough cold water to make a firm dough. Roll out to about ½ inch/1 cm thickness on a floured surface. Cut in a round slightly smaller than the circumference of the casserole, using the pot lid as a guide; lay on top of the meat and vegetables. Replace the lid and simmer for another hour. To serve, cut the pastry in four or five sections, spoon the stew into a round serving dish, and lay the pastry pieces carefully on top.

roast beef with Yorkshire pudding

joint of beef	
5 oz/150 g flour	
1 egg + 1 yolk	
8 fl oz/0.25 litre milk	
pinch of salt	

Sift the flour into a bowl and make a depression in the centre. Break in the egg and the yolk, and put the milk in a jug. Start to beat the egg with a wire whisk, gradually incorporating the flour from around the edges, at the same time pouring in the milk in a slow stream. When all the flour is amalgamated, the milk should also be absorbed. Add a pinch of salt and continue to beat for a minute or two. Stand for an hour before using. Alternatively the batter can be quickly and easily made in a food processor. To roast the beef, preheat the oven to 425°F (220°C, Gas Mark 7). For a standing rib or roast sirloin, allow 10 minutes a pound/0.5 kg. For smaller roasts, boned and rolled, allow 12 to 15 minutes a pound/0.5 kg depending on the thickness; a thin sausage-shaped cut such as a fillet will take less time than a square compact roast. If really well wrapped and enclosed with fat, the meat can be stood directly on the oven rack two-thirds of the way up the oven, with an empty pan underneath. (To prevent a dirty oven, line with aluminium foil.) Remove this pan briefly from the oven before the last 30 minutes of roasting time, pour off most of the dripping, leaving just enough to cover the bottom of the dish, and pour in the batter. Replace the pan under the meat and bake for the final half-hour. The only disadvantage of this method is that all the potential gravy is used up by the Yorkshire pudding. If preferred, at the time of putting in the Yorkshire pudding batter, the beef can be transferred to another roasting tin, and basted with a glass of red wine to mingle with its remaining juices during the last half-hour of the cooking time.

stewed beef

It has taken me literally years to work out a recipe for stewed beef that I am really pleased with; the final period of cooking time without the lid produces a delicious caramelized effect on the top layer of beef, and a thick and tasty gravy. The choice of vegetables can vary according to the season; in summertime, I usually replace the turnip and celery with fennel and green peppers

2 lb/1 kg stewing beef
1 large onion
2 carrots
1 turnip
2 stalks celery
2 cloves garlic
seasoned flour
1 oz/30 g butter
2 tablespoons olive oil
1 tablespoon tomato purée
¾ pint/4.5 dl stock and red wine, mixed
juice of 1 orange
5 sprigs parsley
dash of Tabasco (optional)
salt and black pepper
SERVES 6

Cut the beef in thin square pieces. Cut the celery, carrots and turnips in strips like matchsticks. Chop the onion coarsely. Crush the garlic. Toss the meat in some seasoned flour, coating each piece. Heat the butter and oil in a casserole and brown the meat rapidly on all sides. Remove the meat and put all the vegetables into the pan to brown. Stir around until they are pale golden then replace the meat and stir in the tomato purée. Preheat the oven to 310°F (160°C, Gas Mark 2). Heat the stock and wine in a saucepan—the proportions do not matter—and pour on to the meat with the orange juice, 3 sprigs of parsley, a dash of Tabasco and black pepper.

Cover and cook in the oven for 1 hour, then remove the lid and cook uncovered for another hour, stirring now and then. If the liquid reduces too much, replace the lid. To serve, lift out the meat with a slotted spoon and place in a shallow dish. Spoon the vegetables over it; pour over the sauce and sprinkle with the rest of the parsley, chopped. Serve with mashed potatoes.

beef olives

5–6 thin slices buttock steak or topside
2 oz/60 g shredded suet
1 oz/30 g soft breadcrumbs
½ teaspoon chopped thyme
pinch of mace
2 rashers streaky bacon
1 tablespoon chopped parsley
½ teaspoon grated orange rind
1 egg
1½ oz/45 g butter
1 onion
1 carrot
1 leek
1 stick celery
½ tablespoon flour
½ pint/3 dl hot stock
salt and black pepper
SERVES 5–6

Put the slices of beef between two layers of cling-film wrap and beat with a mallet until very thin. Trim into neat rectangular shapes; chop the trimmings and add to the suet in a large bowl; add the breadcrumbs, thyme, mace and salt and pepper. Chop the bacon and parsley and mince the orange rind and add. Beat the egg and mix well with the other ingredients. Lay the beef slices on a flat surface and put a mound of the stuffing mixture on each one. Roll them up and tie with thin string. Slice the onion, carrot, leek and celery quite thinly. Melt the butter in a sauté pan and add the four vegetables. Brown them quickly, stirring constantly. Remove them, and put in the beef olives. Brown them quickly, turning on all sides. Remove them from the pan, and sprinkle in the flour. Blend, then add the heated stock, then blend again. Add salt and pepper to taste and replace the beef olives. Cover and cook them gently for 1½ hours. To serve, cut the string and lay the olives on a bed of mashed potatoes, and spoon the sauce and vegetables over the top, or serve them separately.

steak with coriander

2 sirloin steaks
1 tablespoon coriander seeds
½ tablespoon butter
½ tablespoon light oil
1 teaspoon sea salt
1 teaspoon black peppercorns
SERVES 2

Put the coriander seeds, salt and peppercorns into a mortar. Crush roughly with the pestle, mixing well. Coat the two steaks with the mixture and leave for about an hour before cooking. Heat the butter and oil in a heavy frying pan and cook the steaks briefly on each side over high heat.

shepherd's pie

1 medium-size onion
3 oz/90 g butter
1½ lb/0.75 kg minced beef
2 teaspoons flour
½ lb/240 g carrots
1½ lb/0.75 kg potatoes
⅓ pint/2 dl milk
salt and black pepper
SERVES 4–5

Chop the onion and sauté slowly in 1 oz/30 g butter in a sauté pan with a lid. When it starts to turn golden, add the minced beef and break up with two wooden spoons. Cook slowly, stirring often, until browned. Stir in the flour and add ¾ pint/4.5 dl hot water. Simmer gently with the lid on, stirring now and then, for about 30 minutes, adding more water if needed. At the end of the cooking time, there should be a small amount of slightly thickened pan juices. Slice the carrots and boil until tender; drain, reserving, if you like, some of the carrot water for adding to the minced beef. Make the potato purée: peel the potatoes and cut in halves. Boil in plenty of salted water until tender, drain and dry well. Push through a medium food mill, return to the pan and stir over low heat to make a dry purée. Melt the remaining butter in the milk, adding lots of salt and pepper. Pour into the potato purée, beating until all is smooth. When the meat is ready, spoon it into a serving dish and cover with the sliced carrots. Pile the potato purée over all, so that it covers the dish completely. Serve immediately, or reheat briefly in the oven if necessary, or brown slightly under the grill. If made in advance, allow 35–40 minutes at 350°F (180°C, Gas Mark 4) to reheat. If preferred, a dryer purée can be made by reducing the amount of milk and browning under the grill.

Meat/beef, pork and ham

steamed meatballs

For this you will need a steamer, or one can be improvised. If using wicker steamers, one or two vegetables can be steamed at the same time on the other tiers. Alternatively, the meatballs can be poached

¾ lb/360g minced pork and veal, mixed
1 onion
pinch of cayenne pepper
4 tablespoons finely chopped parsley
1 tablespoon lemon juice
1 small egg
salt and black pepper
SERVES 4

Put the meats into a mixing bowl. Finely chop the onion, and add, with plenty of salt and pepper, and the cayenne. (Since the steaming tends to make food bland, add more seasoning than normal.) Stir in the lemon juice. Beat the egg and add. Mix well. Fry a small ball to test for seasoning. Shape into small balls the size of a pigeon's egg on a floured board. Steam over boiling water or stock for 20 minutes.

marrow and herb dumplings

1½ oz/45g beef marrow
1 egg
2 oz/60g soft white breadcrumbs
1 tablespoon finely chopped dill or parsley
2 pints/1 litre beef consommé
pinch of salt
SERVES 3

Warm the marrow slightly until it is semi-melted, then beat with a wooden spoon. Beat the egg and stir in. Continue to beat until smooth, adding a pinch of salt. Add the breadcrumbs and the chopped dill a little at a time, mixing until it forms a firm, soft dough. Leave in a cool place for 30 minutes. Form the marrow dough into tiny round balls about as big as the top of your thumb. Bring the beef consommé to the boil, drop in the dumplings, reduce heat, and simmer for 4–5 minutes, covered. The dumplings will float to the surface when cooked. Test one to be sure it is cooked in the centre. Drain, strain the liquid, then serve the bowls of beef consommé with the dumplings floating in them.

pig's trotters

1 pair pig's trotters
1 large onion
1 leek
1 large carrot
3 stalks parsley
dry breadcrumbs
butter
1 lemon
SERVES 2

A day in advance, tie the pig's trotters with string, so they will keep their shape. Put them into a pot with plenty of cold water and the vegetables, cut in large pieces, and the parsley. Bring slowly to the boil and skim until no more scum rises. Add a little salt and cover the pan. Simmer gently for 3½ hours. Meanwhile, spread some dry breadcrumbs on a tray and put them into the oven at a low heat. Stir the crumbs now and then until they are an even golden colour. Lift the pig's trotters from the pot and strain the stock, reserving it for consommé. Remove the string, cut the pig's trotters in half, and roll them in the crumbs to give an even coating. Referigerate overnight. The next day, melt the butter, and paint the pig's trotters with this. Grill them slowly, turning occasionally until nicely browned all over. Serve with mustard sauce (see recipe, page 103).

pork fillets in cider sauce

2 pork fillets
1½ oz/45g butter
1 onion
1 large cooking apple
⅓ pint/2 dl chicken stock
⅓ pint/2 dl dry cider
1 tablespoon cider vinegar or lemon juice
4 tablespoons double cream
2 tablespoons chopped parsley
salt and black pepper

SERVES 5–6

Cut the fillets in small slices and lay between two sheets of cling-film wrap. Beat until thin, like escalopes of veal. Heat the butter gently and sauté the slices in batches, until golden on each side. Keep them hot while the remainder are cooking. Meanwhile peel and chop the onion. When all the pork is done, sauté the onion until golden in the same fat. Peel and core the apple, and slice. Add to the onion. When coated with butter, replace the pork slices. Heat the stock and the cider together, and pour on, adding the vinegar or lemon juice to cut the sweetness of the cider. Cover the pan, bring to simmering point, and cook gently for 35 minutes. Lift out the meat and arrange on a heated serving dish. Blend the apples, onion and sauce in a liquidizer. Reheat, stirring in the cream. Season well and pour over the meat. Sprinkle with parsley.

pork chops with juniper berries

4 large pork chops
4 dessertspoons Dijon mustard
8 tablespoons juniper berries
4 dessertspoons sea salt

SERVES 4

Crush the berries with the salt coarsely in a mortar, or in a blender. Coat the chops with the mustard and press a layer of juniper berries and salt over each surface with a small knife. Grill slowly, turning carefully and trying not to dislodge the coating. Serve at once with a creamy purée of potatoes and a crisp lettuce salad.

boiled ham with parsley sauce

one 2½–3 lb/2.25–2.5 kg back bacon or corner of gammon, soaked overnight if very salty
1 large onion
1 large carrot
1 leek
2 stalks celery
1 bay leaf
3 cloves
1 oz/30g butter
1½ tablespoons flour
4 tablespoons cream
3 tablespoons finely chopped parsley
1 hard-boiled egg, chopped
pinch of mace
pepper

SERVES 5–6

Put the ham into a large pan, cover with cold water and bring to the boil. Unless you have soaked the ham overnight, repeat the process, with fresh water. Skim off any scum that rises to the top. Cut up the vegetables in large pieces and add to the pan, with the bay leaf and cloves. Simmer gently for 1¾ hours, or until tender when the ham is pierced with a skewer. Lift out, slice and keep warm. Strain the cooking liquid. Melt the butter, blend in the flour, then add the strained stock and blend; simmer for 3 minutes, adding mace and pepper. Stir in the cream, parsley and egg. Pour half of the sauce over the ham and serve the rest separately.

Meat/veal, lamb and liver

veal with apricots

6 *slices knuckle of veal, or 2½ lb/1.25 kg boneless pie veal*
3–4 *tablespoons olive oil*
½ *Spanish onion*
2 *cloves garlic*
1 *green pepper*
1 *red pepper*
2 *oz/60g fresh ginger*
pinch of saffron
½ *teaspoon cumin*
½ *teaspoon coriander*
¼ *lb/120g dried apricots, soaked*
1 *oz/30g butter*
1 *tablespoon flour*
juice of ½ orange
salt and black pepper
SERVES 5–6

Brown the veal in the oil in a casserole. When lightly browned on both sides, add the sliced onion, finely chopped garlic, peppers cut in strips, finely chopped ginger, salt, pepper, saffron, ground cumin and coriander. Add enough hot water to almost cover the meat, put on the lid and simmer gently for 1¼ hours, stirring occasionally. Have the apricots soaked if necessary (if they are soft enough to eat raw, do not bother to soak them). Chop them and add to the stew. Cook for a further 15 minutes, until all is tender, then lift out the veal and put into a serving dish. Lift out the vegetables and apricots with a slotted spoon and keep warm in a separate dish. Strain the sauce and reduce if necessary by fast boiling. Melt the butter in a clean pan and stir in the flour. Cook for one minute then stir in the strained sauce. Stir over gentle heat for 3–4 minutes, until smooth and well blended, then add the juice of ½ orange. Pour over the veal in its dish, then scatter the sliced vegetables over the top.

Lancashire hotpot

This excellent old English dish is made with the same ingredients as Irish stew, but Irish stew is cooked covered for the whole time, usually on top of the stove, and ends up a much more liquid dish

2–2½ *lb/1–1.23 kg best end neck of lamb*
2–3 *tablespoons flour*
1 *lb/0.5 kg onions*
½ *pint/3 dl stock—chicken or beef, or made from the lamb trimmings*
1½ *lb/0.75 kg potatoes*
salt and black pepper
SERVES 4

Ask the butcher to divide the best end in cutlets, but not to trim them. Season the flour with salt and pepper and drop each piece of lamb into the flour. Transfer to a buttered fireproof dish. (The traditional hotpot dish was deep and round but a shallower earthenware sort can also be used.) Slice the onions and scatter them over the meat. Make either 1 or 2 layers of meat and onions according to the shape of the dish. Season each layer with salt and plenty of pepper. Add the stock. Preheat the oven to 300°F (160°C, Gas Mark 2). Peel the potatoes and cut in thick slices; lay these over the entire surface of the dish, overlapping to form a sort of lid. Cover the dish with foil or a lid and bake for 2 hours. Remove the cover, turn up the heat to 350°F (180°C, Gas Mark 4), and bake for a further 30 minutes.

bargee's dinner

Place a platform of sticks, or flat stones, in the bottom of a galvanised iron bucket. Half-fill it with water and bring to the boil over a bonfire or simple stove. Fill a large earthenware jar that has a lid with layers of lamb, cut in neat pieces with most of the fat removed, and a selection of vegetables cleaned and cut in large chunks: carrots, leeks, small whole onions, potatoes and turnips. Add salt and black pepper to each layer, and a handful of pearl barley, distributing it evenly throughout the layers, together with plenty of chopped parsley. Pour in enough water to fill the jar by about two-thirds. Make a thick paste of flour and water to seal the lid completely and tie a piece of cloth over the top. Place the jar in the bucket, and after the water regains boiling point, allow 2½–3 hours cooking time. Care must be taken to maintain a good heat, for the water must not go off the boil. A muslin bag, or even two, can be cooked in the pail at the same time. It could contain a pease pudding or haricot beans; these should be soaked beforehand, and will take about 1½ hours to cook, so should be added about 1 hour after the stew has started to cook.

Moroccan lamb with pears

1½ lb/0.75 kg boneless lamb (half a boned shoulder)

½ Spanish onion

1–2 green peppers

1–2 heads fennel

seasoned flour

3 tablespoons olive oil

¾ pint/4.5 dl chicken or veal stock

pinch of saffron

¼ lb/120g dried pears, soaked

2 tablespoons lemon juice

salt and black pepper

SERVES 4

Cut the lamb in neat pieces. Slice the onion, cut the peppers in strips and the fennel in thin slices. Toss the lamb in seasoned flour and brown in the oil. Remove the lamb and add

the sliced vegetables to the pan. Stir while they cook gently, until lightly coloured. Replace the meat and pour on the heated stock. Add a pinch of saffron and salt and pepper to taste. Cover the pan and simmer for 1 hour. Then add the dried pears, cut in strips. (These may not need soaking; if they seem soft and chewy already, do not bother.) Cook for a further 15 minutes until soft, then stir in the lemon juice and serve with a dish of couscous or boiled rice.

liver and bacon

4 thin slices calf's liver

8 rashers streaky bacon

½ lb/0.5 kg rice

3 oz/90g butter

2 large onions

5 tomatoes

salt and black pepper

SERVES 4

Cook the rice in plenty of boiling salted water until tender; drain well. Slice the onions. Melt 2 oz/60g butter in a large pan and sauté the onions slowly until they are well browned. Meanwhile, in another pan fry the bacon. Add the rice to the onions and stir until well mixed, adding salt and pepper to taste. When the bacon is crisp, remove it, add a little butter to the pan and fry the calf's liver briefly; about 2 minutes on each side. Remove the liver and bacon and keep hot. Cut the tomatoes in half and fry them in the same pan. To serve, put the rice on a large flat dish and lay the liver and bacon on it, with the tomatoes around the edges. Serve with broccoli or string beans.

large sausage roll

1 *poaching sausage, about ¾ lb/360g*

½ *lb/240g short pastry (see recipe, page* 126*)*

1 *egg yolk*

SERVES 2–3

Poach the sausage gently by covering it with hot water in a pan that is long enough to allow it to lie straight. Bring to the boil and simmer gently for 50 minutes. Take it out and leave to get cold, when it will stiffen and be easier to handle. Meanwhile make the pastry and chill in the refrigerator. Roll out the pastry into a rectangle and lay the sausage on it. Trim it to fit and wrap loosely round the sausage, sealing firmly and decorating as liked. Beat the egg yolk and brush the pastry with this. Bake for 30 minutes at 350°F (180°C, Gas Mark 4). Serve hot cut in slices, with a mustard sauce (see recipe, page 103). This also makes a good hors d'oeuvre, in which case it will serve 3–4.

toad-in-the-hole

This should be served with chopped cabbage, or a similar vegetable, and some good mustard

1 *lb/0.5 kg pure pork chipolatas*

6 *oz/180g flour*

2 *large eggs*

½ *pint/3 dl milk*

SERVES 4

The batter can be quickly made in a food processor, but if making it by hand, sift the flour into a large bowl and make a hole in the centre. Drop in the eggs, and beat with a wire whisk, pouring in the milk in a thin stream with your other hand as you beat. Gradually incorporate the flour from around the edges into the beaten eggs, still pouring in the milk. When all is amalgamated, continue to beat for

a couple of minutes, then stand in a cool place for 1 hour. Preheat the oven to 400°F (200°C, Gas Mark 6). Beat the batter again well, then pour a thin layer into a shallow rectangular baking dish which has been well greased and put in the oven for 5 minutes, or until set. Lay the sausages on it in one layer, then pour the remaining batter over them. Put into the oven for 30 minutes, then turn down the heat to 325°F (170°C, Gas Mark 3) and bake for another 15 minutes.

sausages with peppers

This excellent dish needs no other accompaniment, except possibly some good home-made bread

1½ *lb/0.75 kg pure pork sausages, mild or highly seasoned, large or small*

1 *lb/0.5 kg peppers, (mixed green, red and yellow, if possible)*

1 *oz/30g butter*

1 *tablespoon olive oil*

2 *shallots*

1 *clove garlic*

½ *tablespoon flour*

¼ *pint/1.5 dl white wine*

¼ *pint/1.5 dl chicken stock*

salt and black pepper

SERVES 4

Heat the butter and oil in a sauté pan. Chop the shallots and sauté them slowly. Mince the garlic, and add. Cut the peppers in strips, and cook slowly for five minutes, stirring. Add the sausages, browning them quickly on all sides. Blend in the flour. Heat the wine and stock together in a small saucepan, and stir in. Cover the pan and simmer for 15–20 minutes. Transfer to a serving dish.

sausages in vegetable sauce

1½ lb/0.75 kg thin pure pork sausages

¾ lb/360 g leeks

½ lb/240 g turnips

¼ lb/120 g carrots

1 small onion

1 oz/30 g butter

½ tablespoon flour

2 teaspoons Dijon mustard

¼ pint/1.5 dl cider

2 tablespoons sour cream

salt and black pepper

SERVES 4

Parboil the leeks, turnips and carrots separately, but in the same water, until almost tender. Keep the cooking water. Chop the onion. Melt the butter in a heavy frying pan and sauté the onion, stirring frequently, until softened. Add the flour and the mustard, and stir in. Measure ¼ pint/1.5 dl of the vegetable cooking liquid, mix with the cider and add to the pan, stirring. Chop the cooked vegetables coarsely in a food processor, or push through a coarse food mill. Stir them into the sauce and blend. Add salt and pepper to taste. Brown the sausages briefly in a lightly greased frying pan, and add to the sauce. Cover the pan and simmer for 20 minutes, stirring now and then. Transfer the sausages to a serving dish. Stir the sour cream into the sauce, pour the mixture over the sausages, and serve with boiled potatoes.

sausages with haricot beans

1½ lb/0.75 kg saucisses de Toulouse
or other large pork sausages

½ lb/240 g dried haricot beans, soissons
or cannellini

1 oz/30 g butter

1 tablespoon olive oil

1 medium onion, chopped

1 clove garlic

one 8 oz/240 g tin peeled Italian tomatoes

salt and black pepper

SERVES 4

Soak the beans for 3–4 hours in plenty of cold water, or put them into a pan, cover with cold water, and bring to the boil; turn off the heat and leave, covered, for 1 hour. Drain and cover with fresh water, bring to the boil, reduce heat, cover and simmer until tender, ¾–1½ hours, depending on the beans. Add salt towards the end of the cooking time. When the beans are tender, drain the water off and reserve it for soup. Cover the pan and leave the beans until the sausages are cooked. Melt the butter with the oil in a sauté pan and sauté the chopped onion until pale golden. Chop the garlic and add it halfway through. Add the tomatoes, and chop them up roughly with a palette knife. Brown the sausages quickly in another frying pan, turning until evenly coloured, then add them to the pan with the tomatoes, and cover the pan. Cook slowly for 30 minutes, turning them from time to time and adding a few drops of stock, tomato juice or water if the pan gets dry. At the end of the cooking time, lift out the sausages and keep warm. Add the beans to the tomato sauce and cook gently for 3–4 minutes, stirring, until well heated through. Add salt and pepper as needed. Pour the sauce into a heated serving dish and lay the sausages carefully on top and serve.

Meat/sausages

pork sausages

10oz/300g lean pork (from the leg)
10oz/300g belly of pork
3oz/90g brown breadcrumbs
6 tablespoons milk
2 cloves garlic
12 juniper berries
¼ teaspoon mace
¼ teaspoon allspice or quatre épices
4 large leaves fresh sage or 1½ tablespoons fresh basil, chopped (or if neither fresh herb is available, use ½ teaspoon dried sage and ½ teaspoon dried oregano)
1½ tablespoons chopped parsley
2 teaspoons sea salt
1 teaspoon black peppercorns
wide casings
MAKES 1½lb/0.75kg

Cut the lean pork in cubes and put through a mincer, or use a food processor (the processor will give a better, coarser texture). Separate the fat from the lean belly of pork and grind or process the lean; chop the fat in tiny dice. Mix the meats together in a large bowl. Put the breadcrumbs into a small bowl and pour the milk over them; leave for 10 minutes, then squeeze out the milk and add the bread to the meat. Mix well. Chop the garlic roughly and put into a mortar with the salt, peppercorns and juniper berries. Mash roughly with the pestle, only until coarsely crushed. Stir into the meat mixture and add the mace and allspice or *quatre épices*. Add the fresh or dried herbs and stir in. When all the mixture is well blended, test for seasoning by frying a little ball of it. Then fill the casings according to the directions. These need slow cooking, under the broiler, in a frying pan or for 30 minutes in a 350°F (180°C, Gas Mark 4) oven.

veal sausages

These sausages can be grilled, fried or roasted. They are a trifle expensive to make, but extremely good for a treat. I like to serve them with a dish of brown lentils, or a purée of spinach, or creamed onions

¾ lb/360g belly of pork
½ lb/240g lean veal, from the leg, loin or shoulder
2oz/60g hard back fat (if available)
4 tablespoons vermouth or dry white wine
4 tablespoons soft white breadcrumbs
1 tablespoon chopped shallot
1½ tablespoons soft green peppercorns
½ teaspoon allspice or quatre épices
¼ teaspoon mace
1oz/30g pistachio nuts
2 teaspoons sea salt
wide casings
MAKES 1½lb/0.75kg

Put the lean part of the belly in a food processor or through a mincer with the veal. Cut the fat part of the belly of pork and the back fat (if you have been able to get it) in tiny cubes. Mix all the meats together. Pour the vermouth over the crumbs and leave for 10 minutes, then squeeze out and add to the mixture. Stir in the chopped shallot, the salt, whole green peppercorns, the ground spices and, lastly, the pistachio nuts, roughly chopped. When all the ingredients are well mixed, force them into the casings.

candied sweet potatoes

6 *sweet potatoes or yams*

6 *oz*/180*g brown sugar*

4 *tablespoons orange juice*

1½ *oz*/45*g butter*

2 *cloves*

SERVES 5–6

Boil the sweet potatoes in their skins until tender, 30–40 minutes. Peel and slice diagonally. Lay them in a buttered gratin dish. Heat the brown sugar, orange juice, butter and cloves in a small pan. Boil gently for 5 minutes. Preheat the oven to 375°F (190°C, Gas Mark 5). Remove the cloves and use the syrup to baste the potatoes while they bake for 30 minutes.

spiced sweet potatoes

Buy the sweet potatoes with red or pink skins and white flesh, rather than the Jamaican variety with orange flesh

1 *lb*/0.5 *kg sweet potatoes*

1 *oz*/30*g butter*

1–2 *tablespoons oil*

allspice

salt and black pepper

SERVES 3–4

Peel the potatoes and cut in thin slices. Fry until golden brown in a mixture of butter and oil, turning them frequently with a spatula so that they are nicely browned and even slightly burnt in places. When soft, season with salt, lots of freshly ground black pepper, and a good sprinkling of allspice.

pommes Anna

1 *lb*/0.5 *kg waxy potatoes*

1½ *oz*/45*g butter*

salt and black pepper

SERVES 4

Thickly butter a round cake tin, preferably with a loose bottom. Peel the potatoes and slice them thinly and evenly. Preheat the oven to 350°F (180°C, Gas Mark 4). Lay the slices of potato in overlapping layers, and dot each layer with butter, salt and pepper. When the tin is full press the mixture down firmly and cover with a buttered piece of foil. Bake for 1 hour, and turn the dish from time to time so that the potatoes cook evenly. Turn out on to a flat platter and serve in slices.

hot potato salad

1½ *lb*/45*g waxy potatoes*

2 *tablespoons white wine vinegar*

½ *pint*/3 *dl sour cream*

1 *oz*/30*g butter*

1 *small onion*

3 *rashers streaky bacon*

2 *tablespoons chopped chives*

salt and black pepper

SERVES 4

Boil the potatoes in their skins and drain. Peel and slice them thickly while still hot. Stir the vinegar into the sour cream and pour over the potatoes. Stir gently. Chop the onion and soften in the butter, adding the chopped bacon. When all is crisp and lightly browned, lift out with a slotted spoon and add to the potato. Add salt and pepper to taste. Scatter chopped chives over and serve immediately.

gratin dauphinois

This is excellent with roast lamb

1½ lb/0.75 kg waxy potatoes

1 egg

¾ pint/4.5 dl milk

1 clove garlic, crushed

grated nutmeg

a little butter

salt and black pepper

SERVES 5–6

Preheat the oven to 350°F (180°C, Gas Mark 4). Peel the potatoes and slice them thinly and evenly. Beat the egg, stir in the milk and the crushed clove of garlic, with salt and black pepper to taste, and a little grated nutmeg. Pour over the sliced potatoes and turn them into a buttered gratin dish. Dot the potatoes with butter and bake for 1 hour.

parsnip and potato purée

Excellent with grilled steaks, lamb chops or roast meat. A purée of parsnips alone is delicious, but must be made with even more care to prevent it being watery; the addition of potato helps to dry it out

1 lb/0.5 kg parsnips

1 lb/0.5 kg floury potatoes

2 oz/60 g butter

salt and black pepper

Peel the parsnips and cover them with cold water. Add salt, bring to the boil and cook until just tender but not mushy. Drain well and dry out by stirring over gentle heat. Push through the medium mesh of a food mill. Boil the potatoes, dry out also, then push through the same mill on top of the parsnips. Mix together, stirring, over low heat until dry and blended. Stir in the butter in small pieces and add plenty of salt and black pepper. Add a little double cream if you have it.

potato gnocchi

1 lb/0.5 kg potatoes

2 oz/60 g butter

1 egg + 1 yolk

2½ oz/75 g flour

grated nutmeg

salt and black pepper

SERVES 4

Boil the potatoes, drain and dry them well, then push them through a food mill. Cut the butter in small pieces and beat the eggs, and add them with the flour, salt, black pepper and a little grated nutmeg. Handle the mixture lightly and form it in little oval shapes about 1 inch/2.5 cm long, and flatten slightly in the middle with a finger. Drop into boiling salted water and poach for 5 minutes, then lift out and drain on soft paper while you cook the next batch. Do not do too many at once. Transfer to a heated dish and cover with a good tomato sauce. Serve with a green salad or a dish of vegetables.

green gnocchi with tomato sauce

1 lb/0.5 kg spinach

1 oz/30 g butter

6 oz/180 g ricotta

3 oz/90 g grated Fontina or Gruyère cheese

2 eggs

2½ tablespoons flour

salt and pepper

sauce:

1 oz/30 g butter

1 small onion

one 14 oz/420 g tin peeled tomatoes

pinch of sugar

salt and black pepper

SERVES 3–4

Cook the spinach in boiling salted water until just tender; drain well. Chop the spinach until reduced to a fine purée. Dry out as much as possible by stirring over gentle heat in a heavy pan. Cut the butter into small pieces, beat the ricotta with a wooden spoon; add them to the spinach with the salt and pepper. Then beat in 1oz/30g of the grated Fontina or Gruyère cheese. When all is smooth, turn off the heat, beat the eggs, sift the flour and stir them in. Beat until smooth, then pour into a shallow dish and leave to cool. Put it, uncovered, in the refrigerator overnight. The next day it will have become thicker and more solid. If not, it means the purée was too moist, so beat in a little extra flour. Shape with two teaspoons, and roll lightly into egg shapes on a floured board. Bring a large pan of lightly salted water to the boil and drop in the gnocchi. Do not put too many in as they are better cooked in several batches. Lift out with a slotted spoon after 4–5 minutes, when they float to the top. Test one to make sure it is cooked through. Drain them on a cloth, then transfer them to a shallow serving dish and keep warm, while you cook the sauce. Melt the butter and cook the chopped onion until a pale golden colour. Stir in the tomatoes, chopping them roughly with the edge of a palette knife. Simmer gently for about 12 minutes or until reduced to a mush, adding salt and pepper and a pinch of sugar. Pour over the gnocchi and serve.

artichokes mornay

1½ lb/0.75 kg Jerusalem artichokes
⅓ pint/2 dl milk
½ bay leaf
1 slice onion
2 cloves
2 oz/60 g butter
3 tablespoons flour
¼ pint/1.5 dl single cream
¼ lb/120 g grated Gruyère cheese
salt and black pepper
SERVES 4–5

Brush the artichokes well under the tap and put into a pan of cold water. Add salt, bring to the boil, and cook until tender when pierced with a skewer. Drain and peel as soon as they are cool enough to handle, reserving ½ pint/3 dl of the cooking water. Cut the artichokes in thick slices and put them into a shallow fireproof dish. Keep them warm. Meanwhile, make the sauce. Heat the milk with the bay leaf, onion and cloves. Cover just before it boils and take off the heat. Leave for 15 minutes. Melt the butter, stir in the flour, and blend with the reserved cooking water and the strained milk. Simmer until thickened and smooth, add the cream, and salt and black pepper to taste. Stir in the grated cheese, keeping a little to scatter over the top, and stir until blended with the sauce. Pour the sauce over the artichokes, sprinkle with the rest of the cheese, and brown under the grill. Alternatively, prepare in advance and reheat for 20–25 minutes in the oven at 400°F (200°C, Gas Mark 6).

Vegetables/greens, peas and beans

cabbage with cumin

1 green cabbage
approx ½ pint/3dl milk
a little butter
⅓ teaspoon ground cumin
salt and black pepper

SERVES 4

Use only the tender heart of the green cabbage. Thinly slice it and cook it in a pan with enough milk to come level. Simmer very gently, allowing about twice as long as usual for the cabbage to become soft. Drain, and add a knob of butter, salt, black pepper and the ground cumin before serving.

green pancakes with tomato filling

batter:
¼ lb/120g spinach
¼ lb/120g flour
1 egg
¼ pint/1.5dl milk
a pinch of salt
filling:
1 lb/0.5kg tomatoes
1 oz/30g butter
2 teaspoons flour
a pinch of sugar
¼ pint/1.5dl sour cream
salt and black pepper

SERVES 4–5

Make the batter in advance. If you have a juice extractor, put the spinach in this, which will give you approximately 4 tablespoons juice. If you have no juice extractor, cook the spinach and push through a fine food mill with the cooking water, to give a thin purée; take 4 tablespoons and cool. Put the flour into a bowl and make a hole in the middle. Add a pinch of salt and break the egg into the hole. Beat with a whisk, drawing flour from the edges gradually into the centre, at the same time pouring on the milk. When all the milk is absorbed add the spinach juice and beat until amalgamated. Alternatively the batter can be quickly made in a food processor. Stand for an hour before using. Meanwhile, make the filling. Skin and chop the tomatoes. Soften them by cooking very briefly, about 5 minutes, in the butter. Add the flour and stir until amalgamated, then add the salt, pepper and sugar. Stir in the sour cream and cook gently until blended and heated, stirring continuously. Cover and put aside in a warm place. Beat the batter thoroughly and make about 10 small pancakes. Roll each one round some of the filling and serve immediately.

dried pease pudding

This is delicious when served with sausages or boiled bacon

½ lb/240g split peas
1½ oz/45g butter
1 large egg, beaten
salt and black pepper

SERVES 4

Split peas do not need soaking, but if you are using whole dried peas soak them for 3–4 hours first. Cover the peas in lightly salted water and cook until tender, or tie them loosely in a muslin bag and cook in the same pot as a piece of bacon for 1–1½ hours, or until soft. Drain them well and push through the coarse mesh of a vegetable mill or put into a food processor. Cut the butter in small bits and mix it in with the beaten egg. Season well with plenty of salt and freshly ground black pepper. Form the mixture in a ball, wrap it tightly in a muslin cloth and tie with a string, leaving long ends to lift it in and out of the pan. Lower the bag into a pan of fast-boiling water, preferably with a piece of bacon already cooking in it, and cook for 1 hour. To serve, untie the cloth and turn the pudding out carefully into a round dish.

three bean salad

¼ lb/120g *French or Italian dried haricot beans*
¼ lb/120g *green dried flageolets*
¼ lb/120g *red kidney beans*
olive oil
white wine vinegar
1 *Spanish onion*
4 *tablespoons chopped parsley*
salt and black pepper
SERVES 4–6

Each of the three types of beans must be cooked separately. Either soak them in separate bowls for 2–3 hours, or bring them to the boil in a pan covered with cold water. Turn off the heat and leave covered for 1 hour. Then drain away the water, cover with fresh cold water and cook until tender, adding salt only towards the end of the cooking. When the beans are tender, drain them in a colander and rinse them briefly under the tap. Mix all the beans together in a bowl and add salt and black pepper. Add enough olive oil to moisten well without leaving a pool in the bottom of the bowl, and about one-third as much wine vinegar. Cut the Spanish onion in quarters, then cut each piece in thin slices, and divide each slice into thin strips. Stir into the beans and mix well. Add the chopped parsley, stirring in some of it, and leaving some on top as a garnish. This salad is best eaten within an hour or so of cooking, before it has completely cooled.

vegetarian casserole

4–5 oz/120–150g *buckwheat or couscous*
2 *tablespoons oil*
1 oz/30g *butter*
1 *large onion*
2 *leeks*
2 *carrots*
3 *courgettes*
½ lb/240g *tomatoes*
1 *egg*
1 *tablespoon flour*
½ pint/3 dl *yoghourt*
salt and black pepper
SERVES 4

Cook the buckwheat or couscous according to the directions on the packet. Put the cooked buckwheat or couscous in the bottom of a buttered casserole. Slice the onion and leeks. Heat the oil and butter in a sauté pan and cook the onion and leeks until soft and lightly coloured. Slice the carrots and parboil them until almost tender; drain. Chop the unpeeled courgettes and add to the onion and leeks; cover the pan and simmer gently for 4 minutes, then add the sliced carrots and a little of their cooking water. Stew gently for another 3–4 minutes. Peel and thickly slice the tomatoes and add. Cook very briefly, then season well with salt and pepper and pour over the grain in the casserole. Preheat the oven to 350°F (180°C, gas mark 4). Beat the egg, stir in the flour and beat into the yoghourt. Add salt and pepper to taste and pour over the vegetables. Cover the pan and bake for 30 minutes. Serve with a green salad.

Vegetables/beans and lentils

haricot beans with garlic butter

This is a delicious accompaniment to a
casserole of beef, with a simple lettuce salad

½ lb/240g *haricot beans, soisson or cannellini*

1 *onion*

1 *carrot*

1 *stalk celery*

½ *bay leaf*

¼ lb/120g *unsalted butter, at room temperature*

2 *cloves garlic*

2 *tablespoons finely chopped parsley, and a few*
parsley stalks

1 *tablespoon lemon juice*

sea salt and black pepper

SERVES 4–5

Put the beans into a saucepan and cover
generously with cold water. Bring them
slowly to the boil, turn off the heat, cover the
pan and leave for 1 hour. Alternatively, soak
the beans for 3–4 hours. In either case, throw
away the water, cover with fresh cold water,
add the halved onion, carrot and celery, the
bay leaf and a few parsley stalks. Bring to the
boil and simmer until tender, adding some sea
salt towards the end of the cooking.
Meanwhile make garlic butter. Pound the
butter in a mortar until it is a smooth cream. If
you have no mortar you can bash it to a cream
in a bowl with the back of a wooden spoon.
Alternatively it can be quickly made in a food
processor. Put the garlic into a press, or mince
it very finely, and add to the butter. Continue
pounding until amalgamated into a smooth
paste. Add the finely chopped parsley, lemon
juice to taste, and freshly ground black
pepper. Scoop into a ball and chill in the
refrigerator until needed. When the beans are
tender, drain them and discard the flavouring
vegetables. Put the beans into a clean pan and
reheat, stirring in the garlic butter carefully in
fairly small pieces.

curried lentils

Any lentils can be used for this dish, except
for the English orange lentil, which I find
tasteless and mushy. Yellow split peas are
excellent cooked in this way. Curried lentils
are good with grilled pork sausages, hot boiled
bacon, or hard-boiled eggs

½ lb/240g *lentils, brown, green, or yellow*

2 *onions*

3 *tablespoons oil*

1 *clove garlic, crushed*

1 *teaspoon garam masala*

½ *teaspoon mustard seed*

½ *teaspoon ground turmeric*

½ *teaspoon ground ginger*

¼ *teaspoon chilli powder*

a few fresh coriander leaves, or

½ *teaspoon ground coriander*

sea salt

SERVES 3–4

Pick over the lentils carefully and put them
into a saucepan with 2 pints/1 litre cold water.
Bring to the boil and simmer until the lentils
are soft, the water almost boiled away. Add
some sea salt halfway through the cooking.
Slice the onions and cook them in a frying pan
in the oil until soft and golden. Add the garlic
and spices and cook for another 5 minutes,
stirring often. When the lentils are ready –
reduced to a thick, soupy consistency – stir in
the onions and spices. Reheat, stirring all the
time. When available, chop a few fresh
coriander leaves and add at this stage.
Otherwise add ½ teaspoon ground coriander
with the other spices.

spiced lentils

These are best served with hot hard-boiled eggs and grilled rashers of back bacon

1 *medium onion*
1½ *oz/45g butter*
1 *large clove garlic*
1 *teaspoon ground coriander*
½ *teaspoon ground cumin*
½ *teaspoon ground ginger*
¼ *teaspoon ground chilli*
¼ *teaspoon ground turmeric*
½ *lb/240g brown lentils*
½ *teaspoon salt*

SERVES 3–4

Chop the onion and cook it gently in butter in a sauté pan that has a lid. Add the crushed garlic and spices, then carefully pick over, wash and drain the lentils and add them also. Stir around now and then for 5 minutes, then pour on 1½ pints/9dl hot water and cover the pan. Simmer for about 35 minutes, until the lentils are soft and the water absorbed. Add salt and more spices if needed before serving.

lentil vinaigrette with smoked sausage

½ *lb/240g continental lentils*
¼ *Spanish onion*
3 *tablespoons olive oil*
1 *tablespoon white wine vinegar*
2 *pepperoni, kabanos or frankfurter sausages*
salt and black pepper

SERVES 3–4 AS A FIRST COURSE OR
2–3 AS A MAIN COURSE

Cover the lentils in water; bring to the boil, then reduce the heat and simmer until cooked; drain well. While they are still hot, add salt and black pepper to taste. Cut the onion in thin slices and stir in. Add the oil and vinegar and mix well. Cut the pepperoni or kabanos in thick slices and stir into the lentils, scattering some over the top. If using frankfurters, heat them before slicing by pouring boiling water over them; stand for 5 minutes, then drain and slice. This dish should be served as soon as possible after making, while it is still warm.

Esau's potage (a lentil and rice stew)

This comforting dish is excellent as an accompaniment to hard-boiled eggs, gammon steaks, grilled sausages or pork chops

½ *lb/240g brown lentils*
¼ *lb/120g long grain rice*
1 *large onion*
3 *tablespoons olive oil*
1 *tablespoon sea salt*

SERVES 4

Pick over the lentils well, and put them into a pan with 2 pints/ 1 litre water. Bring to the boil and simmer. Wash the rice in a colander, and when the lentils are nearly tender, after about 35 minutes cooking, add the rice. Continue cooking until both rice and lentils are soft. Meanwhile chop the onion and fry it in the oil until pale golden, then add to the lentils and rice at the end of their cooking time. Cook for another 5–10 minutes, then serve. It may be necessary to add a little extra water if it gets too thick. This is best eaten immediately, but is also good eaten warm, or even cold. In this case, however, it must be made a lot thinner by adding more liquid, for it thickens considerably on cooling.

hummus

½ lb/240g chick-peas

1–2 cloves garlic

¼ pint/1.5dl tahini

¼ pint/1.5dl lemon juice

1 tablespoon olive (or sesame) oil

paprika

salt and black pepper

SERVES 4–6

Soak the chick-peas for 6–8 hours or overnight. Drain them and cover with plenty of fresh cold water. Bring to the boil and simmer for 2 hours or until they are soft. Keep an eye on them as it may be necessary to add more water from time to time. Add some salt after about 1 hour. When soft, drain them and keep the cooking stock. Push them through the medium mesh of a food mill, or pound to a paste in a mortar. Alternatively this can be done very quickly in a food processor. Add some of the cooking liquid to thin the mixture, which should be about the same consistency as double cream. Crush the garlic and beat it into the paste, then add the tahini and lemon juice alternately by degrees, beating in each addition until blended. When the mixture is well blended, taste for seasoning and add more salt if needed. Adjust the consistency by adding more stock if required, then pour on to a flat dish. Pour a thin film of olive or sesame oil over the top and sprinkle with paprika. Accompany with hot pitta bread. Hummus keeps well and if made in advance should be kept in a covered jar in the refrigerator with a film of oil (or oiled greaseproof paper) over the top. Before serving, beat the oil into the purée, spread on a dish and cover with a fresh film of oil.

fruit curry

1 medium onion

2oz/60g butter

1 tablespoon light curry powder

1 tablespoon flour

¾ pint/4.5dl chicken or vegetable stock

2 tablespoons lemon juice

2 tablespoons orange juice

1 tablespoon red currant or crab apple jelly

1oz/30g coarsely chopped almonds

3 firm bananas

½ honeydew melon

½ lb/240g tomatoes

SERVES 4–6

Chop the onion and cook gently in the butter until golden. Add the curry powder and flour and stir for 2–3 minutes. Heat the stock and pour on. Stir until blended, then simmer gently for 12 minutes, stirring now and then. Push the jelly through a small sieve and add it with the fruit juices and the nuts. Simmer for another 3 minutes. Cut the bananas in thick slices, and the melon in cubes. Peel the tomatoes, and cut them in eighths. Add them to the mixture and simmer for a few moments, until all is well heated and mixed. Serve with boiled rice.

Sauces/mustard and horseradish

mustard sauce

This is particularly good with shellfish

3 *tablespoons single cream*
¼ *pint/1.5dl mayonnaise*
3 *tablespoons Dijon mustard*
1 *teaspoon lemon juice*
dash of Tabasco
pinch cayenne
salt and black pepper
SERVES 4–5

Mix the cream into the mayonnaise, then add the mustard, lemon juice and Tabasco and season to taste as required.

foamy mustard sauce

Serve with English pork sausages, as opposed to continental ones which are too rich for a creamy sauce, or grilled pork chops

1 *oz/30g butter*
1½ *tablespoons flour*
1½ *teaspoons Dijon mustard*
¾ *pint/4.5dl milk*
1 *teaspoon white wine vinegar*
1 *teaspoon lemon juice*
2 *tablespoons double cream*
1 *egg white*
salt and black pepper

Melt the butter, stir in the flour and blend. Add the mustard and stir until smooth. Heat the milk and pour on, stirring until blended. Add salt and pepper to taste, then add the vinegar and lemon juice. Stir in the cream. Pour into a bowl and cool for a moment while you beat the egg white. When stiff, fold it into the sauce and serve immediately.

mustard mayonnaise

Serve with grilled shellfish

2 *hard-boiled egg yolks*
2 *raw egg yolks*
1 *tablespoon Dijon mustard*
½ *pint/3dl olive oil*
1½ *tablespoons tarragon vinegar*
1½ *tablespoons white wine vinegar*
4 *tablespoons sour cream*
salt and black pepper
SERVES 4–6

Mash the hard-boiled egg yolks with a fork and put them in a mortar or heavy bowl. Add the raw egg yolks and pound with a pestle or the back of a wooden spoon until well blended. Add a pinch of salt and black pepper and stir in the mustard. Add the oil drop by drop as for an ordinary mayonnaise, thinning with the vinegars from time to time. When all is mixed in, taste for seasoning; it should be quite mustardy and tart. Stir in the sour cream and blend well.

horseradish and apple sauce

Serve with cold roast goose, duck or pork

2 *Bramley apples*
¼ *pint/1.5dl sour cream*
3–4 *tablespoons grated horseradish*
1 *teaspoon lemon juice*

Make an unsweetened purée with the apples: stew them in a little water then push them through the coarse mesh of a food mill. Cool, then stir in the sour cream. Gradually stir in the grated horseradish until the flavour is strong enough. The apple and horseradish should be evenly balanced so that neither predominates. Add a little lemon juice to taste. Chill and serve.

Sauces/fruit and nut

apple sauce

Serve hot, warm or cold with sausages, pork chops, roast pork or duck

2 Bramley apples

1 tablespoon sugar

1 teaspoon lemon juice

Peel and core the apples and cut them into thick slices. Put them in a small pan with just enough water to cover the bottom. Add the sugar and simmer until the apples are soft and mushy. Either leave as it is, breaking it up with the edge of a wooden spoon, or push through a food mill, or, for a really smooth sauce, put the mixture in a blender. Stir in the lemon juice and a little butter if you like.

cranberry sauce

Serve with hot or cold roast turkey, goose, duck or chicken. It is also good with hot or cold ham, pork and cold spiced beef

½ lb/240g cranberries

¼ lb/120g sugar

1 tablespoon orange juice

1 teaspoon grated orange rind

Pick over the berries and wash well. Put ½ pint/3dl water in a heavy pan with the sugar and boil until the sugar has melted. Put in the berries and simmer for about 3 minutes or until they start to burst. Cover the pan and remove from the heat. Leave for about 15 minutes, then pour into a bowl and add the orange juice and rind. When completely cold, put in the refrigerator. It will keep for weeks if stored in a covered jar.

cherry sauce

Serve hot or cold with duck, goose, turkey, hot or cold ham or spiced beef

one ½–¾ lb/240–360g tin black cherries

¼ pint/1.5dl port or red wine

grated rind of ½ a lemon

grated rind of an orange

3 tablespoons red-currant jelly

1 tablespoon Dijon mustard

2 tablespoons lemon juice

2 tablespoons orange juice

Grate the lemon and orange rind in thin strips with a sharp potato peeler. Drain a tin of black cherries and remove the stones, if not already done. Put the cherries in a pan with the port or wine and add the grated lemon and orange rind. Simmer for 10 minutes, until quite thick and syrupy. Meanwhile melt the jelly in a small bowl over boiling water. Stir in the mustard, then the fruit juices. When the cherries are ready, remove them from the heat and pour the jelly mixture on to them through a small food mill or sieve.

plum sauce

Serve either hot or cold with roast duck, goose, turkey, hot or cold ham or spiced beef

one 1 lb/0.5kg tin plums

¼ pint/1.5dl port or red wine

¼ teaspoon ground cinnamon

¼ teaspoon ground cloves

¼ teaspoon ground nutmeg

¼ teaspoon ground ginger

3 tablespoons red-currant jelly (or crab apple)

1 tablespoon Dijon mustard

1 tablespoon orange juice

Drain the plums of their juice and remove the stones. Put in a pan with the port or wine. Add the spices and simmer for 10 minutes, until slightly thick and jammy. Meanwhile melt the jelly in a small bowl over boiling water and stir in the mustard and the fruit juice. Push the mixture through a small sieve, or food mill, on to the plums and cool. It can be used immediately or stored for a week or two in the refrigerator.

Cumberland sauce

Serve with any kind of cold meat, especially ham, game, cold meat loaf or pâté

1 *shallot or small onion*
2 *oranges*
1 *lemon*
½ *lb/240g red-currant jelly*
1 *teaspoon Dijon mustard*
¼ *pint/1.5 dl port*
2 *teaspoons arrowroot*

Mince the shallot or the onion and put in a small saucepan. Pare the rind of 1 orange and the lemon, cut it in thin strips and add to the shallot in the pan. Cover with cold water, bring to the boil and cook for 5 minutes. Drain, throwing away the water. Put the jelly in a small china bowl set over a saucepan of hot water and stir until it has melted. If there are still lumps, put it through a strainer and return it to the clean bowl over simmering water. Stir in the mustard, the port, the juice of the oranges and the lemons, the blanched rind and the minced shallot. Cook for about 5 minutes, then mix the arrowroot to a paste in a cup with a tablespoon of water and add to the mixture. Simmer for another 2–3 minutes, then pour into a jar and leave to cool. Close tightly and if possible do not eat it for a week. It will keep for about two months but should be kept in the refrigerator once opened.

Malaysian nut sauce

Serve with grilled chicken joints or small skewers of lamb or pork

¼ *lb/120g, unsalted peanuts*
2 *tablespoons oil*
1 *medium onion*
3–4 *oz/90–120g creamed coconut*
1 *tablespoon soft brown sugar*
1 *tablespoon soy sauce*
1½–2 *tablespoons lemon juice*
2–3 *dashes Tabasco*
salt and black pepper
SERVES 4–5

Heat ½ tablespoon oil in a frying pan and fry the nuts until a golden brown, then chop them coarsely by hand or in a food processor. Chop the onion finely and fry in the remaining oil until pale golden; add to the nuts and blend. Pour ½ pint/3 dl water over the chopped or grated creamed coconut and leave for 20–30 minutes. Blend quickly in a blender or food processor (after removing the nuts) and pour through a coarse strainer into a saucepan. Heat, adding the chopped nuts and onions, the sugar, soy sauce, 1 tablespoon lemon juice, a dash of Tabasco and salt and pepper to taste. Bring to the boil and simmer for 5 minutes, adding a little water if it gets too thick. Add more lemon juice and Tabasco as required. Serve hot, and accompany with rice.

Stuffings/nut and bread

nut stuffing

Use to stuff a 4lb/2kg chicken. It is especially delicious when used in a poached chicken, served with boiled rice and a cream sauce made with some of the stock from the boiled chicken. Alternatively, the chicken can be roasted. Allow an extra 20 minutes for the stuffing when cooking the bird

1 oz/30g *chopped onion*
½ oz/15g *butter*
2 oz/60g *minced veal*
2 oz/60g *shredded suet*
1 oz/30g *chopped apple*
1 oz/30g *chopped almonds*
1 oz/30g *chopped pistachio nuts*
pinch of sugar
pinch of mace
pinch of ground coriander
1 *egg*
salt and black pepper
SERVES 5

Brown the chopped onion slowly in the butter. Add the minced veal and cook until evenly browned all over, stirring often. Remove from the heat and allow to cool. Stir in the shredded suet, chopped apple, nuts and seasonings. Beat the egg and stir it in. The stuffing is now ready for use.

celery and breadcrumb stuffing

Use to stuff a goose or turkey or make in half quantities to stuff a capon, duck or large chicken

2 *heads celery*
1 lb/0.5kg *soft white breadcrumbs*
½ *teaspoon ground mace*
3 *large eggs*
4 oz/120g *butter, semi-melted*
1 *tablespoon sea salt*
2 *teaspoons black peppercorns*

Clean and chop only the best parts of the celery quite finely. Mix with the breadcrumbs. Crush the peppercorns roughly in a mortar and add with the salt and mace. Beat the eggs and stir them in, then the semi-melted butter. Mix well.

corn bread stuffing

Use to stuff a medium-sized turkey between 10–14 lb/5–7kg

1 *medium onion*
2 oz/60g *butter*
½ lb/240g *pure pork sausage meat*
1 *turkey liver*
½ lb/240g *corn breadcrumbs*
3–4 *tablespoons chopped parsley*
salt and black pepper

Chop the onion and sauté it in the butter until it is a pale golden colour. Lift out with a slotted spoon, leaving the fat in the pan, and transfer to a large mixing bowl. Fry the sausage meat in the same pan, breaking it up as it cooks with two wooden spoons. When half-cooked, add the chopped liver of the bird and fry them all together. Mix the meat mixture and the onion. Add the breadcrumbs and stir until well mixed, adding salt and black pepper to taste and the chopped parsley. Allow the mixture to cool completely before stuffing the bird.

spaghetti with quick clam sauce

1½ oz/45g butter
1 shallot or small onion
1 clove garlic
one ½ lb/240g tin minced clams
¼ pint/1.5 dl white wine, or clam juice
¼ pint/1.5 dl double cream
2 tablespoons chopped parsley
1 lb/0.5 kg spaghetti
black pepper
SERVES 4–5

Heat the butter and cook the chopped shallot until it is a pale golden colour. Add the crushed garlic and cook for a few moments longer. Open the tin of clams, drain the liquid into the pan and add the wine or clam juice. Simmer gently for 8 minutes. Stir in the cream, reheat, and add pepper to taste. Add the minced clams and reheat without allowing it to boil. Add the parsley and keep warm while you cook the spaghetti in plenty of boiling salted water until tender. Drain well, pour the sauce over and serve.

spaghetti with chicken and vegetable sauce

one 3½ lb/1.75 kg chicken
2 onions
3 carrots
3 leeks
3 stalks celery
2 oz/60g butter
3 tablespoons olive oil
2 cloves garlic, crushed
one 12 oz/360g tin tomatoes
6 oz/180g mushrooms
1½ lb/0.75 kg spaghetti
salt and black pepper
SERVES 6

Half-cover the chicken with hot water in a heavy pot. Cut an onion, a carrot, a leek and a celery stalk in half and put them round the chicken with a little salt. Cover the pot with a tightly fitting lid as soon as it comes to the boil and simmer gently for 1 hour. This can be done in the morning and the bird left to cool in the stock. Later, lift it out and strain the stock. Cut the flesh off the bird in largish pieces and set aside. Melt 1 oz/30g butter and 3 tablespoons oil in a large sauté pan and cook the chopped onion and remaining leeks in it until slightly coloured and softened. Meanwhile, chop the remaining carrots and cook them in a little boiling water for 5 minutes, then drain. Add the carrots to the onion and leeks, with the chopped celery. Stir around now and then, and after about 5 minutes of gentle cooking add the crushed garlic, then the tinned tomatoes, chopped roughly and drained of their juice. Stir around for 3 or 4 minutes then pour on ½ pint/3 dl of the reheated stock, which should be strong and well flavoured. Simmer gently for 20 minutes, adding salt and black pepper to taste. Cut the mushrooms in halves or quarters according to size, and toss them lightly in 1 oz/30g butter until soft. When the sauce is ready, add the chopped chicken and reheat for a few minutes, then add the mushrooms and keep warm while you cook the spaghetti in plenty of salted boiling water until tender; drain and serve with the chicken and vegetable sauce.

Pasta/sauces and garnishes

spaghetti with nut sauce

This sauce can also be served cold in which case the spaghetti should be moistened first with a little extra olive oil, then mixed with the sauce while still hot and left to cool. Tapenade is a paste made from olives, obtainable in jars from some delicatessens

2 teaspoons tapenade or 3 or 4 black olives, finely chopped and mashed to a paste

2 tablespoons olive oil, or olive oil and walnut oil

one ½ lb/240g tin tomatoes

2 cloves garlic

2 oz/60g walnuts

¼ lb/120g mushrooms

4 tablespoons chopped parsley

1 lb/0.5 kg spaghetti

SERVES 4

Stir the olive paste into the oil and heat in a small pan. Chop the tomatoes roughly and add them with the garlic. Simmer for about 3 minutes, then add the walnuts which you have chopped quickly in the blender. Chop the mushrooms and add to the nuts. Stir until all is simmering gently and add the chopped parsley. Keep the sauce warm while you cook the spaghetti in plenty of boiling salted water until tender; drain and serve.

egg noodles with salami

6 oz/180g Italian salami

½ lb/240g frozen petits pois

1½ lb/0.75 kg egg noodles

2 oz/60g butter

½ pint/3 dl single cream

salt and black pepper

SERVES 6

Remove the rind from the salami and chop it in small pieces. Cook the peas and keep warm. Cook the noodles according to the directions on the packet, and drain well.

Return them to the pan over gentle heat and stir in the butter, cut in small pieces, and the cream. Add plenty of salt and black pepper. Stir in chopped salami and peas, reheat for a moment or two then serve.

spaghetti with mussel sauce

Eight large clams can be substituted for the mussels but they will need cooking for 4–5 minutes longer to open the shells

1 quart/1 litre mussels

¼ pint/1.5 dl white wine

1 oz/30g butter

1 shallot

1 clove garlic, crushed

¼ pint/1.5 dl double cream

black pepper

2 tablespoons chopped parsley

1 lb/0.5 kg spaghetti or noodles

SERVES 4

Put the mussels in a deep pan with the white wine. Cook over medium heat with the lid on for 4–5 minutes or until the shells have opened. Lift out the mussels with a slotted spoon and boil up the stock until it has reduced slightly. Strain into a jug – you should have about 8 fl oz/0.25 litre. Take the mussels out of their shells and keep them warm in a covered bowl. Melt the butter in a saucepan, cook the finely chopped shallot until a pale golden colour and add the crushed garlic halfway through. Pour on the strained stock and simmer uncovered for 10 minutes. Add the cream and season with black pepper. Chop the mussels and add to the sauce; reheat for a few moments without allowing it to boil, then add the chopped parsley. Keep warm while you cook the spaghetti or noodles in plenty of salted boiling water until tender; drain, cover with the sauce and serve.

vegetable sauce for pasta

This makes a large vegetable dish in its own right but is delicious when served with noodles or other pasta

¼ lb/120g *small carrots*
¼ lb/120g *small courgettes*
¼ lb/120g *mushrooms*
1 *bunch spring onions*
1 *small cauliflower*
¼ lb/120g *string beans*
½ lb/240g *tomatoes*
3 oz/90g *butter*
1 *tablespoon flour*
½ pint/3 dl *chicken stock*
¼ pint/1.5 dl *single cream*
mace or nutmeg
1½ lb/0.75 kg *noodles or pasta*
salt and black pepper

SERVES 6

Cut the carrots, the unpeeled courgettes and the mushrooms in thick slices. Leave the spring onions whole. Divide the cauliflower into sprigs. Cut the beans into 1-inch/2.5 cm pieces. Skin and chop the tomatoes into large pieces. Cook the carrots, courgettes, onions, cauliflower and beans separately, one after the other, in lightly salted boiling water. Take care that they are quite firm and crisp and not over-cooked. As soon as each vegetable is cooked, drain well in a colander, then transfer to a large bowl in a hot place where they can all be mixed together. Cook the mushrooms in 1 oz/30g of butter in a frying pan, then add them to the rest of the vegetables. Cook the tomatoes in another 1 oz/30g of butter and add to the vegetables. Then make the sauce. Melt the remaining butter and blend it with the flour and the heated stock. Simmer until smooth, add the cream and season with salt and black pepper and a pinch of mace or nutmeg. If necessary, a little of the reserved cooking water can be used to thin the sauce. When it is smooth and well flavoured, mix with the vegetables and keep warm while you cook the noodles or pasta in plenty of boiling salted water until tender; drain and serve with the vegetable sauce in a large dish.

buckwheat spaghetti with vegetable garnish

1 *onion*
1 *carrot*
1 *leek*
1 oz/30g *butter*
2 *tablespoons olive oil*
soy sauce (optional)
½ lb/240g *buckwheat spaghetti*
salt and black pepper
sesame salt

SERVES 2–3

Cut the onion, the carrot and the leek in half and slice each of them thinly. Heat the butter and the oil in a sauté pan and cook the sliced onion until it is slightly softened. Add the leek then the carrot. When all are cooked but still crisp, add salt and pepper to taste and a few drops of soy sauce if desired. Keep warm while you cook the buckwheat spaghetti in plenty of boiling salted water until tender; drain well, spoon the vegetables over and sprinkle with sesame salt.

Grains/rice, wheat and couscous

buckwheat kasha with egg

Serve hot with a bowl of cold yoghourt

1 *egg*
1 *teacup buckwheat*
1 *oz/30g butter*
2 *teacups water*
dash of soy sauce
salt and black pepper

SERVES 2

Beat the egg and stir it into the buckwheat until well mixed. Melt the butter in a heavy pan and put in the buckwheat. Stir around for 3–4 minutes, until coated all over with fat. Heat 1 cup of water until boiling and pour on. Add salt and simmer gently with the lid on for about 15 minutes. Add seasoning to taste and a dash of soy sauce.

cracked wheat risotto

This can be served as an accompaniment to grilled meat, or on its own topped with yoghourt

¼ *lb/120g butter*
1 *onion*
½ *lb/240g cracked wheat*
¾ *pint/4.5dl chicken stock*
salt

SERVES 3–4

Melt the butter in a sauté pan and cook the chopped onion until a pale golden colour. Add the cracked wheat and cook gently over low heat for 10 minutes, stirring often. Heat the stock and pour on enough to cover the ingredients generously. Bring to boiling point, add salt, cover the pan and simmer for 10 minutes or until all the stock is absorbed. If this happens before the wheat has softened, add a little more stock.

cracked wheat salad

6 *oz/180g cracked wheat*
1 *bunch spring onions*
½ *lb/240g tomatoes*
¼ *pint/1.5dl chopped parsley*
4 *tablespoons sunflower seed oil*
2 *tablespoons lemon juice*
salt and black pepper

SERVES 3–4

Soak the cracked wheat for about 45 minutes in cold water, then drain and squeeze out as much moisture as possible with your hands. Chop the parsley and the spring onions, using the best of the green parts as well as the bulbs. Skin and chop the tomatoes and drain them of their juice. Then mix them with the wheat. Stir in the oil and lemon juice and add salt and pepper to taste.

couscous with vegetables

Serve with chicken, lamb cutlets or other vegetable dishes

½ *lb/240g couscous*
2 *lb/1kg carrots*
6–8 *oz/180–240g frozen petits pois*
2 *oz/60g butter*
salt and black pepper

SERVES 4

Pour 8fl oz/0.25 litre cold water over the couscous and leave for 10 minutes, then place it in a strainer over a saucepan. Cook the sliced carrots in lightly salted water in the pan below and cover the strainer. Cook the peas separately, drain and keep hot. When the carrots are cooked, the couscous should be heated through. If not, lift out the carrots with a slotted spoon and leave the couscous for another 10 minutes over boiling water. When all is cooked, mix together and add the butter cut in small pieces. Season to taste.

rice and yoghourt salad

6oz/180g *long grain rice*

1 *medium onion*

2 *tablespoons oil*

½ lb/240g *tomatoes*

2–3oz/60–90g *frozen petits pois*

1 *carton yoghourt*

2 *tablespoons chopped fresh herbs*

juice of ½ a lemon

salt and black pepper

SERVES 3–4

Cook the rice and drain well. Chop the onion and cook in the oil until soft and pale golden in colour. Skin the tomatoes and chop them, discarding any seeds and juice. Mix the onion and tomatoes with the rice. Cook the peas and stir them in, then the yoghourt and the chopped herbs. Season with salt and black pepper and add the lemon juice. For a hot version, use 1oz/30g of butter instead of the oil to cook the onion, and add the chopped tomatoes during the last couple of minutes of cooking to soften them. Season well but leave out the lemon juice.

vegetables with brown rice

1oz/30g *butter*

2 *tablespoons oil*

1 *medium onion*

4 *small carrots*

2 *stalks celery*

4oz/120g *mushrooms*

6oz/180g *brown rice*

¾ pint/4.5dl *chicken stock*

salt and black pepper

SERVES 3–4

Melt the butter and oil in a sauté pan. Chop the onion and cook it gently until it starts to colour. Slice the carrots and cook them gently in lightly salted water for 5 minutes. Drain them and add with the chopped celery and chopped mushrooms. Wash and drain the rice and stir it in. Continue to stir until all ingredients are coated with fat and well mixed. Heat the stock and pour on, add salt and pepper to taste and cover the pan. Simmer gently for 40–45 minutes, stirring occasionally and adding more stock if needed. At the end of this time the rice should be tender and all the liquid absorbed. If it is not, take off the lid and cook until it has evaporated completely.

polenta

This can be served either as a snack with drinks or accompanied by grilled rashers of bacon, fried eggs and kabanos sausages cut in thick slices and heated in bacon fat. It is also good when cut into rounds and topped with a poached or fried egg

¼ lb/120g *polenta*

bacon fat or oil

salt

SERVES 4

Bring ¾ pint/4.5dl lightly salted water to the boil in a saucepan and shake in the polenta. Cook gently for about 4 minutes, stirring constantly. When it has become thick and smooth, turn out on to a wet board and smooth with a palette knife into a rectangle about ½ inch/1cm thick. Leave to cool. Later cut into rectangles about 3 × 1 inch/8 × 2.5cm and fry on both sides, preferably in bacon fat. Serve immediately.

Desserts/puddings

Christmas pudding

1½ lb/0.75 kg seedless raisins
½ lb/240g mixed candied peel
½ lb/240g glacé cherries
¼ lb/120g chopped almonds
¾ lb/360g shredded suet
¾ lb/360g soft white breadcrumbs
8 eggs
¼ pint/1.5 dl Guinness
6 tablespoons brandy
SERVES 6–8

If using large raisins, halve them, then chop the peel and halve the cherries. Mix them all together with the chopped almonds, suet and breadcrumbs. Beat the eggs and stir them in with the Guinness and the brandy. If possible, stand for a few hours, or overnight. Butter three 1½-pint/9dl pudding basins and fill them with the mixture; do not pack it down tightly, and leave at least 1 inch/2.5cm unfilled at the top. Cover each bowl with a buttered piece of foil and tie them in a square of cloth. Stand the bowls on up-turned saucers, without touching each other in a large pan half-filled with boiling water. Cover the pan and bring back to the boil. Keep boiling steadily for 6 hours, adding more boiling water as needed to keep the level of water halfway up the sides of the bowls. When done, lift out the bowls and leave to cool. (One pudding can be eaten straight away, and the others stored in a cool place for up to three months. If storing them, wrap them in clean cloth after cooling.) On Christmas day, steam again for 4–5 hours, or as long as is practicable. Turn out on a flat dish to serve and stick a sprig of holly in the top. Warm 2–3 tablespoons of brandy in a ladle and set light to it. Pour immediately over the pudding and carry to the table flaming. Serve with brandy butter or rum butter.

castle puddings

3 eggs
3 oz/90g castor sugar
3 oz/90g flour
1 teaspoon grated lemon rind
3 oz/90g butter, semi-melted
golden syrup
lemon juice
SERVES 4

Beat the eggs until very light and almost frothy, adding the sugar by degrees and beating continuously. Then shake in the flour, also by degrees, and lastly stir in the semi-melted butter and lemon rind. All this may be speedily done in a food processor. When all is well mixed, pour into small buttered moulds shaped like tiny buckets. Preheat the oven to 350°F (180°C, Gas Mark 4). Stand the moulds on a baking tray and bake for 20 minutes. Turn the puddings out of their moulds to serve, and accompany with a sauce of golden syrup heated with a little lemon juice, and a jug of cream.

queen of puddings

½ pint/3 dl milk
2 strips lemon peel
1 oz/30g butter
¼ lb/120g castor sugar
2 oz/60g soft white breadcrumbs
3 eggs
3 tablespoons raspberry jam
SERVES 4–5

Put the milk in a pan with the lemon peel and bring slowly to the boil. Remove from the heat, cover the pan and leave for 10 minutes. Return to the heat, discard the lemon peel, and add the butter and 1 oz/30g castor sugar. Stir until the butter and sugar have melted. Remove from the heat and stir in the breadcrumbs. Leave to cool for another 10 minutes, then stir in the lightly beaten egg yolks. Preheat the oven to 325°F (170°C, Gas Mark 3). Pour the mixture into a well-buttered pudding dish and bake for 30 minutes. Take out of the oven and leave to cool slightly, turning the oven down to 250°F (140°C, Gas Mark 1). Warm the jam and spread it over the pudding. Whip the egg whites until stiff, and fold in the remaining 3 oz/90 g castor sugar to make a meringue mixture. Cover the pudding completely with meringue. Return to the cooler oven and bake for 30 minutes, or until the top of the meringue is firm and lightly coloured. This pudding can be served immediately, or kept warm for some time without spoiling. Serve with cream. It is also good cold.

seven-cup pudding

1 teacup (6 fl oz/180 ml) soft white breadcrumbs
1 teacup (6 fl oz/180 ml) sultanas
1 teacup (6 fl oz/180 ml) currants
1 teacup (6 fl oz/180 ml) sugar
1 teacup (6 fl oz/180 ml) flour
2 oz/60 g chopped mixed peel
2 oz/60 g coarsely chopped (nibbed) almonds
2 teaspoons ground ginger
1 teaspoon ground cinnamon
1 teaspoon mixed spice
pinch of salt
1 egg
approx ¼ pint/1.5 dl milk
1 teaspoon baking soda
1 teaspoon wine vinegar

SERVES 6–8

Mix all the ingredients together except the egg, milk, bicarbonate of soda and vinegar. Break the egg into a teacup and fill to the brim with milk. Stir into the pudding mixture.

Dissolve the soda in the vinegar for a minute or two, then stir in also. Mix all well together and turn into a buttered pudding basin. Cover with foil and stand in a large pan with boiling water coming halfway up the sides of the basin. Cover the pan and boil steadily, replenishing the water as needed as the level drops. Steam in this manner for 4–6 hours. Turn out on a flat dish and serve with a custard sauce or cream.

bread and butter pudding

3–4 thin slices white bread
approx 1½ oz/45 g butter
2 tablespoons sultanas, or currants and raisins, mixed
½ pint/3 dl milk
1½ oz/45 g vanilla sugar (see recipe, page 126) or castor sugar and ¼ vanilla pod
2 eggs

SERVES 4

If you have no home-made vanilla sugar, heat the milk with the vanilla pod in it. When it reaches boiling point, remove from the heat, cover the pan, and stand for 20 minutes. Do not remove the crusts of bread; butter each slice and cut in four triangles. Lay them in layers in a buttered fireproof dish and scatter the dried fruit over each layer. If using home-made vanilla sugar, simply heat the milk and sugar gently in a small pan until the sugar has melted. If using a vanilla pod, remove it from the milk, add the sugar, and reheat until the sugar has dissolved. Preheat the oven to 325°F (170°C, Gas Mark 3). Beat the eggs and beat in the hot milk. Pour over the bread through a small strainer, into the side of the dish so that the top layer of bread is not submerged. Bake for 1 hour until set and a light golden brown. Serve immediately.

Desserts/puddings, pies and fruits

Eve's pudding

Although not traditional, a most delicious variation is to add ½ lb/240g blackberries to the apples when stewing

1 *lb/0.5 kg cooking apples*	
4½ *oz/135g sugar*	
3 *oz/90g butter*	
¼ *lb/120g self-raising flour*	
2 *eggs*	

SERVES 5

Peel and slice the apples and stew gently in a covered pan with just enough water to cover the bottom, and 1½ oz/45g of the sugar. When soft, turn into a buttered soufflé dish of 1½-pint/9dl capacity. Preheat the oven to 350°F (180°C, Gas Mark 4). Cream the butter and the rest of the sugar together carefully. Beat the eggs, and add them, and the sifted flour, alternately, beating constantly. Alternatively, this may be done in a food processor. Spoon over the apples, being careful to cover them completely. Bake for 30 minutes until golden brown and puffy. Serve as soon as possible after baking and hand round a separate jug of cream.

rice pudding

2 *oz/60g pudding rice*	
1 *oz/30g sugar*	
1 *pint/6dl milk*	
½ *oz/15g butter*	

SERVES 4

Wash the rice and put it in a buttered pie dish. Preheat the oven to 300°F (160°C, Gas Mark 2), add the sugar to the rice and pour on the milk. Mix with a fork, then dot with butter. Bake for 2 hours, or until the top is nicely browned and almost all the milk is absorbed by the rice. Serve hot or cold.

cheesecake

crust:

6 *oz/180g digestive biscuits*	
1½ *oz/45g melted butter*	
1 *heaped tablespoon soft brown sugar*	

filling:

½ *lb/240g castor sugar*	
2 *oz/60g butter*	
2 *egg yolks*	
¼ *pint/1.5dl double cream*	
1 *lb/0.5 kg curd cheese or plain cream cheese*	
1–1½ *tablespoons lemon juice*	

SERVES 6

Preheat the oven to 350° (180°C, Gas Mark 4). To make the crust, break up the biscuits in crumbs (reserving a spoonful) and stir the melted butter and sugar into the crumbs until well mixed. Alternatively, put the biscuits, melted butter, and sugar into a food processor. Use two-thirds of the mixture to line the bottom and sides of a round baking tin, preferably about 2 inches/5cm deep. Bake for 8 minutes, then cool. If you have a food processor, the ingredients for the filling can be put in all together. If mixing by hand, sift the castor sugar and beat into the creamed butter, then beat in the egg yolks and the cream. Beat the cheese in a separate bowl until free from lumps, and beat the first mixture into the cheese. Stir in the lemon juice. Mix well and pour into the case, scatter the remaining crumbs over the top, and chill.

buttered apples

1½ *lb/0.75 kg cooking apples*	
¼ *lb/120g butter*	
3–4 *tablespoons sugar*	
5–6 *slices dry white bread*	
⅓ *pint/2dl double cream*	

SERVES 5–6

Peel the apples and slice them thickly. Melt 1oz/30g of butter in a sauté pan and cook as many of the sliced apples as will fit comfortably in one layer. Add 1 tablespoon sugar and fry the apples gently, turning them now and then, until soft. Then lift them out with a slotted spatula and keep them warm while you cook a second batch, adding more butter and sugar. While the apples are cooking, remove the crusts from the bread, and cut each slice in a round, allowing one per person. When all the apples are done, add more butter to the pan and fry the rounds of bread. Turn them often until they are golden on both sides. Lay them on a flat dish and spoon the sliced apples carefully on to each one. Whip the cream, pour any remaining juice over the apples and top each pile with a dollop of whipped cream.

pumpkin pie

2 lb/1 kg pumpkin

¾ lb/360g short pastry (see recipe, page 126)

2 eggs

6 oz/180g soft brown sugar

½ teaspoon sea salt

1 teaspoon ground cinnamon

½ teaspoon ground nutmeg

¼ teaspoon ground cloves

one 12 fl oz/⅓ litre tin evaporated milk

¼ oz/7.5g fresh ginger, or ½ teaspoon ground ginger

SERVES 6

Preheat the oven to 350°F (180°C, Gas Mark 4). Cut the pumpkin in half, scrape out the seeds, and place the two halves in a baking tin with ½ inch/1cm water. Bake for 50 minutes or until the flesh is soft when pierced with a skewer. Scoop out the flesh and push through the medium mesh of a food mill. Drain for 10 minutes in a sieve. Roll out the pastry and line a pie tin with it. Prebake the pastry for 10 minutes at 350°F (180°C, Gas Mark 4), then cool. Reset the oven to 450°F (230°C, Gas Mark 8). Beat the eggs thoroughly, stir in the drained pumpkin purée (you should have about ½ pint/3 dl) and the sugar, salt, spices and evaporated milk. Peel the ginger, and chop it finely, if not using ground ginger, stir it into the pumpkin mixture and pour into the pastry case. Bake the pie for 15 minutes. Turn off the oven and leave the pie in it. Take out after 45 minutes, and chill before serving.

dried fruit salad

½ lb/240g mixed dried fruit: apples, pears, apricots, peaches, prunes, figs

2 tablespoons raisins

½ teaspoon grated orange rind

½ teaspoon grated lemon rind

2 tablespoons sugar

juice of 1 orange

2 tablespoons coarsely chopped (nibbed) almonds

SERVES 4–5

Soak the fruit if necessary. Cover with cold water (or the water they soaked in) and cook fairly quickly until soft, but not disintegrated. The timing varies widely according to the fruit; soaked fruit of good quality should take about 15 minutes. At the end of the cooking, add the raisins, the grated rind and the sugar. Leave to cool, then stir in the orange juice and the chopped nuts. If there is too much juice after cooking, remove the fruit to a serving dish with the chopped almonds stirred in and boil the juice to the desired amount, then pour over with the orange juice. Serve while still warm, or completely cool, but do not chill. Serve with a bowl of cream.

Desserts/fruits, fools and mousses

a tropical fruit salad

2 *guavas*

4 *kiwi fruit (Chinese gooseberries)*

8 *lychees*

2 *passion fruit*

juice of 2 limes

pinch of castor sugar

SERVES 4

Peel the guavas and cut them in small cubes. Peel the kiwi fruit, cut them in half and then in quite thick slices. Peel the lychees, cut them in half and remove the stones. Mix all the fruits together in a bowl. Cut the passion fruit in half and spoon the interior over the other fruits. Squeeze the juice of the limes and mix it with the fruits, adding castor sugar to taste. Serve in glass bowls.

green fruit salad

1 *small honeydew melon*

½ *large pineapple*

4 *kiwi fruit (Chinese gooseberries)*

juice of 2 limes

SERVES 4

Cut the melon in cubes. Slice the pineapple thickly, remove the centre and cut each slice in chunks. Peel the kiwi fruit and cut them in slices. Mix all the fruits together and pour over the lime juice. Chill and serve.

apricots in white wine

These are delicious eaten at the end of a meal, with coffee. A narrow fork is useful for fishing them out of the jar

Take the best dried apricots you can find and wash them carefully. Pack loosely into jars and cover with a fairly sweet, but good, white wine such as Sauternes. Screw the lids on tightly and leave for a week before eating.

mango fool

This is rather a startling colour, but good

1 *large ripe mango*

juice of 1 large lime

½ *pint/3 dl yoghourt*

SERVES 3–4

Skin the mango and cut the flesh off the stone. Put it into a blender or food processor with the lime juice – approximately 2 tablespoons – and the yoghourt. Blend until smooth, then pour into 3–4 small glasses and chill for a couple of hours before serving.

prune mousse

½ *lb/240g prunes*

cold tea

2 *oz/60g sugar*

2 *tablespoons brandy or 1 tablespoon lemon juice*

½ *pint/3 dl double cream*

3 *egg whites*

SERVES 4–5

Soak the prunes overnight in cold tea, then cook them very slowly in the tea, adding the sugar. When soft, lift them out of the liquid and remove the stones. Put the flesh in a blender with enough of the juice to make a thick purée. Add the brandy or lemon juice to sharpen the flavour. Whip the cream until stiff but not dry, and fold in. Beat the egg whites stiffly and fold in. Chill the mousse in the refrigerator for at least 2 hours.

coffee mousse

6 fl oz/180 ml double strength black coffee
¼ lb/120 g Menier, or other good plain dark chocolate
¼ lb/120 g castor sugar
1½ packets gelatine
3 egg yolks
⅓ pint/2 dl milk
½ pint/3 dl double cream
SERVES 6

Melt the chocolate in half of the coffee, adding 2 oz/60 g castor sugar. Dissolve the gelatine in the remaining coffee. When both the chocolate and the gelatine are melted, mix the two liquids together. Beat the egg yolks with the remaining 2 oz/60 g sugar. Scald the milk and pour on to the egg yolks. Stir, then stand over a pan of almost boiling water and stir until slightly thickened. Pour it into the chocolate mixture and cool it in a sink half-full of cold water, stirring now and then. When quite cold, whip the cream and fold it in. Pour into a soufflé dish and chill until set.

petits pots de crème au café

These are very rich and one only wants a very small amount. They can also be made with single cream, or half milk and half cream, but the smoothness of the double cream is extremely delicious

4 tablespoons double strength black coffee
½ pint/3 dl double cream
2 egg yolks
1½ tablespoons castor sugar
SERVES 4

Heat the coffee and the cream together. Beat the egg yolks with the sugar. When the coffee mixture is almost boiling, pour it on to the egg yolks and sugar. Mix well, then pour through a strainer into tiny fireproof china dishes;

oeufs en cocotte dishes are good. Stand them in a baking tin half-full of hot water and bake for 25 minutes at 300°F (160°C, Gas Mark 2), or until just set.

sauce à la vanille

Serve this delicious sauce with almost all fruit, bread or steamed puddings, stewed fruit, baked apples or ice-cream

½ vanilla pod
½ pint/3 dl milk
2 egg yolks
2 tablespoons castor sugar
SERVES 4

Put the vanilla pod into the milk and heat slowly to boiling point. Remove from the heat, cover the pan and leave to infuse for 20 minutes. Put the egg yolks into a bowl and beat with an electric beater or whisk for about 2 minutes, adding the castor sugar by degrees. When blended into a thick and creamy paste, reheat the milk until almost boiling and pour on after removing the vanilla pod. Continue to whisk by hand as you add the milk. Then put the bowl over a saucepan of just boiling water and stir with a wooden spoon until slightly thickened – it will thicken more on cooling. If it is to be served hot, allow it to cool slightly as it does not want to be scalding hot. It can then be kept warm over hot water. If it is to be served cold, stand in a sink half-full of cold water to cool as quickly as possible and stir frequently to prevent a skin forming.

wheatgerm ice-cream

2 eggs + 2 yolks

2½ oz/75g vanilla sugar (see recipe, page 126) or castor sugar and ½ vanilla pod

½ pint/3dl milk

½ pint/3dl double cream

2 oz/60g sweetened wheatgerm

SERVES 6

If you have no home-made vanilla sugar, put half a vanilla pod in the milk, heat to boiling point, cover, remove from heat, and leave for 20 minutes. Beat the eggs and the egg yolks together with an electric beater. Add the vanilla sugar, or castor sugar, and continue to beat. Heat the milk until just about to boil, removing the vanilla pod if necessary, then pour on to the eggs and sugar. Continue to beat until incorporated. Place the bowl over a pan of simmering water and stir constantly until very slightly thickened, like an egg custard. Then pour the mixture through a strainer into a clean bowl, stand in a sink half-full of cold water and leave to cool, stirring now and then to prevent a skin forming. Beat the cream until semi-whipped and fold into the custard when it has cooled. Pour into an ice-cream machine and freeze for an hour. Then stir in the wheatgerm and continue freezing. Alternatively, if you do not have an ice-cream machine, freeze the mixture in ice trays, covered with foil. After an hour, beat the mixture with a fork and add the wheatgerm before returning it to the freezer.

coffee granita

5 oz/150g sugar

¼ pint/1.5dl water

1 pint/6dl strong coffee

SERVES 4–5

Put the sugar and water into a heavy saucepan and bring to the boil. Boil gently for exactly 5 minutes, stirring until the sugar has melted. Meanwhile make the coffee and cool with the syrup quickly in a sink half-full of cold water. Stir the two together and pour into an ice-cream machine or, if you do not have one, freeze the mixture in ice trays, covered in foil. If you use ice trays, the ice-cream should be stirred every half-hour until set. When set, put it in wine glasses and serve.

hazelnut ice-cream

This can be made with blanched almonds instead of hazelnuts

2 oz/60g hazelnuts, blanched

2 tablespoons castor sugar

2 eggs + 2 yolks

3 oz/90g vanilla sugar (see recipe, page 126) or castor sugar and ½ vanilla pod

½ pint/3dl double cream

SERVES 6

If you have no vanilla sugar, put half a vanilla pod into the milk and heat to boiling point. Cover the pan, remove from the heat, and stand for 20 minutes. Put the hazelnuts in a heavy frying pan with the sugar and cook over a fairly strong heat, stirring constantly, until the sugar caramelizes. The nuts will turn a golden brown and the whole pan will smoke slightly. Turn out on to an oiled surface – marble or glass is best – and leave to cool. Then put in a food processor or blender and chop until reduced to a medium-fine consistency; an uneven texture does not matter, it even improves the ice-cream. Beat the egg and the yolks with the vanilla sugar, or plain castor sugar, if used, until thick. Remove the vanilla pod from the milk, if necessary, and heat the milk until almost boiling. Pour on to the eggs, beating all the time. Stand the bowl over a pan of simmering water and stir constantly until slightly thickened – about 8 minutes. Strain into a clean bowl and stand in a sink full of very cold water, stirring now and then to prevent a skin forming. When cool, whip the cream until semi-thick and fold into the egg custard. Pour into an ice-cream machine and freeze. When almost frozen, fold in the crushed nut mixture and continue to freeze until totally set. If you have no ice-cream machine, freeze the mixture in ice trays, covered with foil. After about 1 hour, beat the mixture well with a fork, then fold in the crushed nuts carefully. Continue to freeze until set.

passion fruit sorbet

12 *passion fruit*
juice of 4 large oranges
juice of 2 limes
¼ *lb/120g sugar*
2 *egg whites*
SERVES 4

Cut the passion fruit in half and scoop out the pulp with a teaspoon. Rub it through the medium mesh of a food mill, keeping back the pips. Squeeze the juice of the oranges and limes and add to the passion fruit. Heat the sugar with 4fl oz/120ml water in a heavy pan until melted, then boil until reduced to ¼ pint/1.5dl thin syrup. Cool slightly and mix with the fruit juices. Pour into an ice-cream machine and freeze until mushy – about 1 hour. Whip the egg whites fairly stiffly and

fold into the semi-frozen ice. Turn back into the machine and continue to freeze until set. If you do not have an ice-cream machine, freeze the mixture in ice trays, covered with foil. When the mixture is mushy, remove from the freezer and beat with a fork. Then fold in the egg whites carefully and continue to freeze until set.

pineapple sorbet

1 *large pineapple*
¼ *lb/120g sugar*
juice of 4 medium oranges
1 *tablespoon lime juice (when available),*
or 2 teaspoons lemon juice
2 *egg whites*
SERVES 5–6

Cut the top and bottom off the pineapple and slice it thickly. Remove the central core from each slice and cut off the rind. Cut the slices in cubes and purée them in a food processor or blender. Push through a nylon sieve. You should have about ½ pint/3dl. Heat the sugar with 4fl oz/120ml water in a heavy pan. Boil it gently until reduced to ¼ pint/1.5dl thin syrup and then cool. Squeeze the juice of the oranges. Mix the orange juice with the pineapple juice and the cooled sugar syrup, adding the lime juice. If fresh limes are not available, use 1–2 teaspoons lemon juice to sharpen the flavour slightly. Pour into an ice-cream machine and freeze for about 1 hour or until mushy. Tip into a bowl and fold in the stiffly beaten egg whites; freeze again as usual. If you do not have an ice-cream machine, freeze the mixture in ice trays, covered with foil. Add the egg whites as above, when the mixture is semi-frozen. Return to the freezer until set.

Breads/plain and savoury

Finnish rye bread

1 oz/30 g *fresh yeast*

3 *teaspoons soft brown sugar*

½ oz/15 g *butter, melted*

1½ *teaspoons salt*

½ lb/240 g *white bread flour*

6 oz/180 g *rye flour*

Put the yeast in a cup with 1 teaspoon of brown sugar. Add 4 tablespoons of tepid water taken from ½ pint/3 dl. Leave in a warm place for 10 minutes, then stir. Pour into a large warm bowl, add the remaining tepid water, 2 teaspoons of brown sugar, the melted butter and the salt. Shake in the white flour gradually, then the rye flour. Knead for 4–5 minutes or until smooth, then sprinkle with flour and leave to rise in a warm place in a covered bowl for 1 hour, by which time it should have doubled in size. Butter a baking sheet and sprinkle with flour. Knead the dough again for 4–5 minutes and pat into a flat round shape, large enough to fit nicely on the sheet. Leave to rise again for 20 minutes, then preheat the oven to 375°F (190°C, Gas Mark 5). Sprinkle the dough with rye flour and bake for 1 hour watching to make sure it does not become too brown. If this happens, cover with a sheet of foil. Cool on a wire rack, but eat while still very fresh.

corn bread

2½ oz/75 g *maize meal*

1 oz/30 g *fresh yeast*

2 *teaspoons castor sugar*

8 fl oz/0.25 *litre milk*

2 *teaspoons salt*

4 *tablespoons soft brown sugar*

1¾ lb/860 g *white bread flour*

Measure 8 fl oz/0.25 litre of water into a small pan and bring to the boil. Shake in the maize meal gradually, stirring all the time. Boil gently, continuing to stir for about 3–4 minutes or until thick and smooth. Tip into a large mixing bowl and leave to cool. Put the yeast in a cup with the castor sugar and 4 fl oz/120 ml tepid water. Leave in a warm place for 10 minutes. Warm the milk until lukewarm. When the yeast is bubbly, stir it into the cool maize meal. Mix as smoothly as possible, then add the milk, the salt, the brown sugar and start adding the flour, a cupful at a time. Beat in each addition well with a wooden spoon. Stop adding the flour when the dough clings together nicely, and start to knead on a floured board, adding as much of the remaining flour as is needed to give a smooth elastic dough. After 6–8 minutes, leave to rest, wash and dry the mixing bowl and rub it well with softened butter. Put the dough in the bowl, turning it over so it gets a light coating of fat all over, cover with cling-film wrap or a cloth and leave in a warm place for about an hour, until double in size. Punch down, knead again briefly and divide in two. Form the dough into loaf shapes, put in two buttered tins and leave them to rise again for another 30 minutes or so, until again doubled. Bake for 10 minutes at 425°F (220°C, Gas Mark 7) then turn down the oven to 350°F (180°C, Gas Mark 4) and bake for a further 20 minutes. Tap to see if the loaves are done – they should sound hollow – if not, tip them out of the tins and lay them on the oven rack on their sides for another 5 minutes. When done, cool on a wire rack.

white loaf

1 lb/0.5 kg white bread flour
½ oz/15 g fresh yeast
1 teaspoon sea salt

Put the flour in a large bowl and leave in a warm place. Crumble the yeast into a cup and add 2 tablespoons of warm water. Put in a warm place for 10 minutes. Crush the salt and dissolve in a little hot water. Make this amount up to ½ pint/3 dl with lukewarm water. When the yeast has started to become bubbly, make a hole in the centre of the flour and pour the yeast in. Add the warm water, stirring with a wooden spoon. (You may need slightly more or less than ½ pint/3 dl depending on what flour you use.) When it begins to hold together, turn out on to a floured surface and start to knead, sprinkling with more flour until it no longer sticks to the working surface. Continue to knead for about 5 minutes in all. By this time it should be smooth and elastic and no longer sticky. Wash out the bowl and dry it. Put back the dough, sprinkle with flour and cover with a cloth. Leave to rise for 2 hours in a warm place by which time the dough should have doubled. Punch the dough down with your fist and turn out with a rubber spatula. Knead for another 5 minutes, then form it into a loaf shape and roll it into a greased tin sprinkled with flour. It should fill it by about half, perhaps slightly more, but by no more than two-thirds. Leave it to rise again for another half-hour. After 25 minutes preheat the oven to 420°F (220°C, Gas Mark 7). After 5 minutes more sprinkle the top with flour or brush it with beaten egg yolk for a shiny crust. Bake in the centre of the oven for 45 minutes. Test by turning it out of the tin and knocking it on the bottom; it should have a hollow sound.

potato bread

This is excellent when toasted and served with cheese or simply with butter. It keeps well and when stale can be used to make a delicious stuffing

½ oz/15 g fresh yeast
¼ lb/120 g sugar
8 fl oz/0.25 litre milk
6 oz/180 g butter
2 eggs
6 oz/180 g freshly mashed potato
2 lb/1 kg white flour
1 tablespoon sea salt

Put the yeast with 1 tablespoon of the sugar and 4 fl oz/120 ml tepid water in a large bowl in a warm place. After 5 minutes, warm the milk with the butter cut in pieces. When lukewarm and semi-melted, add to the yeast with the remaining sugar, the salt and the beaten eggs. Stir well until mixed, then beat into the freshly mashed potato. When smooth, start adding the flour, one cupful at a time. Beat it in with a wooden spoon, stopping as soon as the dough clings together. Knead for 10 minutes, adding flour as is necessary to give a smooth springy dough. Clean the bowl, rub with butter, and put in the dough. Cover tightly with cling-film wrap, and leave in a warm place for 2 hours to rise. Punch down, turn out, and knead again for another 5 minutes. Divide it in two, shape into loaves and turn into buttered loaf tins. Put the dough to rise again for 1 hour, then bake for 45 minutes at 375°F (190°C, Gas Mark 5). Tap the bottom of the loaf to see if it is cooked; it should sound hollow. Stand on a wire rack to cool completely before eating.

Breads/sweet and savoury

onion bread

This bread is delicious served with pâté

1 *lb*/0.5 *kg white bread flour*

½ *oz*/15 *g fresh yeast*

1 *lb*/0.5 *kg onions*

2 *oz*/60 *g butter*

2 *egg yolks*

salt and pepper

SERVES 6–8

Put the flour in a warm bowl with 1 teaspoon salt. Put the yeast in a cup with 3 tablespoons tepid water and stand in a warm place for 10 minutes. Make a well in the centre of the flour and pour in the yeast mixture, which should be bubbly. Add ½ pint/3 dl tepid water and mix with a wooden spoon. As soon as it holds together turn it out on to a floured board and knead briskly, sprinkling with more flour as necessary, for 5 minutes. Return to the bowl, cover with a cloth and stand in a warm place for 2 hours. Punch down, turn out and knead again for another 5 minutes. Pat into a flat round shape and lay on a greased baking sheet sprinkled with flour. Leave to rise again for 45 minutes while you prepare the onions. Slice them quite finely and cook gently in the butter in a covered sauté pan until soft and a pale golden colour. Add salt and pepper and pile the onions on top of the bread when it is ready to go in the oven. Preheat the oven to 450°F (230°C, Gas Mark 8), beat the egg yolks and brush lightly over the onions. Bake for 15 minutes, then turn the oven down to 425°F (220°C, Gas Mark 7) and bake for a further 30 minutes. Watch to see that the onions do not burn; if they start to become brown cover them lightly with a sheet of foil.

saffron bread

This beautiful golden-yellow bread is delicious when served with hot or cold mixed vegetable dishes

1 *lb*/0.5 *kg white bread flour*

1½ *teaspoons salt*

½ *oz*/15 *g fresh yeast*

¼ *pint*/1.5 *dl milk*

2 *packets saffron*

2 *eggs*

1 *egg yolk (optional)*

SERVES 6–8

Put the flour in a warm bowl with the salt. Put the yeast in a cup with 4 tablespoons tepid water and leave in a warm place for 10 minutes. Heat the milk with the saffron to boiling point, then leave to cool until luke-warm. Beat the eggs. Make a well in the flour, pour in the yeast mixture, cover with flour, then add the saffron milk and the beaten eggs. Mix well with a wooden spoon, adding a little extra milk or water if needed. Turn out and knead for about 5 minutes. Return to the bowl, cover with a cloth and leave for 1 hour to rise. Punch down, turn out and knead again for 4–5 minutes. Turn into a buttered loaf tin and leave to rise again for 45 minutes. Preheat the oven to 375°F (190°C, Gas Mark 5). Bake for 30 minutes. For a shiny crust, brush with a beaten egg yolk before baking.

spiced fruit bread

1¾ lb/360g white bread flour

1 teaspoon salt

1 oz/30g fresh yeast or ½ oz/15g dried yeast

3 oz/90g lard

2 eggs

6 fl oz/180 ml milk

½ lb/240g raisins

¼ lb/120g sultanas

2 oz/60g mixed peel

6 oz/180g sugar

1 teaspoon allspice

1 tablespoon black treacle

Warm a large bowl, put in the flour with the salt and return to a warm place. Put the yeast in a cup with 2 tablespoons of tepid water and leave for 10 minutes. Cut the lard in small pieces and rub it into the flour. Beat the eggs in a measuring jug and add enough milk and water in equal quantities to make ¾ pint/ 4.5 dl. Make a well in the middle of the flour and tip in first the yeast, then the eggs, milk and water mixture. Mix briefly and return to a warm place for 30 minutes. In the meantime, measure the dried fruit into another bowl and put in a warm place also. After 30 minutes, turn out the flour mixture and knead until smooth, then return to the bowl and stir in the dried fruit, the sugar, the allspice and the treacle which you have warmed in a cup. Mix thoroughly, then put back in a warm place for 2 hours. Divide the mixture in half and place in two well-buttered loaf tins, sprinkled with flour. (To be on the safe side they can be lined with buttered greaseproof paper.) Put back in the warm place for 20 minutes. Preheat oven to 350°F (180°C, Gas Mark 4). Bake the loaves for 1¼ hours and turn out on a rack to cool. The loaves can be wrapped in a cloth and stored in an airtight bread crock. To serve, cut in slices and spread with butter.

pirog

This Russian bread is light in texture and similar to brioche but less rich. It is traditionally filled with a layer of vegetables such as cabbage, carrots and mushrooms (see recipes, overleaf)

1 lb/0.5 kg white bread flour

1 teaspoon salt

¾ oz/22.5g fresh yeast

pinch of sugar

¼ lb/120g butter

1 egg + 3 yolks

¼ pint/1.5 dl tepid milk

SERVES 6–8

Put the flour with the salt into a large warm bowl. Put the yeast in a cup with the sugar and ¼ pint/1.5 dl water. Stand for 10 minutes in a warm place until it starts to bubble. Soften the butter slightly, until almost melted, and beat the egg yolks with the milk. Make a well in the middle of the flour, pour in the yeast and cover with the flour. Pour on the eggs and milk and mix well. Turn on to a floured board and pat out into a rectangle. Dot the butter over the dough in small pieces, then roll it up and knead it to mix well. Only knead for a moment or two, then return to the bowl and cover with a cloth. Leave in a warm place for 2 hours, or until doubled in volume. Punch down, turn out and knead again; it should be slightly easier to work now. Continue to knead, sprinkling with extra flour, until smooth. Roll out in a large oval shape and lay the cooled filling over half of it. Cover with the other half, like an omelette in shape, and seal the edges with beaten egg, pinching together with floured fingers. Preheat the oven to 400°F (200°C, Gas Mark 6) and return to the warm place to rise for another 20 minutes, then bake for 20 minutes. Serve while hot, cutting across in slices.

mushroom filling for pirog

½ lb/240g flat mushrooms
2 oz/60g butter
juice of ½ lemon
4 tablespoons chopped parsley
salt and black pepper

Slice the mushrooms and cook them gently in the butter. When almost softened, add the lemon juice, parsley, and plenty of salt and black pepper. Allow to cool before using.

cabbage and onion filling for pirog

1 medium onion
1½ oz/45g butter
1 green cabbage
salt and black pepper

Chop the onion and soften it in the butter. Remove the outer leaves of the cabbage and cut the heart in quarters. Cook them briskly in boiling salted water, until just tender. Drain well and chop, squeezing out all the water as soon as it is cool enough to handle. Add to the softened onion and stir well, seasoning with plenty of salt and black pepper. Cool before using.

potato and apple cake

This is an Irish teatime dish and is surprisingly good
1 lb/0.5 kg floury potatoes
1 oz/30g butter
1 teaspoon castor sugar
pinch of salt
¼ lb/120g flour
¾ pint/4.5 dl stewed apple

Boil the potatoes until tender; drain. Mash them while they are still hot and beat in the butter. Add a level teaspoon of sugar and a pinch of salt. Shake in the sifted flour bit by bit and beat with a wooden spoon until smooth. Knead lightly and divide it in half. Butter a small cake tin with a removable bottom and roll out each half of dough to fit. Preheat the oven to 350°F (180°C, Gas Mark 4). Lay one circle in the tin and cover with a layer of juicy stewed apple. Cover with the second circle and bake for 50 minutes. Sprinkle with castor sugar and serve while still hot with plenty of cream.

spiced cookies

10 oz/300g flour
9 oz/270g butter
2 medium eggs, or 1 large egg and 1 yolk
6 oz/180g soft brown sugar
2 teaspoons ground cinnamon
½ teaspoon ground ginger
½ teaspoon ground nutmeg
½ teaspoon ground cloves

Sift the flour into a large bowl. Soften the butter slightly, cut it in small pieces and rub into the flour. Beat the eggs; add the sieved sugar to the eggs, beating it in gradually until smooth. Mix the ground spices into the egg mixture and combine with the flour and butter. Stir well with a wooden spoon until smooth. It will be soft and must be chilled before rolling. Leave overnight in the refrigerator; if it is still too soft, put for 20 minutes in the ice compartment. Roll out carefully until about ¼ inch/0.5 cm thick and cut into shapes with a floured star-shaped cutter. Preheat the oven to 350°F (180°C, Gas Mark 4). Lift up the little shapes with a palette knife and lay them on a buttered baking sheet. Bake for 8 minutes and when cool lift them off the sheet.

Drinks

sloe gin

This is delicious when served as an aperitif

2 *bottles dry gin*

2 *pints/1 litre sloes*

¾ *lb/360g lump sugar*

Get a large earthenware crock or jar big enough to hold 6 pints/3 litres. Prick each sloe with a strong needle stuck in a cork and drop them into the jar. Add the gin and the sugar and close the jar tightly. Leave for 2½–3 months, turning round and shaking from side to side every two or three days. When the time is up, pour into bottles, discarding the sloes, and seal tightly.

Monaco

This delicious and virtually non-alcoholic cocktail can be made quickly and easily

dash of grenadine

light lager

fizzy lemonade

SERVES 1

Put a dash of grenadine into a tall glass. Add several ice-cubes and fill up with equal parts of lager and fizzy lemonade. Mix lightly and serve immediately.

lemon vodka

Chilli vodka can be made by substituting 4 or 5 small hot chillis for the lemon rind, and tarragon vodka by substituting a branch of tarragon

1 *lemon*

1 *bottle vodka*

Use a pretty bottle holding roughly 1¼ pints/ 7.5 dl, preferably in clear glass, with a well-fitting stopper or cork. Alternatively, use 2 bottles holding about ¾ pint/4.5 dl each. Pare the rind of the lemon thinly, being careful to take only the yellow part. Cut it off the lemon lengthwise in thin strips. Put 7 or 8 strips into a large bottle, or 4 or 5 into each smaller bottle. Fill them up with vodka and seal tightly. Leave for at least 10 days before drinking. This is best drunk very cold and can be kept safely in the freezer, since the high alcohol content stops it actually freezing.

Irish coffee

2 *teaspoons sugar*

2 *measures Irish whiskey*

2 *cups strong black coffee*

¼ *pint/1.5 dl very cold double cream*

SERVES 2

Warm two glasses and put a teaspoon of sugar into each. Next add a measure of whiskey to each, then the hot coffee. Stir gently, then pour into each some very cold double cream over the back of a spoon, so that it floats on the top of the coffee. Serve immediately.

Turkish coffee

1 *heaped teaspoon ground Turkish coffee*

1 *teaspoon sugar*

2–3 *cardamom seeds (optional)*

SERVES 1

Put the coffee and the sugar into a traditional coffee pot with a narrow neck, or use a very small saucepan. Add 2 tablespoons cold water and set over a high flame, stirring until well mixed. Bring to the boil, removing from the heat when the froth rises. Stir briefly, return to the heat and allow to boil up a second time, then pour immediately into a small cup, allowing the froth to lie on the surface. Serve hot, but allow the grounds to settle before drinking. You can add 2 or 3 cardamom seeds to the coffee halfway through the brewing.

Basic recipes

basic white sauce

½ pint/3 dl liquid: milk, chicken, fish or
vegetable stock
1 slice onion
2 cloves
¼ bay leaf
1½ oz/45g butter
2 tablespoons flour
pinch grated nutmeg
salt and black pepper

If no other flavouring is to be used in the
white sauce, the milk (if used) should be
infused before adding. Put it into a small pan
with the onion, cloves and bay leaf. Bring
slowly to the boil and immediately remove
from the heat. Cover the pan and stand for
20 minutes, then strain before using. Melt the
butter slowly in a heavy pan. Remove from
the heat and shake in flour, stirring until
amalgamated. Return to the heat and cook for
1 minute, stirring constantly. Remove from
the heat again and add the heated milk or
stock gradually, mixing until each new
addition is blended. When all is absorbed,
return to the heat and bring to the boil,
stirring. Simmer gently for at least 4 minutes,
stirring now and then. Add salt and pepper to
taste and the grated nutmeg. Grated cheese or
cream should be added at this stage, chopped
herbs only at the last moment. This sauce can
be served immediately or kept warm over a
pan of hot water until needed; in this case
beat well before serving.

vanilla sugar

3–4 vanilla pods
castor sugar

Half-fill a large glass jar with castor sugar and
stick a few vanilla pods upright in the sugar.
Fill up the jar with more sugar and close
tightly. Leave for at least a week before
using, if possible, to allow the flavour to
permeate the sugar. Some people cut the
pods in half lengthwise, which increases the
flavour, but gives a sticky brown substance to
the sugar, which I find unattractive. If
required, a pod can be taken out of the sugar
and used to flavour a dish, then carefully
washed, dried and replaced in the jar. This is
rarely necessary, however, as I do not often
seem to need the flavour of vanilla without
the sweetness of the sugar. As it is used up,
the sugar can be replenished. The pods will
only need replacing after a year or so.

short pastry

Where a recipe calls for ½lb/250g pastry, use
the quantities given here. Where a recipe calls
for 6oz/180g pastry, make this quantity,
reserving the leftovers for another use. Where
a recipe calls for ¾lb/360g, make double the
quantity and reserve the rest. For a sweet
dish, omit the salt and add a pinch of castor
sugar and a squeeze of lemon juice

½ lb/240g flour
pinch of salt
¼ lb/120g butter
2 oz/60g lard
iced water

Make sure the fats are very cold indeed before
starting. Sift the flour with the salt in a large
bowl. Cut the fats in small pieces. Rub them
into the flour very quickly, then add just
enough iced water, mixing with the blade of a
knife, to make a soft dough. Form into a ball,
handling as little as possible, wrap in cling-
film wrap and chill for 30 minutes in the
refrigerator before using.

Index

The VOGUE
Summer
COOKBOOK

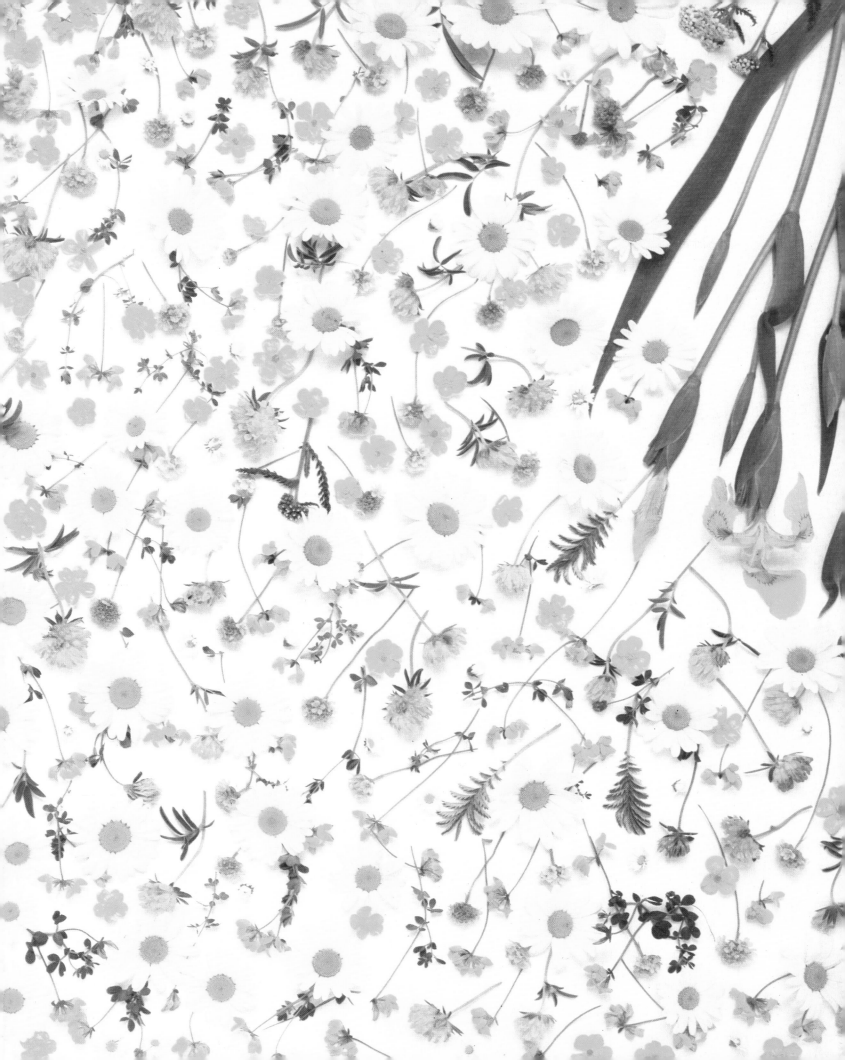

The VOGUE
Summer
COOKBOOK

Arabella Boxer and Tessa Traeger

Mitchell Beazley

Editor	*Fiona Grafton*
Art Editor	*Val Hobson*
Assistant Editors	*Jane Garton*
	Helen Scott-Harman
Assistant Art Editor	*Ingrid Mason*
Art Assistant	*Flick Ekins*
Executive Editor	*Alexandra Towle*

The Vogue Summer and Winter Cookbook was edited
and designed by Mitchell Beazley Publishers Limited,
Mill House, 87-89 Shaftesbury Avenue, London W1V 7AD

© Mitchell Beazley Publishers Limited 1980
Text © Arabella Boxer Photographs © Tessa Traeger and
Condé Nast Publications Limited
All rights reserved
No part of this work may be reproduced or utilized in any
form by any means, electronic or mechanical, including photo-
copying, recording or by any information storage or retrieval
system, without the prior written consent of the publisher

ISBN 0 85533 216 6

Typeset by Pierson LeVesley Ltd
Reproduction by Gilchrist Bros Ltd, Leeds
Printed in Great Britain by Morrison and Gibb Ltd

The publishers and authors would like to thank the following:
Vicarage Herbs, East Claydon, Buckinghamshire;
Mr Vincent at Enton Hall Health Centre, Godalming, Surrey;
Stephen Long, 348 Fulham Road, London SW10; Pat
Walker of the Doll Shop and all the stallholders of
Antiquarius, King's Road, London SW3; Elizabeth David of
46 Bourne Street, London SW1; Elijah Allen and Son and
J.W. Cockett, Butchers, of Hawes, Yorkshire; Justin de
Blank Provisions, 42 Elizabeth Street, London SW1; Justin
de Blank Herbs, Plants and Flowers, 114 Ebury Street,
London SW1; L'Herbier de Provence, 341 Fulham Road,
London SW6; Still Too Few, 300 Westbourne Grove,
London W11; Anglers' Retreat, Stall 93, Chelsea Antique
Market, King's Road, London SW3; Giovanni Filippi of
Lina Stores Ltd, 18 Brewer Street, London W1; Chattels,
53 Chalk Farm Road, London NW1; Bernard Gaume of the
Carlton Tower Hotel, Cadogan Place, London SW3.
Our special thanks to Jan Baldwin, Tessa Traeger's assistant,
and to Oula Jones who compiled the indexes.

Contents

How to use this book . . . . .
The Summer and Winter Cookbook is presented as two books
bound together under one cover. Each book is divided into two sections.
The illustrated text on seasonal cookery themes is cross-referenced to the recipe section.
The index for the Summer Cookbook begins on page 127.

Introduction

The foods that appeal most in summertime are so varied as almost to defy classification. In short, it is easier to define the foods that do not appeal: the heavy dishes, with a high starch content, or those rich in fat which we need in winter to keep us warm. Almost all my favourite foods are summer foods. I have a strong inclination, almost a passion, for light, fresh-tasting, fruity foods: leafy vegetables, dishes in aspic, grilled and poached foods and salad of all sorts.

Another appealing aspect of summer eating is the opportunity of using fresh herbs; although loath to offend the devotees of dried herbs, I must honestly admit I can find little to recommend them. Fresh green herbs, on the other hand, have just about everything in their favour. They are like the distilled essence of fresh food; full of health-giving properties, they add to our capacity to digest foods, as well as giving them delicate taste and visual appeal. They also have the advantage of distinguishing clearly the essential difference between freshly cooked and packaged food, for there is no way that their freshness of flavour can be either preserved or duplicated in any fashion.

Many of our favourite dishes change their character in summer; new potatoes, for instance, are a quite different vegetable from the floury old ones of the winter months. While these are also good, indeed better for some purposes, they cannot rival the first new potatoes, fresh from the garden, with their summery taste. Summer spinach, with its soft, almost silky texture and tart taste, is another example of a food that reaches its peak at this time of year. Crisp fresh lettuces, even the soft-leaved and tender varieties, are totally dissimilar to their winter cousins, the limp products of greenhouses and artificial heat. Young spring chickens have a character all their own, although they may lack some of the flavour of the older birds. A spring lamb, especially one that has fed on the salt marshes of France, Kent or Wales, makes one of the best dishes of all time, especially when served with fresh mint sauce or fruit jelly—crab apple, red currant, or quince. Salmon trout is another of our summer delights, although its cousin, the salmon, appears in late winter and very early spring.

In very hot weather—late summer for instance—we hardly feel the need for solid food, but this can be misleading. It becomes dangerously easy to neglect our diet in muggy weather, when appetites wane and the urge to cook disappears almost altogether. Yet liquid food can be nourishing as well as appetizing and there

are many delicious drinks, often speedily made in a food processor or blender, that are also full of vitamins. Fresh herbs combined with buttermilk; vegetable juices alone or mixed with yoghourt; fruit juices; consommés of beef or chicken, drunk chilled, or jellied; thin purées of cooked vegetables enriched with a little cream—all these can add nourishment to our diet without weight. I am not often an advocate of tinned foods but in hot weather they do prove their worth. Tinned clam juice makes an excellent cold soup, while for those without a juice extractor, tinned vegetable juices and tomato juice are worth their weight in gold. Tinned tomatoes also make good quick sauces, even uncooked, for spaghetti is often served cold in Italy, well moistened with olive oil and covered with a fresh spicy sauce. A nut sauce is also very good.

Ice-creams and sorbets make a perfect close to a summer meal, just as chilled soups make a good beginning. The home-made ice-creams of childhood memories taste better than even the best commercial varieties. I find these have become so complex in their diversity of flavours as to make one long for simple tastes: the acid fruits like black currants make the best ice-cream, in my opinion, since they can withstand bland additions of cream and egg yolks without losing any of their pungency. Sorbets, on the other hand, seem more suited to mixtures of fruit; many of the tropical fruits make delicious water ices when combined with orange and lime juice. Citrus fruits do not on the whole combine well with cream; lime, lemon, orange, grapefruit—and pineapple as well—are all much better when they are made into tart iced sorbets. One of the delights of summer is eating fresh fruit quite simply, whether berries, currants or the stone fruits like apricots, peaches, plums and nectarines. This is how they have been served for hundreds of years in English country houses: as a separate course, following the cheese, which itself followed the dessert. Straight from the garden, which was usually well supplied with greenhouses to compensate for the vagaries of the English summer, the fruit course had its own special china and even its own knives and forks, often in silver gilt to avoid the unpleasant effect of acidity on steel, accompanied by a silver sugar castor and cream jug. As young children in our home in Scotland, for our birthdays the head gardener would contrive to produce the first peach, raspberry, or nectarine of the year for each of us in turn. In this way I learnt to appreciate the joys of eating fruit early, but already in season.

8

The indispensable egg

The egg has played an important role in our culinary history, and today we recognize it as one of the most complete and economical of foods

All eggs are edible and have probably been eaten at some time or other. Swans' eggs were once used for wedding cakes, while plovers' and quails' eggs have been considered a delicacy in England for hundreds of years.

Almost all wild birds' eggs are now protected by law. Among the few exceptions are the eggs of most of our gulls. The eggs of the black-headed gull fetch high prices in London during their short season in late May and early June. Surprisingly enough, the eggs of the lapwing or green plover may be gathered, but only up to April 14. But the eggs can only be used for home consumption; their sale is prohibited. Pheasants' eggs are supposed to be extremely good to eat, but these birds, also, are too valuable for the eggs to be eaten, as indeed is often the case with the eggs of ducks and geese.

All domestic birds' eggs can be eaten and this now includes quails'. Quails' eggs can be bought imported, in jars, but the fresh eggs have more flavour and are more decorative. Like gulls' eggs, they are sold already cooked, and need only to be served as they are, in their shells, with thinly sliced brown bread and butter, celery salt and cayenne pepper. Pullets' eggs, like bantams', are full of flavour in spite of their small size.

Doves' eggs were once much used, for the dovecote was not just a decorative addition to a country house but had a sound practical value. With all the facilities of modern life one tends to forget the exigencies in previous times of feeding large families through the winter months. With a dovecote a supply of fresh eggs and the occasional bird was assured. Dovecotes were never artificially set up; the dovecote was simply built and left empty, whereupon flocks of wild doves would arrive to fill it. Nowadays doves' eggs are protected, with the exception of the collared dove in Scotland.

It comes as a surprise to realize how much birds' eggs vary in shape, size and colour. The egg of the owl, like that of the dove, is very nearly a perfect round, while the guillemot's egg is long and pointed, like an avocado pear. This is a form of protection, for the guillemot lays its eggs on precipitous ledges on the sides of cliffs and if caught by the wind the egg does not roll but swings round on its axis to face into the wind.

Although early English cookery books, from the fourteenth century onwards, contain many recipes for cooking eggs—in pastry, with vegetables, as omelettes, fritters and custards—they are rarely mentioned in accounts of meals. I could find only three mentions of actual egg dishes as part of a meal, which puzzles me somewhat. They were certainly used in large numbers; until the seventeenth century, for example, hard-boiled eggs formed the basis of most stuffings, in the way that breadcrumbs do today. Perhaps egg dishes did not figure in the sort of grand meals that were considered worthy of recording. The earliest account that I was able to find was of an elaborate dinner of 68 dishes given in 1730; included were pheasant dressed with its eggs and another dish called Portugal eggs. Thirty years later, in *The Diary of a Country Parson*, Parson Woodforde records a simple dinner consisting of roast mutton, veal cutlets, a selection of cold meats and boiled eggs.

In the nineteenth century the egg made its first appearance at the breakfast table. Until then a heavy meal of meat dishes with cheese and beer had been the custom among country folk while a few more sophisticated people had taken to a light breakfast of rolls with hot chocolate. Now the traditional cooked English breakfast as we know it established itself.

In this century, England's consumption of eggs doubled just before World War I began; then it doubled again before World War II. In both cases, restrictions interrupted what would otherwise have been a steady growth. Then for the first time in hundreds of years, the English started to eat less; the heavy meals of the eighteenth and nineteenth centuries gave way at last to a totally new approach to food, encouraged by the emergence of smaller households, and fewer children and servants. In this era of lighter meals the egg gained a new importance. Certainly by the 1920s and 1930s an egg dish was considered acceptable as a first course for a simple luncheon or dinner, while some years later it would be thought of as a possible meal in itself. Nowadays egg dishes have become almost a way of life. As Cole Lesley recorded in his biography, all Noël Coward wanted to eat in the evening was "a little eggy something on a tray".

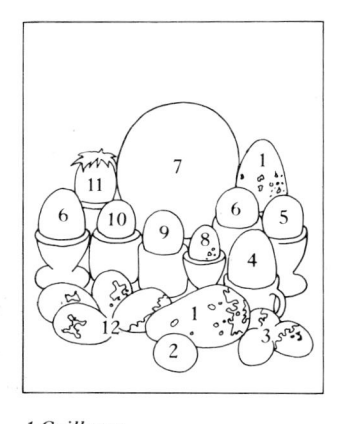

| 1 Guillemot |
| 2 Dove |
| 3 Quail |
| 4 Herring gull |
| 5 Black-headed gull |
| 6 Duck |
| 7 Ostrich |
| 8 Moorhen |
| 9 Guinea-fowl |
| 10 Pullet |
| 11 Chicken |
| 12 Plover |

eggs in green peppers p74
stuffed eggs p74
egg croquettes p75
baked eggs with
  cheese p75
tomato sauce 1 p103

Hot-weather soups

Small china bowls of attractively garnished creamy purées, golden consommés or blends of raw vegetables, served hot or icy cold, make an appetizing start to a summer meal

1 *Cold cucumber soup*
2 *Beetroot and fennel soup*
3 *Carrot and tomato soup*
4 *Gaspacho*
5 *Cold watercress soup*
6 *Crème Sénégale*

Summer soups are as different from winter soups as summer frocks are from winter dresses. For a start, they are less substantial, and never form the main part of a meal, as a minestrone might in wintertime. Their purpose is quite different, and they are intended more as a prelude to a meal than as part of the meal itself. In really hot weather they may be almost more like a cocktail, or a sort of liquid salad, than solid food. In Spain, for instance, gazpacho originated as the food of the poorest peasants in Andalusia, a sort of simple salad eked out with water and eaten with bread for the midday meal. From there it travelled to the tables of smart restaurants in Madrid, London and New York, popular for its very lack of nourishment, its refreshing quality that helps to revive a flagging appetite. Iced consommés are also delicious in hot weather: cold bortsch, madrilène, or simply a well-made beef tea or chicken broth. When preferred, any of these may be served jellied, which makes them even more appetizing, especially when served with fresh lemons. The jelly should not be too firm, nor set solid; it should be roughly broken up and piled up in small cups.

Only slightly more filling are the light vegetable purées; a cream of green peas is one of the best known, but more unusual is one of broad beans. Thin purées of watercress, cucumber or spinach are also good; in varying shades of green, these look pretty with a blob of lightly whipped cream floating on the top, or partly stirred in. Another good purée can be made with sweet corn, or an unusual one with courgettes. Purée of potato can be enriched with cream and flavoured with one of the most delicate summer herbs: chervil, dill or burnet. All of these soups can be served hot or cold as desired; when cold, I like to purée them to a smooth texture, and add a garnish at the last minute. A green pea soup could have a few small peas floating in it, while some slivers of broad beans can decorate the bean soup. A few kernels of corn look pretty in the corn soup, while the watercress soup needs only a little sprig of its own leaves. The soups of courgettes and of spinach are best garnished with a little sour cream, or some chopped herbs. When these soups are served hot, I like to have a slightly coarser texture, and leave them ungarnished.

One of the most popular hot-weather soups is vichyssoise, with its obligatory garnish of chopped chives. It is not easy however to find leeks in midsummer, in fact leeks and chives rarely overlap for more than a few weeks at a time. Spring onions can be substituted for the leeks, but are not quite so good. Cold soups are always popular in America, where vichyssoise made its reputation. One which I like even more, but never see outside New York, is crème Sénégale. This I ate for the first time at the Knickerbocker Club in New York, and have since made it often myself. A chilled cream of chicken soup, lightly flavoured with curry powder, it is a most appealing colour, very refreshing, and more than delicious.

Some refreshing and unusual soups can be made by using a combination of cooked and raw ingredients. I have devised a soup of cooked and puréed cucumbers with chopped raw tomatoes stirred in at the last moment; in this way one combines the digestive qualities of the cooked vegetable with the sharp acidity of the raw one. The same technique can be used with just one vegetable; a cream of cauliflower can be enhanced by the addition of some raw chopped florets, scattered in at the last moment to add a contrasting texture.

Some soups that we connect more often with wintertime can be adapted to make interesting summer soups. A lentil soup made with buttermilk for instance, makes a most delicious and unusual cold soup, more sustaining than most. I often use buttermilk for adding to cold soups, for it gives a smoothness and tart flavour, increased with lemon juice when desired, without the bland richness of cream. It is not suitable for hot soups since it separates as the temperature nears boiling point; to achieve a similar effect in a hot soup it is best to use a mixture of sour cream, milk and lemon juice.

A light fish soup can be excellent in hot weather, particularly when made with prawns, crayfish and other shellfish. A version of crème Sénégale, substituting shellfish for chicken, is one of the nicest and most appetizing. If preferred, saffron can be used instead of curry powder as a flavouring.

Just as the soups themselves differ from their winter versions, so should the method of serving vary. Whether hot, cold or jellied, all summer soups are best served in small cups or bowls, preferably of thin china. Only a small amount per person is required, and since a garnish is often an intrinsic part of the soup, they are not suited to serving in a tureen. Whether of small vegetables, leaves, herbs, or simply cream, a garnish always looks better contained within a cup rather than floating about in a large soup plate.

Freshwater fish

Their excellence too often underrated, fresh fish from rivers and lakes are delicious hot or cold with the simplest of accompaniments, and so easy to cook

Fishing is apparently the favourite sport of the English, surpassing even football in popularity. Yet despite this, freshwater fish are sadly neglected by English cooks. (In one classic English cookery book some thirty-five pages are devoted to recipes for sea fish, and only six to freshwater fish.) Apart from salmon and trout, river fish are rarely found on the table in either houses or restaurants; probably the only people who ever eat pike, shad, perch or grayling here are the anglers themselves. Yet in France there are many classic dishes based on river and lake fish, including *quenelles de brochet*, *matelote* of mixed river fish, *anguilles au vert* and many dishes of *écrevisses*, the freshwater crayfish.

While sea fish vary widely from ocean to ocean and many Mediterranean fish simply have no equivalent in Great Britain, freshwater fish seem to vary little, except possibly in flavour. The rivers of European countries and even Russia are filled with salmon, trout, pike, perch, shad, grayling and crayfish, as are our own, while even the char, which I thought existed only in Derwent Water, a mysterious relic from the ice age, turns out to be well known in Lake Annecy and other deep lakes in France and Switzerland. Known as *omble chevalier* in French, this was formerly a highly rated fish in England, before becoming so rare as to be almost extinct. Potted char was a much-loved breakfast dish in country houses before the First World War, and pretty shallow china dishes called "char dishes" can till be found in antique shops.

Today, the trout is probably the best and most popular of river fish, apart from the salmon, which has now joined the ranks of luxury foods, thus acquiring an unjustified reputation in my opinion. In days gone by, Scottish labourers used to stipulate in their contracts that they were not to be fed salmon more than a specified number of days each week.

There are two sorts of trout native to England, salmon trout and brown trout; and a third, rainbow trout, has been introduced from America. Salmon trout, or sea trout, approaches salmon in price, but is in many ways superior in flavour. It is a pretty fish, weighing from 1½ to 6 pounds, with a delicate light pink flesh that is paler and less rich than that of the salmon. It divides its life as the salmon does, between river and sea, and is usually caught by netting the estuaries. It is best poached in plain salt water and served either hot or cold, but never chilled. When hot, it is exquisite, served with sauce mousseline or hollandaise; when cold, a green mayonnaise is a good accompaniment.

The brown trout, very similar to both the European trout and the American brook trout, can be found in fast-flowing streams and rivers and in deep lakes. Its flesh varies in colour and flavour according to the water it inhabits. It has delicate flesh and very tasty skin. It can be grilled, fried or poached, baked in the oven, or filleted and fried in oatmeal as it is in Scotland. It is also a fish that is really good when it is smoked.

The rainbow trout is widely raised here on fish farms, and will live happily in waters that the brown trout will not tolerate. Its flesh varies from white to pale salmon pink; the pink ones in particular are very good, although not so delicious as the wild brown trout.

Pike are rarely seen in shops, yet they are ideal for pounding into quenelles, mousses and moulds. They are also good poached whole in a court bouillon and served with a wine-flavoured sauce or a *beurre blanc*. Roach and perch, though lacking in any special interest, are good when freshly caught and fried, while shad is an excellent fish much loved in the United States. Grayling is never seen in shops, yet this is a useful fish, like a cross between a grey mullet and a trout, which comes into season just when salmon and trout go out: it is available from mid-June to mid-March.

In terms of food values, fish is probably better value for money than almost any other food. Trout, in particular, is rich in protein, calcium and iron. Yet half of the fish eaten in this country is bought from fish and chip shops, which is a sad reflection on our cooking. England has probably never been a great fish-eating country, unlike Scotland which, despite the excellence of its beef, has always consumed vast quantities of fish. In Celtic times, eating fish was forbidden since the rivers were thought to be sacred. With the coming of the Romans this changed, and as Christianity spread, fish-eating days were introduced and later enforced by law. Devout church-goers did not eat meat at all during Lent, or on any Friday or fast day throughout the year. In inland areas this meant that large supplies of freshwater fish were essential, especially for the large households of the time. In many ways, the well-stocked fish ponds of the monasteries were like the forerunners of our modern fish farms. As early as 1100, the monks had succeeded in reproducing the conditions necessary for encouraging the fish to spawn successfully. These ponds were stocked mainly with carp, some of which were reputed to be more than a hundred years old.

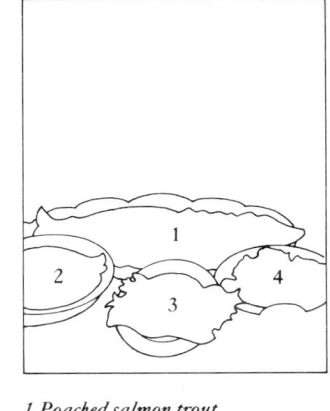

1 Poached salmon trout
2 Grilled trout
3 Cold trout en gelée
4 Trout in oatmeal

Fish from the sea

Take a fresh look at fish—their delicate flavour and texture gives endless variety to many of our best-loved dishes, and there is a fascinating range to choose from

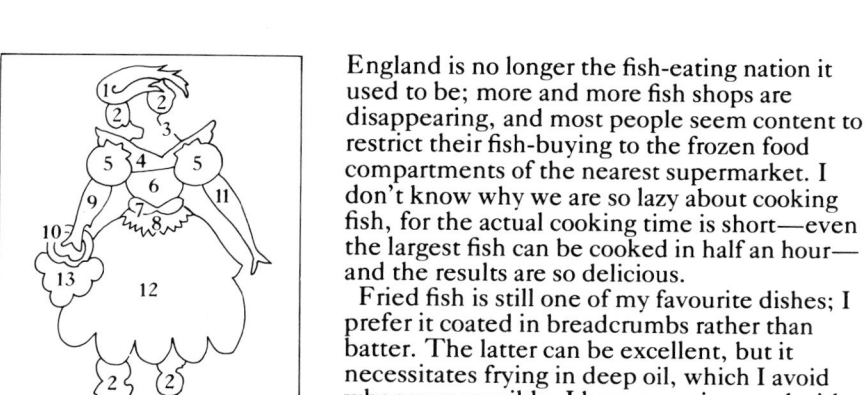

| 1 Lobster |
| 2 Oysters |
| 3 Whitebait |
| 4 Whiting |
| 5 Scallops |
| 6 Sardines |
| 7 Mussels |
| 8 Sprats |
| 9 Trout |
| 10 Eel |
| 11 Mackerel |
| 12 Smoked haddock |
| 13 Clams |

goujons of sole p85
baked cod p85
fish in aspic p86
tomato sauce 2 p103
mayonnaise p104
herb sauce p105
horseradish sauce p107
curry sauce p107
easy hollandaise
  sauce p108

England is no longer the fish-eating nation it used to be; more and more fish shops are disappearing, and most people seem content to restrict their fish-buying to the frozen food compartments of the nearest supermarket. I don't know why we are so lazy about cooking fish, for the actual cooking time is short—even the largest fish can be cooked in half an hour— and the results are so delicious.

Fried fish is still one of my favourite dishes; I prefer it coated in breadcrumbs rather than batter. The latter can be excellent, but it necessitates frying in deep oil, which I avoid whenever possible. I have experimented with frying all sorts of fish in shallow fat and find it perfectly satisfactory, although the results do not always look quite so professional.

When I first started cooking, I used to make endless dishes of fillets of fish baked in the oven, with various garnishes; now I much prefer fish cooked absolutely plainly, either grilled, fried or poached, and served with a separate sauce. I think almost all white fish is good fried: little strips of Dover sole are exquisite, but even quite dull fish such as dab or lemon sole are also good. I make a huge platter of several different sorts and shapes of fried fish and serve them with two or three sauces. In a restaurant I like to seize the opportunity to have *beurre blanc*, or hollandaise sauce, as I find these too nerve-racking to make, but there are many simple and delicious sauces that can be quickly made instead; I like a creamy horseradish sauce with fried fillets of plaice or sole, while a sorbet of tomatoes and sour cream is quite delicious with *goujons* of sole. A herb sauce made with dill, tarragon or chervil is ideal with a poached white fish, while a béchamel made from fish stock and cream is far better than a cheese sauce for *gratins* or fish pies. A curry sauce with white fish is excellent, as is saffron sauce. Herb butters cannot be improved upon; parsley butter sharpened with plenty of lemon juice is probably the best of all with grilled Dover sole, but more unusual herb butters can be made with tarragon or chervil.

We rarely eat cold fish dishes in this country, and I find this sad for they are among my favourite summer dishes. Fillets of poached fish in aspic jelly with a light curry sauce make a good first course, as does a fish salad of poached halibut dressed with olive oil and lemon juice, and plenty of chopped herbs. Fillets of sole in *chaudfroid* sauce garnished with tarragon leaves look pretty, while a cold fish mousse with a contrasting sauce makes a good main course for a light meal. I have a passion for solid white fish such as American swordfish and pompano and I love the Mediterranean dishes of *loup de mer* and *daurade*, although I know that they cannot match our own Dover sole and salmon trout for delicacy of flavour and of texture.

Halibut is my favourite local fish, because of its firm texture and excellent flavour. I like it cut in steaks and grilled, or baked in the oven with strips of bacon. Turbot is a close rival; this soft and delicate fish responds best to poaching, and the ideal accompaniment is hollandaise sauce. Bass is a nice firm fish, good served cold with tomatoes, onion and herbs, or baked with bacon.

Sadly the oily fish like mackerel and sardines are only really good when eaten within hours of being caught. Herrings are one of our cheapest and most nutritious of fish, yet are not prepared by many home cooks. It may be the bones that put people off; the only way I like them is filleted, coated in coarse oatmeal, brushed with melted butter and grilled.

Whiting is another cheap fish. It used to appear invariably as the first course at dinner parties, deep fried with its tail in its mouth. It does not have much special character, but I find it quite good with head and tail removed, dipped in egg and breadcrumbs and fried with a sharp, strong horseradish sauce.

I rarely buy cod now as it no longer has even the merit of being cheap; I have always preferred haddock, except for two excellent dishes that demand cod. One is a piece of cod poached and served with a wide variety of boiled vegetables and *aïoli*, a garlicky Provençal sauce. The other is a less well-known Belgian dish of cod baked in the oven with butter and lemon juice; it is surprisingly good.

All dishes of hot poached fish are improved by the addition of steamed or boiled potatoes, particularly when they have a sauce. I find that little else is needed except perhaps a glass of good white wine.

Beachcombing

Take a stroll along the beach at low tide and discover a veritable wealth of delectable food: it is a true gourmet's paradise, and all for free

The sea-shore has been a rich hunting ground for scavengers since time began, especially during the winter months, when little nourishment was to be found on land. In the Hebrides strange conical mounds were found near the shore which, on excavation, turned out to be the garbage tips of the very earliest settlers, and furnished abundant proof that they lived entirely on the sea-shore. This was probably for two reasons: first as a source of food, and second as protection from the wild animals that inhabited the thickly wooded interior.

During a week in Wales with my son, I was amazed by the abundance of food to be gathered on the beaches. On an estuary in North Wales, armed with only a child's bucket and spade, we had found enough food within a couple of hours to last us for a few days, had we been desperate: three huge clams, each bigger than my fist, dozens of mussels, cockles and tiny crabs. There were also shrimps and fish to be caught, and some edible seaweeds.

Shrimping has long been a favourite occupation of both those who live near the sea-shore and holiday-makers. Proper equipment is vital, for without the right sort of net it is almost impossible to catch the tiny transparent shrimps as they dart about. The net must be of the finest possible mesh, quite deep, with a flat end bound with wood and a long handle. This is pushed through the shallows when the tide is farthest out and just on the turn. The shrimps must be transferred from the net to a bag with a flap to stop them jumping out; this is usually worn slung round the neck or waist. On getting home they are flung into swiftly boiling water, when they will immediately turn bright pink, and are cooked for one minute. Shelling them is a fiddly business for they are so small, but quite delicious.

Cockles are also found at low tide, but a little earlier, as the tide is receding. They either lie on the surface of the sand or just under it, where their presence can be detected by holes, sometimes with jets of water spurting from them. The ones on the surface must be carefully inspected, for they are often dead. Cockles are best eaten raw, but they are very hard indeed to open, the only way being to twist one against another. They can be easily opened by boiling for one minute, when their shells open, but their fresh raw taste is lost. They are always sold cooked, for this produces the sterilization required by law. Clams are found in the same way, although they are sometimes deeper in the sand. They can also be eaten raw or cooked, but the large ones we found in Wales would certainly have been too tough to eat raw.

Mussels can be found with no difficulty, often clinging to pipes and piers, but they must not be eaten unless they come from clean water with no sewage outlets in the vicinity. I have never eaten whelks, but I am told they are quite good, although inclined to be tough. Limpets are another mollusc that I have yet to try; their cone-like shells can be found clinging to rocks, from which they can be detached as the tide rises, when they may relax their grip to move away.

Winkles are always sold cooked, and are eaten with a pin; sometimes they are dipped in oatmeal and fried, but they can also be eaten raw. A friend of mine remembers sitting on the beach at Ramsgate with her nanny, who was eating raw winkles with her hatpin. This must have been sometime before World War I and she says firmly that all nannies did this.

There are three main edible seaweeds which grow on the western shores of the British Isles: dulce, carragen and laver. Dulce is a red algae, still occasionally eaten in parts of Scotland. Carrageen, or Irish moss, is usually dried and sold in health food shops. It is a natural form of gelatine, with little taste of its own, and rich in iodine and other minerals. It can be used for making sweet or savoury jellies, or as a thickening agent for soups, stews or jams. If prepared at home, it must be washed for several hours in fresh water, then laid out to bleach in the sun and, ideally, showers of rain, over a period of some days. When dry, it must be stored in a completely dry place or it will absorb moisture from the atmosphere.

Laver, or sloke as it is called in Ireland, is still made much use of in South Wales. It is a large brownish seaweed, almost transparent, which lies over the rocks like a fine net. It must be pulled from the rocks and washed for several hours, preferably in a mountain stream, then boiled for five or six hours, until it is reduced to a blackish pulp, slightly slimy in texture, like over-cooked spinach. It can be bought in Wales in this form known as "laver bread". It is then usually mixed with ground oatmeal to make flat cakes, which are then fried in bacon fat. Cooked simply as a vegetable, it is the traditional accompaniment to the delicious Welsh lamb, which can be seen grazing on the salt marshes along the beaches.

| 1 Scallops |
| 2 Dulce |
| 3 Gut laver |
| 4 Shrimps |
| 5 Prawns |
| 6 Sprats |
| 7 Oysters |
| 8 Mussels |
| 9 Crab |

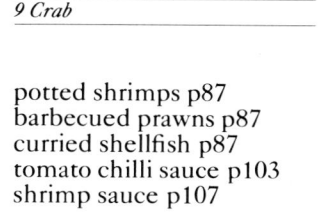

potted shrimps p87
barbecued prawns p87
curried shellfish p87
tomato chilli sauce p103
shrimp sauce p107

Chicken supreme

Whatever your mood or resources, chicken is endlessly adaptable. Hot or cold, mild or spicy, unadorned or in a creamy sauce, for picnics or parties, chicken reigns supreme

Since time immemorial and in almost every culture, the chicken has found its way into the pot. Not long ago it was regarded as something of a luxury, and had to be ordered specially from the butcher; a roast chicken was many families' Sunday lunch, in preference to roast beef. The spread of factory farming has resulted in the general availability of cheap and tender birds, but there has been an inevitable deterioration in flavour. I bought a chicken in a small town in Tuscany recently and was horrified by its appearance. It was a terrible colour with mottled orange flesh, huge misshapen legs, and bright yellow feet of vast size—not exactly high in "eye appeal". I bought it none the less and cooked it with a bunch of herbs from the garden and melted butter mixed with orange and lemon juice. It was the best-tasting chicken I have eaten for a long time, in spite of the fact I neglected to remove its innards so that it took an amazingly long time to cook, a fact which gave great pleasure to the other cook in the household. "Fancy writing all those articles and not knowing enough to take the innards out of the chicken." This shaming experience taught me two things: first, always to check the innards and second, to make a point of buying farm-bred chickens from time to time to remember how a real bird tastes.

I have given up buying poussins for the same reason; however carefully I cook them, they remain virtually tasteless although quite appealing in appearance. Any tender little bird is edible when grilled to a crisp golden brown, but a larger farm bird, cut in joints and grilled, or cooked whole on a spit, is a far better dish. As a cook, I would be lost without chickens, for I find them one of the most versatile of foods. Their very lack of strong flavour means that they can be used as a vehicle for myriad different tastes, scents and colours. They can be flavoured with oriental spices, with saffron or with mustard; they can be scented with fresh summer herbs, with tarragon, basil or thyme. They can be grilled over charcoal until crispy and almost charred, or poached and served in a delicate cream sauce. They can be devilled, a popular breakfast dish of the 1920s, set in dishes of jellied aspic, or braised with aromatic vegetables. They can be stuffed with mixtures of breadcrumbs, shallots and herbs, or with a layer of delicate farce, like a mixture of sorrel and cream cheese (*à la cuisine minceur*) pushed between the skin and the flesh.

Slices of black truffle are sometimes inserted in this way; the bird is then steamed in a chicken broth and served with a velouté sauce. Chickens can be made into a spicy curry, or something bland such as chicken à la king, that great favourite of the American women's clubs.

As an alternative to roasting I prefer to cook a bird slowly in a covered dish in the oven, with butter and lemon juice and a bunch of mixed herbs—marjoram, basil, rosemary and thyme. Another chicken dish of which I am very fond is the Belgian *waterzooi*: a semi-liquid dish of neat fillets of chicken, covered in a thick sauce made from the many vegetables with which it has been poached, enriched with cream and egg yolks. I have a great affection for these sorts of dishes, a cross between a soup and a main dish, eaten in soup plates with knife, fork and spoon, but they are not to everyone's taste.

The tender flesh of the chicken combined with its crisp skin makes it ideal for barbecues, as it cooks quickly and is improved by a degree of intense heat to char the skin; thus it is also well suited to grilling and spit-roasting. It can be first marinated in a mixture of yoghourt, or oil and lemon juice, spices and herbs, or it can be simply painted with mustard and basted with olive oil and lemon juice. Boneless chicken can be cut in neat pieces, threaded on skewers, and basted with a mixture of melted butter, lemon juice and minced garlic. Drumsticks are excellent for picnics or barbecues where they are to be eaten in the fingers. I like to baste them with the same barbecue sauce I use for spareribs. The wings can be used in an elegant dish—a *chaudfroid* of chicken, or a *poulet à l'estragon*. The breasts alone can be fried in butter for a delicious quick and very simple dish.

A whole bird is best for a dish of chicken in aspic, or for a chicken pie, sometimes in small individual dishes, which I find very appetizing. One whole bird can be made into two related dishes; the best of the flesh can be cut up for skewers, for instance, while the carcass and scraps can be made into a most excellent soup, combined with young vegetables and rice or noodles. Chicken livers are useful as the basis for a quick pâté, or as an addition to a risotto. Last of all, the chicken gives us the most useful and delicate stock without which I would be lost. So many dishes depend on a good chicken stock, and substitutes, though useful, are not the same.

Making more of lamb

Plain roast lamb is so good that few of us experiment further. Yet lamb has a natural affinity with many herbs, spices and vegetables which should not go unexplored

English lamb is probably the best in the world, yet apart from the admittedly delicious roast leg of lamb, and grilled lamb cutlets, surprisingly little use is made of it. The cheaper cuts are still occasionally seen, in Irish stew, Lancashire hotpot and Scotch broth, but there seems to be no middle range of lamb cookery in this country. There is no equivalent, for example, to that most delicious of all casseroles, the *navarin d'agneau*, where tender lamb is simmered in broth with a variety of tiny vegetables, each added to the pot at carefully graduated intervals so that all are tender at the same moment. In England, stewing, as it is called, is only considered suitable for tough cuts of meat requiring long, slow cooking. There is no understanding of dishes like *boeuf bourguignon*, where top rump is cooked slowly in good red wine to make a really delicious dish. I published a recipe for this once and received an angry letter asking what was the point of using rump steak in a stew? In the same vein, a friend, who is a good and inventive cook, once said sadly that when she had spent hours simmering a chicken in bouillon with myriad different vegetables, her husband would simply look in the pot and say, "Oh, stew again." A saddle of lamb is the best of all roasting joints, but one can cook the same piece of animal in a smaller and less expensive form, as in a *carré d'agneau*. This useful little joint is made from the best end of neck, with the chine bone removed and the bones neatly trimmed. The English term for this is a rack of lamb, but few butchers will prepare it in the French way. Usually consisting of seven bones, it will serve three people, or four at a pinch. In some New York restaurants, a six-bone carré is served for two people, and carved lengthwise like a saddle of lamb, in thin strips. The bones are cut up and served separately.

A shoulder of lamb is a joint I like immensely. Cheaper than the leg, it is more fatty and not really suitable for roasting. I like to braise it with lots of vegetables and serve it with a sauce made from the cooking liquid enriched with a roux or egg yolks. It is also excellent cooked slowly in the oven and served on a bed of haricot beans well flavoured with garlic.

In the country I cook a boned leg of lamb on a rack over the fire; the only drawback is the shrinkage, for the flavour is extraordinary. I tried doing this in town recently, starting it off under the grill and finishing in the oven. It was almost as good, and took only thirty-five minutes to cook a large leg. The secret is to get your butcher to cut out the bone in such a way that you are left with a rectangular slab of meat, roughly even in thickness. Another good way of cooking a boned leg, and even quicker, is to treat it like a steak and serve with parsley butter. Ask the butcher to cut out the bone leaving the meat as intact as possible; then you need only cut it across in thick slices, as many as you need, brush with olive oil and lemon juice, and grill. In the Middle East, almost all the meat dishes are made from lamb, for beef is almost non-existent. *Moussaka*, for instance, meatballs, and *kafta*—rolls of ground meat pressed round skewers and grilled—are all far more tasty when made with lamb, which seems to have much greater affinity with spices than beef. It certainly goes admirably with the other Middle Eastern accompaniments, the salads of chopped herbs and cracked wheat, and the dishes of cucumber in yoghurt. I think the best of all skewered dishes is the Greek *souvlakia*, where tiny pieces of lamb are threaded on thin sticks, marinated in oil and lemon juice, grilled and served three or four to each person. Nothing else is added—no bay leaves, onion rings or halved tomatoes—and with the accompaniment of hot pitta bread, *tsatsiki* and the inevitable Greek salad, this is a meal of which I never tire. In London now the doner kebab houses are rivalling the pizza houses in popularity. Huge mounds of lamb, revolving vertically on a spit, are carved downwards in thin strips and stuffed into steaming hot pitta.

Though it is not highly thought of, I find cold lamb excellent, particularly when a whole leg of lamb has been roasted and left to get cold before carving. When accompanied by a rice and herb salad, mint sauce made with lemon juice instead of vinegar, and some apple and quince jelly to replace the usual red currant, it makes an impressive and delicious summer meal.

1 *Braised shoulder of lamb with vegetables*
2 *Sauce for braised lamb*
3 *Spicy meatballs*
4 *Mint sauce*
5 *Stuffed aubergine*
6 *Carré d'agneau*
7 *Yogurtlyia*
8 *Pitta bread*
9 *Souvlakia*
10 *Quince jelly*

braised lamb with
  vegetables p91
navarin d'agneau p91
skewers of lamb p92
carré d'agneau p92
Irish stew p92
meat loaf p92
yogurtliya p93
spicy meatballs p93

Substantial salads

Shellfish, poultry, eggs, nuts, cheese, crisp fresh vegetables—combine whatever you choose and create a colourful salad that makes a wholesome meal in itself

| 1 Shellfish salad |
| 2 Rosemary; mint |
| 3 Prawns |
| 4 Scallops |
| 5 Chives |
| 6 Garlic |

shellfish salad p77
chicken salad p77
avocado, tomato and
  mozzarella salad p78
spinach, bacon and
  mushroom salad p80
pitta salad p80
pine kernel salad p81
potato and vegetable
  salad p81
mayonnaise p104
herb sauce p105

In the days when I used to cook proper meals of two or three courses it always annoyed me that I did not have enough time to spend on the salad. There were always other more important things to attend to. Now, for a variety of reasons, I prefer to do the opposite. I like to take one thing which used to be considered as a mere part of the meal, a detail, and by spending a lot of care and thought on it, turn it into a meal in itself. I started to do this with cooked vegetable dishes; now I do it with salads. A salad can be a whole meal in microcosm; it may contain meat, poultry, fish, cheese, eggs, nuts, as well as a huge variety of vegetables, both raw and cooked, and even bread, or crisp croûtons.

A fairly substantial salad seems to me a perfect lunch. Even if I am alone, I almost always have a meal of some sort in the middle of the day; I find it as hard to work all afternoon on an empty stomach as I do after a large lunch with half a bottle of wine. A salad is the obvious answer— not a simple green salad, which would be my first choice if eaten as an accompaniment to another dish—but a *salade composée*, that is to say, a salad made up of a mixture of ingredients, some cooked, some raw—like a salad Niçoise.

I love these sorts of dishes: light, appetizing and nutritious, they are neither too expensive nor troublesome to make. During the summer months a salad of this sort, accompanied by a crusty loaf of bread and followed by some home-made yoghourt, makes a perfect light meal. In colder weather, you can start with a hot soup.

I refuse to give up eating certain foods just because they have become too expensive, but I don't mind eating them less often, and in smaller quantities. Another advantage of these sorts of salads is that they are a good way of using small amounts of costly materials, and making them into a proper dish. Shellfish has become too expensive for most of us to contemplate buying in large quantities, but we can still afford a few crawfish tails or a handful of giant prawns occasionally. Quite apart from the expense, it is important that the "solid" part of the dish be kept down in relation to the leafy content, or the dish will change its character entirely. I remember reading a stricture of Elizabeth David's years ago about not over-filling an omelette; two tablespoons was, I think all she would allow for a three-egg omelette—and I realize now how right she was. A similar formula could be adopted for salads.

Although a salad is by its nature a mixture of things, it must be a carefully chosen mixture, not just a heap of remains. The cooked part must be freshly cooked, and should be either just one thing or a group of closely related things: a mixture of shellfish for example, or a combination of new vegetables. There are a few exceptions: hard-boiled eggs go well with fish, or with a mixture of cooked vegetables; fried bacon and mozzarella cheese make a delicious combination with finely shredded summer spinach and sliced avocado. The ingredients should be cut in similar-sized pieces; whereas in a simple lettuce salad I leave the leaves whole, in a mixed salad I usually cut them in strips.

As far as I am concerned, a salad is composed mainly of raw vegetables, most of them green and leafy: raw spinach or sorrel, lettuce, endive, batavia, chicory, watercress, cucumber, fennel and radish. The numerous Italian dishes of cooked vegetables dressed with oil and lemon are sometimes called salads, but, good as they are, they do not really fit into this category.

Last, there is the choice of dressings. With a quite elaborate salad, one containing chicken or fish, I think the best solution is to have two dressings: one very simple to mix with the dish itself, possibly a little beforehand; the other quite different, more of a sauce, creamy and quite thick, which is served separately. If a thick sauce of this type is poured over the salad it spoils the appearance and gives a slightly gluey consistency; another advantage in keeping it separate is that those on a diet can avoid the richer sauce altogether. With a shellfish salad, for instance, I would first marinate the fish in lemon juice for an hour before serving, then I would dress the assembled salad with the best olive oil and more lemon juice. When serving, I would have a mayonnaise in a separate bowl. With a chicken salad, I would marinate the chopped chicken briefly in lemon juice, then dress the assembled salad with a light sunflower-seed oil and more lemon; I would accompany it with a creamy sauce flavoured with tarragon or dill.

With the simpler salads, those containing dried bread, cheese or nuts, a creamy sauce is not wanted, but with salads of mixed cooked vegetables, or of hard-boiled eggs, it can be an optional extra. The addition of the second sauce will, however, turn the whole dish into something more special, quite elegant enough for a lunch party.

$\mathcal{M}$outhwatering salads

Light, moist, cool, alluring and properly dressed to enhance their flavour, salads can be as ravishing to the eye as they are appealing and appetizing to the palate

Descriptions of salads in books always make my mouth water. The other day I came across an account of a meal the author had eaten at Sissinghurst including "a delicious salad I never had before—watercress, orange sections, chopped shallots, with a little orange in the lemon oil dressing". I couldn't wait to try it, for it seemed to promise the fruity, semi-liquid quality which I love so much, and it certainly proved worthy of its description.

Whereas the French and Italian *salades composées*, dishes of cooked vegetables in a vinaigrette, provide meals on their own, raw salads make a perfect accompaniment to many main dishes. These light, moist dishes composed of green leaves and fruity vegetables—tomatoes, avocados, cucumbers and peppers—make up some of the most appealing, as well as the most nutritious of dishes. My favourite among salads is made from the thinnings of the rows of salad vegetables in my own garden. A mixture of tender young leaves of lettuce, sorrel, spinach, rocket, mustard and dandelion, this salad is very similar to one found in Italy, made from wild salad greens gathered in the fields, and needs only the lightest of dressings.

I like to make each salad dressing to suit the individual salad, and with the rest of the meal in mind. With a tender salad of thinnings, I usually make a light dressing of sunflower seed oil, a few drops of lemon juice, and a light sprinkling of sugar and black pepper. With a more robust mixture of leaves, perhaps including watercress, batavia, endive or chicory, I would use olive oil, white wine vinegar, garlic, sea salt, sugar, black pepper and Dijon mustard. I usually mix the dressing in the empty salad bowl while the leaves stand in their drainer. I often put a peeled clove of garlic in the bowl and leave it to stand for an hour before serving when I discard the garlic, or keep it for the next salad. Alternatively, I use garlic or shallot vinegar. When fresh herbs are available, I chop them at the last moment, just before tossing the salad. If added earlier to flavour the dressing they lose their bright colour, which is part of their appeal. My favourite mixture is equal parts of tarragon, chervil and chives; I also use each of these singly, or mixed with parsley. With tomato salads I prefer basil alone, while with cucumber salads I use dill, chervil, burnet or mint. The only dried herb I use is oregano, which adds a Mediterranean flavour, and is particularly good with salads containing avocado, tomato or mozzarella.

The choice of oils and vinegars is wide. I always have a variety of oils in my kitchen which usually includes a large can of light-flavoured Italian olive oil, a green "virgin" oil brought back from Tuscany, French arachide oil, sunflower seed oil and a small can of walnut oil. For the most part I use the light olive oil, with the fruity Tuscan oil as an alternative. In early autumn I make a salad with fresh green walnuts, using the curious walnut oil. For the acid element I use Dufrais white wine vinegar, lemon juice, or a mixture of the two. I also have a selection of home-made herb vinegars. The best of these are flavoured with burnet, shallot, basil and garlic, and garlic alone. The shallot and garlic vinegars can be made all year round, and are both a short cut and an economy since peeling and chopping shallots and garlic for each salad is a fiddly and wasteful business. Basil alone does not make a good vinegar; its warm sweet taste is better used to flavour olive oil, which can then be used for tomato salads. Steeping herbs in vinegar has a twofold effect; they flavour the vinegar and render it milder and more palatable.

One of the most important aspects of a salad is the visual one, as anyone who has eaten Japanese food is well aware. Spring onions, radishes and celery can be carved into exquisite shapes and left in a bowl of iced water in the refrigerator overnight to create a ravishing effect, while carrots and cucumbers can be cut into flower shapes, and curly endive added for its lacy effect. A small amount of food beautifully arranged on a plate is more appealing than a huge quantity of food, however good. For me, the prettiest salads are a mixture of different shades of green, ranging from the dark watercress to the pale ice-green of peeled cucumber. I also love a mixture of green and white with a little red, which is supplied by thinly sliced radishes, or finely chopped tomato.

After all, probably the best salad is lettuce alone with a simple dressing; I agree with June Platt, who says in her *Plain and Fancy Cookbook*: "Best of all I like a plain green salad with a well-seasoned French dressing, eaten, not as a separate course, but as the sole accompaniment to hot roast chicken or roast veal, the clear syrupy gravy mixing with the salad on the plate being my idea of a heavenly dish."

1 Radishes
2 Spring onions
3 Carrot
4 Celery

A bouquet of herbs

Fresh, fragrant, subtle or pervasive, herbs have always been praised for their magical, medicinal and culinary properties and are today indispensable to the creative cook

Reading through early cookery books, one is constantly reminded of the important part herbs once played in English domestic life. Every manor house and monastery had its own herb garden, many of them very large indeed, and it was not until the sixteenth century that the separate flower garden was conceived. This was mainly due to the immigrants from Flanders, fleeing from Spanish persecution, who carried with them advanced methods of cultivation, as well as many new fruits, flowers and vegetables.

For several centuries before this, the herb garden reigned supreme. The meaning of the word "herb" then was more loose, and the large gardens included many plants we do not think of in that context. Today the Oxford Dictionary still gives as one of its meanings: "plant of which leaves . . . are used for food, medicine, scent, flavour. . . ." According to this definition the wide range of plants grown in many of the fourteenth- and fifteenth-century herb gardens was perfectly correct, for each had its special use; there were onions, leeks, garlic, lettuce, beetroot, nettles, sorrel, radishes and spinach; also roses, lilies, peonies, carnations (known as gilly-flowers), violets, mallows, primroses, marigolds, honeysuckle, lavender and daisies.

The usual form of the herb garden—that of an enclosed rectangular plot laid out in geometric form— is a descendant from the old monastic herb gardens, which were usually surrounded with high banks of earth, walls or tall hedges. Our modern garden is also an extension of this plan with its herbaceous borders—the word "herb" in this context meaning any plant whose stem dies down after flowering.

The history of herbs goes further back than the earliest English records, for they are among the most ancient of plants; many of them were well known to the ancient Persians and Egyptians, Greeks and Romans. The Egyptians put bunches of herbs in the hands of their mummies, while in the fourth century BC Hippocrates compiled a list of four hundred herbs relating to matters of health. The Romans were responsible for introducing many of their favourite herbs to the British Isles, such as chives, parsley, rosemary, chervil and sage. After the departure of the Romans, the cultivation of herbs was taken over by the monasteries. Yet there must have been some knowledge of herbs in Britain even before Roman times, for they were used by the Druids, who performed secret ceremonies of propitiation before picking them. As Christianity

ousted these practices, the monks substituted prayers for the earlier incantations. Some of these prayers still survive and are very beautiful, but it is sad that their pagan antecedents were destroyed. As modern life, with its insistence on common sense, took over, the magical qualities of herbs were forgotten, although some of their mystery still persists in the beliefs, strongly held although hard to prove, of their curative powers.

As flavouring for food, herbs have been neglected in this country for many years. I rarely have the pleasure of eating dishes where the herb is an intrinsic part, as opposed to a mere garnish, unless with friends who have herb gardens or at one or two imaginative restaurants. Our classic dishes are poor in this respect, in comparison with those of other countries; we have little to offer on a par with the French *poulet a l'estragon*, *jambon persillé*, or the Provençal *pistou*. The Belgians have their *anguilles au vert*, the Italians their *salsa verde*, their pizzas aromatic with oregano, and their many dishes of veal flavoured with sage or rosemary. In the Middle Eastern countries there are salads of parsley and mint, sauces of *tahini* and parsley, and cucumbers in yoghourt lavishly seasoned with dried mint.

The greatest value of herbs, in my opinion, is for the creative cook. Herbs lend themselves to imaginative treatment, and once one understands a herb and its affinities, it is hard to go wrong. Among my favourites are basil and tarragon, chervil and dill, all with good culinary qualities.

Basil is delicious with tomatoes, eggs and vegetable dishes; tarragon is at its best used with chicken or eggs. Chervil is like a more subtle and delicious form of parsley and one of the few that mixes well with other herbs. I am especially fond of dill, combined with mustard in a creamy sauce for boiled beef or chicken, with hard-boiled eggs, boiled potatoes, cucumber or beetroot. I like to have two or three varieties of mint in my herb garden: spearmint for cooking, apple mint for its pretty variegated leaf, and eau-de-cologne, or pineapple mint, for its delicious scent which is released when crushed.

If I were now starting grown-up life, as I did twenty years ago, in a small terraced house with a tiny rectangular south-facing garden, I could think of no better use for it than as a herb garden. Herbs will flourish in the poorest of soils so long as they get plenty of sun, and with the addition of a glass frame even the more delicate varieties, like basil, which needs heat to develop its true flavour, can be grown successfully.

28

The first vegetable harvest

In spring, vegetables are in the prime of their youth. Enjoy them at their best—raw or lightly steamed, on their own or with a variety of dips and sauces

Unlike animal foods, vegetables gain little by being allowed to reach maturity. In almost every case, they are at their best when small, with a fully developed flavour and a firm, crisp texture. At the start of the season, we should take advantage of this, for later in the year we have no choice but to eat them fully grown. As often happens, the French have a term for these young vegetables which describes them exactly: *les primeurs*. This means literally "the first", in other words the first of the season, not out-of-season produce which has been flown in from the other side of the world. That is a different matter.

The younger the vegetable, the more it has to lose by being long out of the ground. No early vegetable—or fruit either—keeps well; even early potatoes do not have the keeping properties of the later varieties, while early apples must be eaten soon after picking, although the later-maturing strains may be kept for weeks, or even months. There used to be running battles between the cook and the head gardener in large country houses, for their aims were diametrically opposed. The cook was crying out for young vegetables while the gardener could not resist growing each one to its proper size. Needless to say, this is a problem that few of us have to face nowadays: those lucky enough to be both cook and gardener will see the advantages.

When very young, vegetables are best treated as simply as possible. We should keep for later the soups and soufflés, purées, and quiches.

Preparing *crudités* is a matter of presentation, not cooking. All one needs is a pleasing combination of very fresh young vegetables that complement each other in colour and in texture, and a pretty dish on which to serve them. After being cleaned scrupulously, they should be chilled briefly in the refrigerator, then cut in appropriate shapes and arranged on a dish, with a few ice cubes scattered among them to preserve their crispness. One or two complementary sauces, thick enough for dipping, should be served at the same time. This makes a perfect start to a summer luncheon.

The same method of presentation can be applied to a selection of spring vegetables which have been very lightly cooked, just enough to render them more digestible, and served while still warm. Large spring onions, for instance, are delicious cooked briefly with their leaves still on, and served with mange-tout peas and steamed mushrooms, accompanied by a garlicky mayonnaise. A number of good sauces can be made from combinations of cream cheese with yoghourt or sour cream with chopped herbs or tomato purée added. These are quickly and easily made in a food processor.

The cooking of young vegetables is best done by boiling in the minimum of lightly salted water for the shortest possible time, just long enough to soften them slightly without losing their firmness, then draining and tossing them in melted butter; the butter should not be allowed to overheat, or change its colour. Second, they can be steamed, which suits most vegetables with the possible exception of string beans, which lose some of their intense colour. Here again the timing is vital, for if left a moment too long they develop an unpleasant taste. My third suggestion may seem strange, but I cannot recommend it too highly. It is to cook whole vegetables, even the youngest, in a pressure-cooker. It works remarkably well, especially with courgettes. The timing varies from two to four minutes, and is soon learnt with practice.

Special pans for steaming can be bought, but I use a gadget in stainless steel which opens out like the petals of a flower to fit almost any saucepan. The Chinese wicker steamers are pretty and easy to use, especially if you have a wok over which to stack them. I love the old-fashioned French pots for steaming potatoes, in shiny brown china, but they are fragile. Steamed potatoes are far superior to boiled, peeled potatoes, especially for eating with fish, or any dish with a delicate sauce. Sprigs of dill can be laid among them as they steam and sea salt added after cooking. Young vegetables are best steamed over plain water, although older root vegetables may benefit from cooking over a meat stock.

May and June are the best of all months for eating young vegetables, for even the root vegetables, which we associate with winter, can be lifted and eaten while still tiny. I have always loved a whole course of vegetables. Two or three hot vegetables served together can be delicious after a cold first course or a hot fish, which is best eaten alone. In this way, they take the place of the salad that often follows a hot meat dish. I usually prefer to keep each vegetable separate, especially when very young, but later in the season I often mix three together—broad beans, carrots and courgettes, for example—in a creamy béchamel sauce which is made from the liquid in which the vegetables have cooked, slightly enriched with cream.

1 Cabbage leaves
2 Carrots
3 Broad beans; peppers; red cabbage
4 Onions
5 Aubergine
6 Tomatoes
7 Red peppers
8 Broad beans; peas
9 Fennel
10 Cauliflower
11 Runner beans; broad beans
12 Red cabbage
13 Spinach
14 Onion tops

pistou p106
tomato sauce 3 p103
mustard sauce p106
green sauce p107

ℳ litany of leaves

Sorrel, rocket, Good King Henry, purslane, corn salad, orach, chard, mustard leaves, watercress, dandelion, buttercrunch, ruby beet and curly kale

1 Chinese cabbage
2 Green cabbage
3 American land cress
4 Watercress
5 Lettuce
6 Spearmint
7 Good King Henry
8 Orach
9 Ruby beet
10 Endive
11 Beet leaves
12 Curly kale
13 Cress
14 Sorrel
15 Purslane
16 Buttercrunch lettuce
17 Dandelion leaf
18 Red cabbage seedlings
19 Webb's Wonder
20 Spring onions

Three hundred years ago, many more salad vegetables were grown in this country than nowadays. In a cookery book of the period the first chapter is devoted to salads, for they are rated "of the first importance". Rocket, for example, once grew so widely in England that it threatened to overrun the City of London after the Great Fire.

Although many of these vegetables have been forgotten, seeds of some are still available; they are easily grown and add a special flavour to one's food. Some are widely used on the Continent, where stronger tastes are still popular. Rocket is still very popular in Italy, where it is known as *rucola*, *rugola*, or *rucetta*. It has a strong, rather bitter taste, and is thought to have medicinal qualities; it is at its best when added in small amounts to a green salad.

Dandelion leaves are popular in France and Italy: the cultivated dandelion has larger leaves than the wild one; seeds can be bought in England, but the leaves are never seen in the shops. Good King Henry, or Mercury, is an old English plant, similar to spinach, that is still grown in France. Purslane is another good vegetable that has fallen into disuse. I only see it now in Greece, but it can be bought at Greek-Cypriot shops in London, although not by that name. It is easily recognized by its fat juicy stem with a rosette of round green leaves at the top. It can be used in salads, or cooked, in the Greek way, with eggs. Corn salad is something found in our shops but is much more common in France, where it is called *mâche*. Orach has been forgotten everywhere, yet this pretty plant with heart-shaped leaves of red and green is easily grown. It is cooked like spinach, and tastes like a mixture of spinach and sorrel. Those with a liking for slightly bitter leaves should try the red-leafed lettuce—*trevigiana* in Italy. Milder than rocket, it looks very pretty when mixed with a green lettuce salad.

Those with their own gardens should try growing mustard. This is the true mustard, with yellow flowers, not the mustard and cress variety. The young leaves have a hot, peppery taste that is delicious in a mixed green salad. Another worthwhile thing to grow, even in a small garden, is a few rows of unusual lettuces. Two of my favourites come from America, but seeds can now be bought here. Salad Bowl, also called Oak

Leaf in America, is a loose-headed lettuce with long narrow leaves of emerald green, indented like large oak leaves. Buttercrunch is a firm, crisp lettuce with a good flavour, and very slow to bolt. My favourite salad is made from the last two or three thinnings of these lettuces, mixed with a few young leaves of sorrel and mustard. This should be dressed with the lightest of dressings, made with sunflower seed oil and lemon juice, or simply with lemon juice and a sprinkling of sugar.

Sorrel is also well worth growing, even in small quantities, and I prefer it mixed with spinach or lettuce to eating it on its own. Even a handful of leaves will give a lift to a dish of cooked spinach or a salad. The young leaves of summer spinach also make a good raw salad, especially when combined with crisply fried diced bacon, their hot fat replacing the usual oil. Other good combinations with spinach are sliced raw mushrooms, avocado pear and mozzarella cheese. The older leaves are best cooked *en branches* or made into soups, quiches or timbales.

Even easier to grow than spinach is spinach beet, for it has an apparent resistance to frost. Basically a tougher form of spinach with a well-developed central stem, it is much used in France, where it is called *bettes*. There are many varieties—sea-kale beet, chard, ruby beet and ruby chard. In the case of chard the central stem is the main point of the plant, and is cooked like sea-kale. In others, where the leaf and the stem are equally well developed, they can be cooked together while still very young, but if picked later on, are best cooked separately. The leaves can be treated like spinach, while the stems are cut in thick chunks and will require about five minutes longer cooking.

Watercress is widely grown in England, but for some reason it is considered as a garnish and rarely cooked. It is rich in minerals and vitamins and I love its peppery taste. I use it often, in hot and cold soups, salads, sauces for soft-boiled eggs, or as a substitute for mint sauce during the winter. Chinese cabbage is a recent import to Great Britain, although it has figured in Chinese cooking for centuries. It is like a cross between a cos lettuce and a green cabbage, and is good either cooked or raw. I use it mostly in stuffed cabbage dishes, for the leaves combine the size and strength of the cabbage leaf with the delicate taste of the lettuce.

The magic of mushrooms

The wildest of wild foods, the most mysterious and magical, mushrooms can be cooked in so many imaginative ways or eaten raw in salads or sandwiches

"If red mullet are the 'woodcock of the sea' on account of their delicate taste, mushrooms might be called the 'oysters of the fields', for no other food has quite the rare flavour of these elfin-like mysteries that grow by the light of the moon, or, to be more accurate in darkness."

So wrote Mrs Leyel in her enchanting book *The Gentle Art of Cookery*, first published in 1925. She goes on to suggest using a silver spoon in the cooking, as a way to guard against poisonous fungi; in the case of inedible varieties the spoon will turn black. I would not place much confidence in this, or in other ways of distinguishing between safe fungi and their alarmingly similar poisonous cousins. The only one I feel totally confident about is the common field mushroom, which is also my favourite. Where I live, surrounded by woods, they are rarely found, for they prefer to grow on open land in meadows and pastures. The fungi that grow under trees are altogether more exotic, more colourful and more dangerous.

Mushrooms are to me the wildest of wild foods, the most mysterious and magical. I used to find it hard to understand how they could spring up so rapidly, with a life-cycle only slightly longer than that of the butterfly, and of what tissue they could be made, that grew and died away so quickly. I have now learnt that what we call the mushroom is in fact only one of the external growths of the full mushroom, which is a mass of tangled spores below the surface of the ground. These growths are thrown up at variable distances and intervals when the climatic conditions are suitable.

For those who feel squeamish about unusual fungi, or who are too lazy to look for wild mushrooms, there is always the cultivated variety, which can be bought all the year round. Mushrooms are a good source of nourishment despite their rapid growth, in that they contain a high amount of vitamin D and very few calories. On the other hand they act like blotting paper in cooking, and absorb huge quantities of butter or oil. For those on diets, they can be grilled without fat, or simmered in stock. They can also be steamed using the minimum of fat: lay a few mushrooms between two plates, dot them with butter and season them and cook them over a pan of boiling water for 20 minutes. A larger amount can be cooked in a double boiler.

Mushrooms should never be peeled, just wiped with a damp cloth, for most of the flavour lies in their skin. The stalks are tougher than the caps and should be left out of delicate dishes. They can always be used for flavouring stocks and sauces. My favourite way of cooking mushrooms is to put them (whole, sliced or chopped) in a small covered pan with a piece of butter and a little lemon juice, and stew them gently for about 12 minutes, shaking the pan from time to time, until they are soft and tender in a delicious juice. They are also good deep fried: the caps only dipped into a good batter and fried for a few minutes in very hot oil, then served with fried parsley and a tart mayonnaise.

Mushrooms are also good eaten raw, but they must be very fresh. They make an excellent salad, dressed with plenty of olive oil and lemon juice, either alone or combined with shredded raw spinach, sorrel or cos lettuce. They also make an unusually good sandwich. Cooked mushrooms are an excellent filling for pastries of all kinds. Crisp fried bacon makes a good contrast to their bland flavour, which also combines well with spinach and tomatoes. Mushrooms have an affinity too with onions, shallots and garlic; and most herbs complement them, especially tarragon, dill, chervil and parsley. In winter and summer alike they can be made into delicious soups and sauces, and they go well with chicken, fish, beef and lamb.

Wild mushrooms take slightly longer to cook than the cultivated ones; I usually stew them gently in butter in a frying pan, adding finely minced onion, garlic and herbs. The more delicate field mushroom does not need strong flavouring; the onion and garlic can be omitted and some cream added at the end. Dried mushrooms, usually a variety of cep or boletus, should be soaked for two to four hours before cooking (the water can be used in stocks or soup). They have an excellent flavour and are a useful addition to the store cupboard.

1 Ceps
2 Chanterelles
3 Non-edible fungus
4 Field mushrooms
5 Oyster mushroom
6 Beefsteak mushroom
7 Puff balls

A glut in the vegetable garden

Rows of bolted lettuce, a greenhouse full of overripe tomatoes and beds of elderly marrows are a dread sight for the gardener and a challenge for the cook

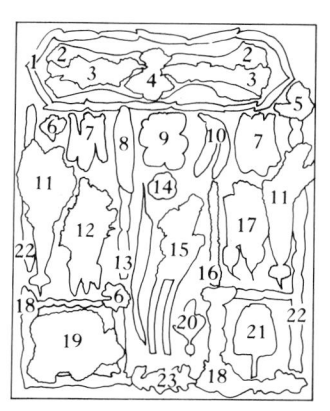

1 *Peas in pods*
2 *Spring onions*
3 *Variegated lemon balm, radishes, sage leaves*
4 *Gooseberries, parsley and chives*
5 *Dill leaves*
6 *Variegated lemon balm*
7 *Courgettes*
8 *Cucumber*
9 *Tomatoes*
10 *Broad beans*
11 *Turnips*
12 *Carrots*
13 *Sage*
14 *Green pepper*
15 *Rhubarb*
16 *Dill tops*
17 *Beetroot*
18 *Apple mint*
19 *Lettuce*
20 *Radish*
21 *Spinach leaf*
22 *Spearmint*
23 *Ginger mint*

Even in the smallest garden, high summer tends to produce a glut. Every gardener is only too familiar with the dread sight of the courgette that got away, yet another vast marrow skulking under its own large leaf like a plump Eve trying to hide behind her fig leaf. Lettuces start to bolt *en masse*, for however carefully one tries to stagger the sowing, a spell of hot weather tends to bring them on together anyway. My efforts to avoid wastage by eating lettuces past their prime reminds me of my Scottish grandmother, who used to irritate my father inordinately by always insisting on eating the bruised peach each evening at the dinner table. He used to try to convince her, but in vain, that if she would only ignore it just once, it would be thrown away and each evening thereafter she could have a perfect peach. I now feel rather the same about lettuce, for the very fact that some have bolted means that there are others about to bolt, and only by relegating a few of the worst to the compost heap can one hope to catch up. In fact, although they produce a bitter taste when eaten raw, bolting lettuces can be cooked quite successfully; even their stalks can be boiled and eaten with butter.

Most of us can be divided somewhat summarily into Marthas or Marys by our habits. When it comes to coping with garden produce, I am most definitely a Mary. The Marthas are never caught out; nothing is allowed to spoil in their well-run gardens, for they simply rush out and spend hour after tedious hour picking, blanching and packaging for their vast freezers. I have a deep resistance to freezing fresh vegetables, probably because it bores me. Instead, I try to use as much as I can by making dishes to be eaten straight away, or in a few days; luckily nothing much is wasted, as my garden is minute. I prefer to use my freezer—also miniscule—for special things: young black currant leaves for making sorbets later in the summer, red and white currants in tiny bags for garnishing the same sorbets and

other fruit desserts, and little bunches of my favourite summer herbs. I am convinced that the freezing of fresh vegetables only makes economic sense when done on a large scale, and for those of us who work in other ways this is just not practical, since our time is also valuable. This concept does not stop me doing things I enjoy, like cooking some time-consuming dishes, but it comes in useful when faced with tasks I dislike!

In recent years, much work has been done to produce varieties of plants that are slow to bolt, but these are not always as delicious as the old varieties. Spinach beet is much easier to grow than true spinach, being frost resistant and slow to run to seed, yet it lacks that tender and delicious quality. In some cases, it is possible to choose a variety that has more than one use; with string beans, for instance, the unusual looking blue beans will produce a most excellent inner bean like a fresh haricot if allowed to reach this stage of maturity. If grown in sufficient quantities, these beans can be dried and stored for the winter. Old runner beans, on the other hand, are simply inedible, but they can always be picked beforehand and stored in the refrigerator, where they will keep their crispness for a week. Courgettes also can be stored in this way, although they lose their delicious earthy taste within hours of picking. They should really be picked when no larger than a man's finger, with the flower still clinging to them, but they are still perfectly edible when larger. Old peas can be made into purées, soups and pease pudding.

Many of these summer vegetables make delicious gratins, or fillings for quiches, or soups. For the latter they can be used alone or in combinations, with added chicken stock, buttermilk, milk or cream. Some of the more unusual herbs and vegetables can be made into purées and frozen in small cartons for future use: sorrel and spinach are two of my particular favourites for frozen purées.

Midsummer vegetables

With all the flavour of exotic lands and the charm of foods ripened in the hot sun, midsummer vegetables share a Gallic affinity with olive oil, garlic and each other

There is a group of vegetables which is so closely related to fruit that it is hard to tell where one ends and the other begins. These are the juicy midsummer vegetables, the tomatoes and aubergines, the peppers in all their various shapes and colours; the cucumbers, courgettes, squashes and marrows; the giant pumpkins and decorative gourds; and the avocado pear. They have all the charm of foods that ripen in hot sun, with a flavour of the Mediterranean and other even more exotic lands. They contain fewer vitamins than leaf vegetables, for their water content is high, but they are none the less delicious for that. The exception is the avocado pear, which is strictly speaking a fruit, but a most unusual one in that it contains vast amounts of protein and of fat. It is extremely nourishing, but is best avoided by those on diets. The other members of this group are suitable for diets, except the aubergine which absorbs large quantities of oil in cooking.

Apart from the avocado, the other vegetables in this group have much in common; they share an affinity with olive oil, garlic and each other. None of them should be cooked in water, for they already contain so much. Courgettes can be par-boiled briefly, before baking in a gratin, or serving cold in a vinaigrette. They are most often fried, whole or in slices, in shallow fat or else in deep oil, in which case they are first coated in batter or simply dipped in seasoned flour. An elegant midsummer dish is a platter of mixed vegetable fritters—aubergines, courgettes and tomatoes dipped in a light batter and fried in deep oil, and served with *skordalia*, the Greek garlic sauce, or simply with lemons. Green peppers are good either raw in salads, or cooked in oil in garlicky dishes such as *piperade* or ratatouille. Tinned red peppers are extremely good, and are useful for combining with tomatoes in Provençal dishes. Skinning fresh peppers is a lengthy business, although it can be done by charring them all over under the grill.

Cucumbers are not often cooked, but in fact they can be substituted in many recipes for courgettes, and are very good. The many different shaped squashes that are popular in the United States are not known in this country, with the exception of the round custard marrow. Their shells make pretty dishes for stuffing with rice and minced meat, or for baking small soufflés. As far as flavour is concerned, however, I much prefer our own small courgette. The larger vegetable marrow is best used for stuffing, for it tends to be watery. It can be good, though, when peeled and cut in chunks and stewed gently in butter in a lidded sauté pan, with some peeled and roughly chopped tomatoes added half-way through. Fresh basil or marjoram improves this simple dish enormously.

Aubergines are almost always fried in oil before being combined with other foods. They can be grilled or baked whole in the oven; grilling in particular gives a delicious smoky taste. Aubergines and tomatoes go well together, but unfortunately the English tomatoes just don't have the strong, sharp yet sweet flavour they acquire in really hot countries. Sometimes I find it best to drain away the seeds and juice, and replace them with a little tinned Italian tomato juice. A delicous dish is made with layers of fried aubergines, onions and tomatoes, baked in the oven with sliced mozzarella cheese melting over the top. I ate this regularly one summer in a little restaurant in Morocco, where the tomatoes are really good, and it has remained a firm favourite with me ever since.

Hot chilli peppers are delicious but they must be used with caution. They are very strong indeed, and only one, or two at the most, should be used in any dish. If they are to be part of an uncooked dish, such as guacamole for instance, they can be blanched by dropping into boiling water for two minutes, which takes away some of their fiery hotness. They must be carefully cleaned, for if any of the white seeds are left they will scorch the roof of your mouth. When added to curries, these little chillies give a lovely fresh hot taste as opposed to the dry hotness that the other spices give.

1 Marrows
2 Courgettes
3 Tomatoes
4 Watermelon
5 Aubergines
6 Cucumbers
7 Chilli peppers
8 Squashes
9 Honeydew melon
10 Peppers
11 Avocado
12 Soursop (custard apple)
13 Mangoes
14 Ogen melon
15 Musk melon

eggs in green peppers p74
vegetable fritters p98
stuffed aubergines p99
spiced courgettes p99
aubergine spread p100
avocado relish p104
skordalia p104

Berries, cherries and currants

Enticing desserts made from succulent strawberries, raspberries and currants are as much a part of summer as the lazy drone of bees and the clink of ice in tall glasses

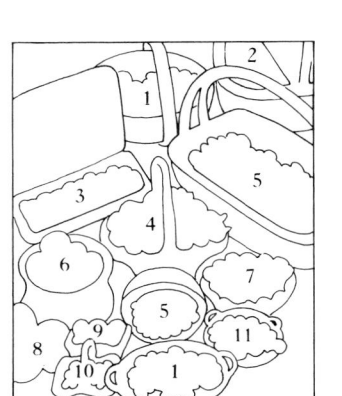

1 *Black currants*
2 *Green gooseberries*
3 *Blueberries*
4 *Strawberries*
5 *White currants*
6 *Dessert gooseberries*
7 *Raspberries*
8 *Chinese gooseberries (Kiwi fruit)*
9 *Loganberries*
10 *Wild strawberries*
11 *Red currants*

black-currant leaf
  sorbet p113
black-currant ice-
  cream p114
apple snow p116
blueberry slump p116
vacherin of red
  currants p118
raspberry and red-currant
  tart p118
blueberry pancakes p119
currant cordial p125

In summer, the café windows in Florence and other Italian towns are lined with rows of large glass goblets, filled to the brim with cut strawberries. These delicious-looking *coppe* are served with scoops of ice-cream in mouth-watering colours, with dollops of whipped cream, or simply with lemon juice. So much of the pleasure of soft fruits lies in their appearance, it seems only sensible to display them in this way as often as possible. Large wine goblets in thick glass are ideal for this purpose; prettier by far than bowls, they are also useful as drinking glasses at other times.

Raspberries are so fragile that they are best treated in a different manner. I think they look prettiest served piled on a lining of vine leaves in a shallow basket, with a fresh cream cheese on a separate dish, and cream and sugar. Except in fools, ice-creams and jams, strawberries are disappointing when cooked, but cooked raspberries lend a delicious tart flavour to many dishes. They combine well with red and white currants, and make a good tart when simply piled into a pre-baked pastry case and warmed through in the oven. Strawberries can be treated in this way; in this case care should be taken that neither fruit is actually cooked.

Red and white currants are not widely grown in the United States and American visitors to England think of them as truly "English". They can be folded into mixtures of beaten egg whites, cream and yoghourt, flavoured with vanilla sugar, for a pretty, light dessert, or used to cover a layer of meringue and whipped cream. Their juice is excellent for adding extra flavour and colour to cooked fruit puddings.

An unusual compôte can be made from a mixture of soft fruits such as strawberries, raspberries and red and white currants, by making a thin syrup of sugar and water and simply pouring it, still boiling, over the prepared fruit. Cherries can be included, but they should

be cooked briefly in the syrup first. The compôte is best served while still warm, or shortly after it has been allowed to cool.

A similar mixture of fruit can be made into an excellent jam. The Swiss make several mixed fruit jams, including one of raspberries and red currants, which is my favourite. From Paris I buy an excellent *confiture des quatres fruits rouges*, as well as concentrated purées of various fruits, including strawberry, raspberry and black currant, which provide a quick and easy base for making ice-creams and sorbets. There is no reason why we should not make similar purées at home and store them in the freezer.

On the whole, I prefer to leave black currants out of these mixed fruit dishes, for their very strong flavour tends to overpower the other more delicate ones. On their own, however, they make the best of all ice-creams, for their acidity cuts through the bland mass of cream, and they make an excellent fool for the same reason. The young leaves of the black currant bush, used to flavour a thin syrup of lemon juice, sugar and water, make an exquisite and delicate sorbet.

Like the black currant, the green gooseberry is best cooked on its own. It is delicious made into a fool with double cream, baked in a tart or pie, or made into ice-cream. An unsweetened purée of gooseberries used to be the traditional accompaniment to mackerel, and I find it good with roast pork as a change from apple sauce.

Cultivated blueberries, bigger and sweeter than their wild variety, are a comparatively recent development in Great Britain, though they have long been a staple in the United States. Delicious eaten raw for breakfast, they can also be mixed into batters and cooked as pancakes, muffins or waffles. Blueberries freeze well, simply packed in plastic bags after washing. The same method works well with currants of all sorts, and with gooseberries. In this way, their short season can be extended for much longer.

40

All about plums

Fresh juicy plums are always a treat, and when cooked their plump flesh and tart flavour bring a sharp sweetness to a rich variety of spicy and unusual dishes

There are some fruits that seem to improve on cooking, and plums are among them. Not, perhaps, the delicate greengages and dessert plums, but both the imported plums that appear in the shops from January onwards and the English Victoria plums of late summer seem to gain flavour when they are cooked.

One of the best of all sweet-sour pickles for eating with cold meats and curries can be made from plums. They also make one of my favourite jams, for the plum skin lends a certain substance to the jam which few other fruits can equal. There is always a particular pleasure in combining seasonal foods, and I find that plums make a delicious cold sauce for eating with the game birds of early autumn. They are an obvious match, for the plums add their own juicy texture to the occasional dryness of game, and their special tart sweetness to the meat's flavour.

Plums combine well with spices, notably cinnamon, cloves and sometimes ginger. Cider vinegar complements them, as do honey, brown sugar and orange juice. Anyone with a juice extractor can make delicious fruit juice from ripe plums; this can be slightly thickened with cornflour to make a version of the Danish *rødgrød*.

For those who like to combine fruit with meat, not added at a late stage (as in the American way of serving glazed ham with pineapple slices) but integrally, the plum is the ideal choice. There are many North African dishes of chicken and lamb cooked with dried fruit of various kinds, and I now find that Russian cookery extends this range still further. In the Caucasus, the part of Russia bordered by Turkey and Iran to the south, and by the Black Sea and the Caspian Sea on either side, there grows a sour plum called the *albukhara*, which forms a central part of the regional cooking. It is combined not only with lamb and chicken but also with pork, duck, goose, beef and even fish. In most cases it is used in the form of a sour plum sauce, with the surprising inclusion of garlic, and this sauce is then used either as an accompaniment to cooked dishes, or as an integral part of the dish itself. I read about Caucasian food after weeks spent experimenting with dishes of meat and fruit, and, as so often happens, my reading confirmed what I had already learnt. The cooking of that part of Russia demonstrates clearly the only satisfactory way of combining two such intrinsically different elements as meat and fruit, which is by adding a number of other ingredients which are complementary to both; these act as a bridge between the two flavours. Thus many of these dishes also include chestnuts, quinces, spices and fresh herbs, just as the ever-popular saffron in Morocco helps to blend the *tagines* of lamb and dried apricots or chicken and prunes. The Russians also make use of dried fruits, and use prunes interchangeably with their sour plums.

The accompaniment to these dishes is vital, as anyone who has ever tried to serve this sort of fruit dish with potatoes will understand. (Sweet potatoes, on the other hand, make a good combination, especially when cooked with spices.) Although rice seems the obvious choice, there are other grains whose nutty flavour and slight sweetness are even better with these dishes. In Morocco, couscous, and in Russia *bulgur* (cracked wheat) or *kasha* (buckwheat) are the most common choices.

I often put the ingredients for a dish together on the table and study them, for this guides me about what to add and what to take away. When confronted with a lump of raw meat next to a pile of fruit it is hard to comprehend they are to be merged into one dish, but with the addition of nuts and spices, grains, garlic and yoghourt, the whole takes on a more homogenous look.

Like all basically tart fruits, the plum goes well with pastry, whether in the continental fashion of the open tart, or the old English closed fruit pie. Both have something to be said for them; the open tart is prettier, but the pie has the advantage in that the pastry does not become saturated with the juice from the fruit, but is merely flavoured by the steam.

The Austrians are very fond of plums, and cook them in a variety of ways. One of the most unusual is a hot plum dumpling; each plum is enclosed in dough, poached in boiling water, and rolled in crisply fried breadcrumbs before serving. These are not easy to make well, for like all dumplings they can be heavy, but when they are successful they are delicious.

Damsons are even better for cooking than plums, for like all fruit which is too bitter to eat raw, they seem to develop their true flavour during cooking. They are at their best in a tart, or combined with double cream (after cooking) in a fool. They also make a good ice-cream, and an excellently flavoured jam.

Bullaces and sloes are the wild relatives of plums and damsons; they are really too bitter for anything but making sloe gin, which is delicious and fun to make as long as you can afford the initial outlay in gin.

Gaviota plums

Cooking with fruits

Make the most of a delectable crop and as the days shorten recall the heat of high summer with the undiminished delights of sun-ripened fruits cooked in pies and puddings

In the early summer, in June and early July, the pleasure of eating the first of the season's fruit is so intense that it seems foolish not to enjoy it in its purest possible form. Home-grown strawberries and raspberries cannot be bettered than when eaten simply with sugar and cream, but as the season wears on the first joy diminishes, and one is ready to appreciate them in other forms. Strawberries and raspberries make the most delicious desserts: fools, mousses, ice-cream and sorbets. They can also be made into an excellent tart; the secret is not actually to cook the berries but to lay them in a pre-baked pastry case and simply warm them through for seven or eight minutes in a very low oven. The strawberry is at its best in an American shortcake, which should be made with the minimum of sugar; the tart raspberry, on the other hand, is a good foil for the sweetness of meringue, as in a *vacherin*. A most useful sauce can be made with raspberries; their acidity makes a good combination with the sweet strawberry and the bland white peach, while the contrast of colours is really exquisite.

Although red and white currants are among my favourites of the soft fruits, both for the sake of their delicate translucent appearance and for their flavour, they are not satisfactory eaten raw owing to their acidity. This applies even more strongly to the black currant: all three are best cooked.

Dessert gooseberries, those delicious plump and juicy berries of dark red, white and golden yellow, are seldom seen nowadays. They can be grown in standard form, like rose trees, and make a charming addition both to the kitchen garden and to the table. The ordinary green gooseberry is I think best cooked and made into pies, fools and mousses. Plums and damsons also make excellent desserts; the delicious greengage, however, is best eaten as it is. Apart from the classic dish in red wine, pears are not very satisfactory for cooking purposes; their bland taste does not go well with pastry or sponge.

Apples, on the other hand, are the best of all fruits for cooking; the range of varieties is vast, and the crisp flesh of the apple makes a perfect foil for bread, pastry, suet and cream. The cooking apple hardly exists outside England; in France, for instance, a tart dessert apple is used for the *tarte tartin* and other apple dishes.

The Morello cherry is another example of good cooking fruit; too acid to eat raw, it can be made into excellent pies, tarts and jams. Its acidity prevents the birds eating it off the trees before it has time to ripen, unlike the sweet cherry. The giant blueberry, which is now grown commercially in the West Country, is so good eaten simply with sugar—and so expensive—that I rarely cook it. But it can be made into pies, as it often is in America, and muffins or pancakes.

The fruit pudding seems to me a typically English thing. Indeed, the first English settlers in America were so distressed to find no apples with which to make their beloved apple pie that they had apple trees brought out from England. Although in the United States this love of fruit desserts, sometimes called strange names like "apple slump" and "berry grunt", has persisted, there are nothing like so many different kinds as in England. Most other countries seem to have one or two; in France and Italy one rarely finds more than a tart of apples or sometimes pears. A favourite dish of mine is a Russian one called *Les Quatres Fruits*; a most beautiful dish of translucent glowing red. It is composed of a mixture of four soft fruits: halved strawberries, stoned red and white cherries and red currants. Simply piled in a glass bowl and sprinkled with castor sugar, the fruit is left for three or four hours in the refrigerator, during which time it slowly produces its own juice.

Surely the best of all fruit puddings is summer pudding; this supremely English creation can be made with any combination of soft juicy fruits, within a casing of bread. My favourite version is filled with raspberries and red currants.

44

Delicious desserts

Fruit tarts, foamy mousses, refreshing sorbets, snowy, white meringues and home-made ice-creams make a cool and tempting finale to a languid summer lunch

It must be years since I ate a dessert in a restaurant, at least from choice, and not just to be polite—since the days when I was at school, and used to be taken to the Etoile or the White Tower for treats in the holidays. I loved the Etoile's fruit salad, made with lots of lemon juice, while at the White Tower I ate yoghourt for the first time, for it was virtually unknown in England then.

Being a pastry chef in some restaurants must be sadly unrewarding, for it seems I am not the only one who treats the sweet trolley, however appealing, merely as part of the restaurant's visual effects. Yet a meal for several people in one's own house seems curiously unfinished without some sweet dish to end with, particularly in the summertime, when there are so many delicious fruits available. This is the moment for light, frothy dishes, tart with the juice of limes or lemons, without either the weight of starch or the richness of large amounts of cream. As an alternative to stiff whipped cream, I like to make a lighter mixture of cream with equal parts of yoghourt and beaten egg white. When served as an accompaniment to acid fruit, such as fresh apricots, it can be slightly sweetened with home-made vanilla sugar, or plain castor sugar. The same mixture without sugar can be drained overnight in muslin to make a fresh cream cheese for serving with soft fruit.

Home-made ice-creams are delicious, but when using fruit like strawberries and raspberries, which provide a purée, I think semi-frozen fools are almost as good, and less trouble to make. (When using liquid flavourings such as coffee, vanilla or chocolate this is not possible, for the mixture is too thin unless totally frozen.) In Italy they serve *semi-freddo* desserts—also, as the name implies, half-frozen. With these very cold dishes, a biscuit is almost obligatory to stop one's teeth aching: they can be bought, but more delicious are the ones made at home. My favourite is the lacy *tuile*, the pretty curved biscuits the French make by rolling them, while still warm, round a bottle. (French recipes specify a wine bottle, English ones a rolling pin!)

Sorbets are more refreshing than ice-creams, and fun to make in one's own original flavours. A lemon-flavoured syrup can be used as the base for making infusions of different flavourings, according to whatever may be growing in the garden. This is the way the black currant leaf ice is made, and an equally delicious sorbet of elderflowers. The different varieties of mint each give their own character to an ice, as will the scented leaves of certain geraniums.

All foamy desserts can gain immeasurably by the manner in which they are served. Sorbets are particularly suited to serving in glasses, since they melt so quickly. I have seen sorbets served in large bowls moulded of ice, which are both attractive and practical. Pretty glass bowls, some in the shape of leaves or flowers, are worth buying if you like to serve this sort of dessert. I remember a lunch given by Maxim's at the Inn on the Park at which the dessert was a most delicious raspberry ice-cream garnished with strawberries, served in individual dishes made from a crisp biscuit mixture in the shape of a folded square of cloth. A truly extravagant gesture, for no one ate the container beyond nibbling at a corner. But it did look extremely pretty anyway.

Mousses that have been set with gelatine are best served on a flat dish. I have been told of an English house where the chef used to serve fruit mousses and moulds surrounded with little frosted branches of red and white currants, still with the leaves on, the whole sprigs first dipped in beaten egg white and then in powdered sugar. No one could deny that much of the pleasure of eating is visual, especially towards the end of a meal, and these details can increase the diners' enjoyment enormously.

There are two old-fashioned desserts too light to be called puddings which I particularly like in the summer. Both of these are based on a *sauce à la vanille*, the true custard. Floating island is a meringue baked in a caramel-lined mould, then turned out on to a "sea" of custard. The other dessert is *oeufs en neige*, a meringue mixture poached in large spoonfuls and served floating in a shallow bowl on the custard sauce. In this one the contrast between the snowy white meringue and the creamy yellow sauce makes it one of the prettiest dishes I know. One of my favourite flavourings is caramel, but it is tricky to make: the timing must be very precise, to prevent the liquid caramel forming into hard toffee when it comes in contact with a cooler substance. It also makes a very pretty garnish: pour a thin layer of caramel into an oiled tin, let it harden completely, then shatter it into a million tiny golden shards, and scatter over the finished dish.

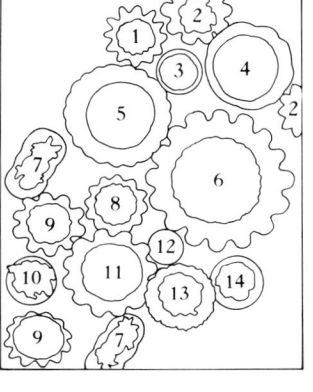

1 *Apple snow*
2 *Mint sorbet*
3 *Orange Boodles fool*
4 *Chocolate apple cream*
5 *Oeufs en neige*
6 *Fruit Salad*
7 *Nectarine, grape, strawberries, mint*
8 *Sliced nectarines in lime juice*
9 *Raspberry ice cream*
10 *Coeur à la crème*
11 *Blackberry fool*
12 *Caramel mousse*
13 *Strawberries in cream*
14 *Prune whip*

Jams and jellies

Black currant, blackberry, crab apple, greengage, damson and plum, red currant and quince; the very names of the berries summon up the taste of summer, so simply preserved

1 *Black currants*
2 *Fraises des bois*
3 *Marmalade*
4 *Mint jelly*
5 *Lemon curd*
6 *Four fruit jelly*
7 *Apricot jam*
8 *Red-currant jelly*
9 *Raspberries*

plum jam p109
rhubarb and ginger
 jam p109
red-currant jelly p109
crab-apple jelly p110

It is only in the past few years that I have become addicted to the joys of eating bread and jam—probably since I started making my own bread. My favourite jams are inevitably those made by myself or my friends, although we do have one or two excellent commercial jams. It is not economical to make your own unless you have fruit from your own garden, but it is none the less a very rewarding task.

Bread and jam, especially when combined with the best unsalted butter, is my favourite snack. Some of my most successful jams have been made with quite commonplace fruit, such as an excellent rhubarb and ginger jam which I make from a friend's recipe. Plum jam has become a favourite in our household, while both greengage and damson jams are even better. A jam made from an excess of red dessert gooseberries turned out to be most delicious. I have since tried to repeat it with green gooseberries but it was not nearly as good.

I like fruit jellies almost better than jam. They are easier to make but more extravagant. They can be eaten as jam, or as a garnish to meat dishes, or as a glaze for fruit tarts. Crab-apple jelly, which I make with fruit from a friend's garden, is good both for eating with bread and as a substitute for red-currant jelly, in cooking or for serving with roast lamb, many game dishes, or baked ham.

Apple and quince jelly is another economical and easily made preserve, with a lovely pinky-golden colour. Quince jam is delicious with *petits suisses* or other cream cheese. Black currants make a very good jelly, as do blackberries, so long as they are not water-logged. All the currants are better in jellies rather than jam, for the tiny pips are irritating unless strained. The juice of red currants can with advantage be added to other fruits in both jams and jellies, for it lends a tart flavour to sweet berries such as strawberries and raspberries, while increasing the pectin content. White currants make an exquisite jelly, also useful as a glaze for white fruit tarts. A jelly made from green gooseberries makes a much less expensive alternative.

Having only begun making jams recently, I am still a novice, but I have gathered various tips from friends and relatives who have been doing it for years. One is to use preserving sugar rather than any other; it is more expensive but does seem to make better jam. My only piece of advice is to make relatively small amounts at a time, at least until you know you like the finished products, and to put it in small jars. I find we get bored before finishing a huge jar, and long to start another while the first sits uneaten on the shelf. For jellies I use tall, narrow, relish jars; these look very pretty, but are only practical if you have a tall jam spoon (we use American iced tea spoons). The Swiss make the best jams in the world, in my opinion, and the French also produce excellent jams, including probably the most expensive jam in the world. This is an exquisite white-currant jelly sold in tiny octagonal glass jars. These jars, filled with a greenish-white jelly with some of the currants suspended in it, have always seemed to me a symbol of luxury. I found a recipe for making this jelly recently in the *Tante Marie Cookery Book*. It involves picking each tiny seed out of every currant with a goose feather, without breaking the skin. The recipe ends with the sound advice, "Do not try to make too much of this at one time." Like all true luxuries, this seems to me a good example of something better bought than made at home.

LES CONFITURES

Pickles and preserves

A larder stocked with jars of neatly labelled chutneys and pickles is the satisfying reward for the traditional housewifely virtues of foresight, economy and industry

The pickling and preserving of food is one of the oldest of culinary arts. Among the California Indians, preparations for the winter were already underway by September. The men would go off on extended hunting trips, while the women spent most of their time collecting acorns and grinding them into flour. This acorn flour formed their staple winter diet, either cooked as a mush or baked into bread. When the men returned with slaughtered deer, most of the flesh would be dried for the winter, while many nuts, roots and seeds were put in store. These practices continued with little change, from the Stone Age up until the beginning of this century.

In contrast, but different only in degree, is the vast range and amount of food customarily stored for the winter in a north Michigan farmhouse in the 1870s. This was probably the most prolific time for storing food, since much of the knowledge that had been acquired through centuries was shortly to be rendered almost valueless by the technological developments in canning, freezing and freeze-drying. Before these developments, the farmer's wife and her helpers would have been occupied for many months, indeed almost continuously throughout the year, in "putting food by". Barrels of flour and dried beans were stored in the larder, as well as sacks of brown and white sugar, buckwheat and cornflour. Jugs of molasses were always at hand, with plentiful supplies of coffee, tea and other bought groceries. In the cellar squash, turnips and cabbages would be heaped, while potatoes and apples were stored in bins. Barrels would be filled with cucumbers in brine and sauerkraut. Jars of preserved fruit would be set out in rows on the shelves: cherries, plums, peaches and pears. There would also be giant crocks of pickles, notably mustard pickle, chow chow, piccalilli and watermelon rind, and crocks of preserved citron, quince, and gingered pears. Bottles of ketchup and chilli sauce would be accumulated in profusion, since they were much used in conjunction with the staple winter dish of dried beans. Salt pork and pickled pigs' trotters would be stored in barrels, while hams hung in the cellar after curing. High in the attic would hang strings of peppers and dried apples, nuts and bunches of herbs.

Although the art of pickling is less vital now than in previous centuries, it has lost none of its emotive appeal. Of all the domestic arts, none has more significance, for it acts as a symbol of all the housewifely virtues: foresight, economy and industry. Even from a purely practical point of view, there is a lot to be said for making some preparations for the winter: despite modern technology, we are still at the mercy of power cuts, strikes and the occasional freak snow storm, and it would seem foolish to rely exclusively on electricity for something as vital as nourishment. None the less pickling plays a rather different rôle in our lives nowadays, being used mainly to add variety to our winter diet, and to make use of garden produce when it is cheapest and at its most plentiful.

Strangely enough, the pickles I like best are those preferred by the Michigan farmer: chow chow, piccalilli, and mustard pickle. Other favourites of mine are pickled beetroot and two chutneys: mango for serving with curries, and mint chutney for eating with crusty French bread and Cheddar cheese.

All in all, making pickles is a very rewarding thing to do, and can be the source of much admiration. As a professional beauty living in New York once told me: "Men are enormously impressed by beautiful girls making pickles; if you're plain it's not worth the effort. Homely girls should find something more exotic to do."

1 Chow chow
2 Pickled eggs
3 Pickled onions
4 Pickled cucumbers and onions
5 Pickled red cabbage
6 Mango
7 Cranberry relish
8 Green tomatoes
9 Pickled corn and red peppers
10 Mango chutney
11 Pickled green beans
12 Pickled eggs in beet juice

Fresh from the dairy

Buttermilk, curd cheese, skimmed milk and soured cream, the traditional products of the home dairy, can enhance breads, soups and sauces to great effect

1 Cream
2 Butter being weighed
3 Eggs
4 Butter churn
5 Butter to be shaped
6 Parsley butter balls
7 Butter in decorative shapes

In former times almost every country house had its own dairy. Even cottagers kept a cow, until the abolition of common grazing grounds by the Enclosure Act of the eighteenth century deprived them of this right. Farmers often leased out a cow to more prosperous families, who would return it when it was dry.

The dairy was a pleasant room, cool and quiet, with that strange milky smell which has strong childhood associations for many of us. It was well ventilated, with a roof of thatch or slate to insulate it against the summer heat. The floor was of stone slabs, the shelves invariably of slate or stone. The windows were slatted to keep out the sun, and the visual effect was a pleasing contrast between the warm golden yellow of butter, milk and cream and the cool grey of slate and stone. There was a feeling of peace and cleanliness. Each day the floor was scoured with fine sand, the containers and implements were scalded with boiling water, rinsed in fresh cold water and left to dry in the open air. Cloths were forbidden and soap was never used. In some of the grander establishments, the ladies of the house made a habit of visiting the dairy to drink milk fresh from the cow and to taste the syllabub; in these cases the dairy was likely to be prettier and less utilitarian, with sprigged china on the shelves. There was usually a separate room for cheese-making, opening off the dairy, which was kept for making butter.

With the setting up of the Milk Marketing Board in 1933, the home dairy all but disappeared. All milk sold through the Board must be pasteurized by law; now children's images of dairy foods are more likely to be of fruity yoghourts in bright-coloured cartons than the old butter churn or Scotch hands, those wooden implements like rectangular ping-pong bats for rolling pats of butter. Once a knowledge of this sort goes, it is hard to re-create a feeling for the products it relates to. How many people nowadays can tell the difference between buttermilk and skimmed milk, or curd cheese and cottage cheese? What were curds and whey and what was Miss Muffet doing on that tuffet?

Curds and whey were, of course, a much-loved English dish, often given to children. Without pasteurization, the milk would form naturally into curds; nowadays the separation must be achieved by adding a cheese starter and bacteria to replace those destroyed by sterilization. The curds were served with some of the slightly sweetened whey poured over them. In Wales, curds were sometimes made from buttermilk, which made a less rich dish.

The first step in the dairy was to separate the milk from the cream. This was done by hand, for cows' milk separates naturally, and after standing for some hours in broad pans, the cream was easily lifted off with a skimmer.

Butter is made by causing the fat globules in the cream to form into a solid mass. This is done by agitation at a controlled temperature as in churning. There are various types of old wooden churns still to be found; some were operated by a plunger, others by turning the whole churn over and over. One was worked by a dog running over the surface of a large wheel. Once it had formed into a mass, the buttermilk was drained off and the butter was well washed.

It was then kneaded, either by hand or with a wooden roller, and washed again frequently until all the buttermilk had been forced out. If any buttermilk were left in, the butter would soon turn rancid. Packed into barrels and heavily salted, with all the moisture and air driven out, it could be kept for months, then the excess salt washed off before eating.

The three main dairy products—cream, cheese and butter—leave us with a residue of three by-products: skimmed milk, whey and buttermilk. Skimmed milk is made into cottage cheese and is valuable for those on diets as it contains many of the properties of milk with almost none of its fat. Whey is usually fed to pigs, calves or chickens, although in Italy and some Scandinavian countries it is made into a soft cheese. Buttermilk is the most interesting from the cook's point of view. Fresh buttermilk has a foamy, slightly acid quality. It is the best liquid ingredient for baking scones and soda bread. Sour milk makes a good alternative, but this is also hard to come by even in Ireland, the home of soda bread. There, I was told that the best solution is to make up skimmed milk from powder and sour it by adding yoghourt or a cheese starter. Cultured buttermilk is thicker, and slightly sourer. I use it constantly, especially in summertime, for making cold vegetable soups and sauces.

Cream from pasteurized milk will not sour safely and simply goes bad, but cultured sour cream can be bought without difficulty. I use it more and more frequently in cooking, for it adds smoothness and richness to food without the accompanying blandness of thick fresh cream.

Hightea

Somewhere between an afternoon snack and an early supper is the English institution of high tea – simple cooked dishes with bread and butter, tea and cakes

The traditional English tea-table must be almost a thing of the past. Usually served in a sitting-room, or the nursery, as opposed to the dining-room, this informal meal must have been one of the pleasantest aspects of grand country house life. Each house had its own tradition, but the actual dishes served were probably similar. As Lady Sysonby said in her cookbook published in 1935: "The ideal tea-table should include some sort of hot buttered toast or scone, one or two sorts of sandwiches, a plate of small light cakes, and our friend the luncheon cake. Add a pot of jam or honey, and a plate of brown and white bread and butter—which I implore my readers not to cut too thin—and every eye will sparkle."

On family holidays in Ireland, we sometimes used to compromise with a high tea for adults and children alike, which we ate about six o'clock. Ireland is the perfect place for informal meals of this sort, for its best food seems particularly suited to them. The cooked part of high tea usually consisted of eggs, bacon, potatoes, tomatoes, mushrooms or cheese, which when combined with the delicious Irish soda bread and many varieties of "brack", or fruit bread, and marvellous farm butter and fresh milk, made an almost perfect meal.

Many of these simple cooked dishes would be equally good for a light lunch or supper, or breakfast. They are mostly quickly cooked, usually in a frying pan, and made of ingredients either already in the larder or easy to buy. Slices of potato cake with fried eggs and bacon, mushrooms on toast, corn beef hash with poached eggs, gammon rashers with grilled tomatoes; these are ideal dishes for a high tea. Then the hearty sandwiches: the *croque monsieur* of toasted cheese and ham; the delicious

American "BLT"—a bacon, lettuce and tomato sandwich, spread thickly with mayonnaise; or toasted bacon sandwiches. And the more elegant sandwiches: watercress or cucumber, potted shrimps with brown bread, shredded lettuce with Marmite, cream cheese with greengage jam. A plate piled with buttered toast cannot be improved upon, especially when served with Gentleman's Relish, Marmite or home-made kipper paste. Pancakes of all sorts are a good idea; rolled round thin chipolata sausages of pure pork with a bowl of apple sauce; thick American pancakes with maple syrup; bacon pancakes made by crumbling crisply fried bacon into the batter before making the pancakes; or the Scottish pancakes, more generally known as drop scones, spread thickly with unsalted butter.

There is a variety of scones to choose from: plain white ones eaten with butter and jam, cheese scones and fruit scones. A home-made loaf of bread will make any tea-table welcoming, especially soda bread, or the potato bread you find in Ireland—so good fried in bacon fat for breakfast. For a cake, I generally rely on American brownies, because they are easy to make and so good. I also love flapjacks for the same reason; these crisp flat cakes made from what we used to call rolled oats and now know as breakfast oats are literally child's play to make. All that is needed now is a huge pot of tea with which to wash down all these good things; my favourite is Lapsang Souchong, although with cooked dishes an Indian tea would probably be a more appropriate choice.

Even writing about these meals makes me feel nostalgic, and I am resolved to bring back the custom of high tea if only occasionally during a holiday or over a weekend.

1 *Flapjacks*
2 *Cinnamon toast*
3 *Potato scones*
4 *Brownies*
5 *Marmalade toasts*
6 *Drop scones*
7 *Cheese scones*
8 *Chasse*
9 *Potato pancakes*

potato cake with
 onions p100
potato pancakes p101
chasse p101
cheese scones p124
brownies p124
flapjacks p124

*W*hen less is best

Shake off the winter's excesses and slim into shape for summer. Ignore gruelling regimens and start to enjoy your diet with light, nutritious and temptingly presented dishes

1 Radishes
2 Grapes
3 Lentils
4 Chilli peppers
5 Bay leaves
6 Mint
7 Rosemary
8 Peppers; cherry tomatoes
9 Capelli d'angelo pasta
10 Marzipan
11 Okra
12 Wild strawberries; Italian
   parsley; fennel leaves
13 Cherry tomatoes
14 Brussels sprouts
15 Quails' eggs
16 Cauliflower; rice crackers; rice
17 Cress

mixed salad p78
sole with watercress
  sauce p85
grilled sirloin with
  garnishes p94
mustard sauce p106
horseradish sauce p107
lemon jelly p122

The cold windy days of early spring seem an odd time to go on a diet, but it is not so foolish as it appears. We can eat masses of warming, comforting food—dishes like *osso buco*—which may well cheer us up at the time, but leave us feeling bloated and overweight, and consequently depressed, or we can choose to go on a diet; this I recommend in anticipation of the spring. As I get older I find I become more and more aware of how I feel, and am just not prepared to put up with feeling less than well. The brain is far more active on a light diet, while large amounts of heavy food dull one's awareness and make one feel uncomfortable.

Although "new" diets are sometimes fun to try out, the more eccentric ones are almost impossible to fit in with normal life, particularly as far as family and friends are concerned. In the long run the best diet is a flexible one based on general principles and one's own tastes. I prefer to concentrate on boiled and grilled food, together with lots of raw fruit and vegetables.

During the summer months, light food presents few problems; there is such a wide range of salads and cold dishes, and so much delicious fruit. In winter and early spring it is a little more difficult. I favour a series of dishes made from boiled beef, chicken and poached fish which provide stock for making clear soups and are the basis of a number of hot and cold dishes. One can learn to do without pasta, rice or potatoes and instead plan to eat a variety of boiled or steamed green vegetables, dressed simply with lemon juice. Instead of bread, stock up on a selection of crisp biscuits and use only minute amounts of sunflower-seed oil for cooking instead of butter or olive oil, and lemon juice instead of vinaigrette. I combine yoghourt, mustard, lemon juice and a very little sour cream to make substitute sauces for mayonnaise and béchamel. Beaten egg white folded into yoghourt and very slightly sweetened can take the place of whipped cream, for serving with fruit compôtes. The only alcohol I drink when dieting is white wine mixed with Perrier, and I attempt to give up coffee, at least in the evenings. Sugar and milk should be omitted, but one soon becomes used to black coffee.

It helps to remember that good habits are just as addictive as bad ones; I know people who have become totally dependent on their daily bicycle riding, swimming or jogging, and the hope is that one can succeed in becoming so attached to one's diet that one chooses to continue with it, at least during the week; then one might eat normal meals at the weekends. It is our general eating habits that matter, not the odd meal. In any case, after a few weeks of eating simply, the craving for fattening food does diminish, or possibly disappears altogether. Until then, I think it is more sensible to give in to one's cravings now and then, to eat the cream cake or chocolate bar without undue guilt, or the forbidden image can become a total and ridiculous obsession.

The most important lesson is simply to eat less. This can be made easier in a number of ways: first by buying best-quality ingredients in small quantities, which increases our pleasure in eating without costing us much more. Second, we can use smaller plates than usual and serve clear soups in small cups instead of bowls. The dishes should be prettily garnished, partly in order to make them look appealing, and partly to camouflage the actual amount of food. It is a good idea to serve the food on individual plates, avoiding the temptation for second helpings. Whenever time permits, and particularly in the evening, serve two or three light dishes instead of just one. A three-course meal takes longer to eat and is more interesting, thus surmounting two of the great problems of dieting.

As an encouragement, I suggest buying a new piece of equipment, something especially relevant to this sort of cooking. If you don't already have one, my first choice would be a pressure-cooker; I use this for all boiled food, from large joints of meat to tiny vegetables. (As a rough guide for beginners, divide normal cooking times by three.) A yoghourt-maker is economical, since one tends to use large amounts of yoghourt as an alternative to cream. (Those who cannot buy low-fat cream cheese can make a good, simple substitute using yoghourt and sunflower-seed oil. A cast-iron grill pan is best for steaks, and non-stick pans best for cooking without fat.

55

56

Freezer food

More than simply an extra larder, the freezer can become a treasure chest of good things to be produced with a flourish when time is short, or when a treat is in store

As with most useful inventions, the freezer can be adapted to many different individuals' needs. For someone with a large garden the obvious use is the freezing of garden produce. To me, with a kitchen garden the size of a pocket handkerchief, its other possibilities become apparent. My freezer is in a cottage where I spend weekends and holidays and I use it in three different ways. First, as a last resort in case I forget to bring even the most immediate essentials from London, so I always have a loaf of bread and a packet of butter in the freezer, which with instant coffee provide at least a scanty breakfast.

Second, I aim to have on hand some first-class basic ingredients for a few main meals: sausages; bacon; a couple of pounds of best steak, minced and wrapped in half-pound packs, for making hamburgers, and sauce Bolognese; a chicken cut in half and wrapped separately for grilling. Usually I have some kipper fillets for making pâté; smoked cod's roe for *taramasalata*; a carton of chicken livers for a smooth pâté; and potted shrimps or king crab meat for making shellfish cocktails. On a simpler level, frozen cod steaks are useful for making fish pie.

In the realm of frozen vegetables, I find spinach one of the most useful, both leaf and chopped. It can be used as a base for *oeufs mollets*, for fillets of sole, for a green sauce to pour over poached eggs, or a creamy soup. Frozen corn is also delicious, both on the cob and off; it makes the basis of corn chowders, succotash, egg dishes, fritters and corn puddings. Finally, I like ratatouille, either commercially frozen or home-made, petits pois, whole green beans, broccoli, broad beans and brussels sprouts.

Yet from my point of view the main advantage of having a freezer is as a sort of extended larder, a storage place for cooked dishes, which I make when I have time and eat when I don't. I use it in a relatively short-term way, often cooking a dish one week for the next, and this seems to work well. I am sure that food does deteriorate, in flavour at least, over long periods (although it is still perfectly safe) and I tend to eat most things within a month at the most.

The dishes I make are mostly simple family meals, like pies, pasta, soups. The best ones for freezing are undoubtedly those covered with a lid of some sort, a covering to protect the interior from the inevitable dehydrating effect of the extreme cold. Thus pastry dishes are ideal and the so-called pies covered with a purée of potatoes are also extremely good: both fish pie and shepherd's pie come in this category. Dishes of pasta are good so long as they are well covered with sauce: noodles, either green or white in a béchamel sauce flavoured with tomato purée and enriched with cream; lasagne, layered with alternate fillings of minced meat and tomato sauce, and covered with a cheese sauce; even a simple macaroni cheese can be good.

Pancakes freeze well, and are extremely useful; so long as no sugar is added to the batter, they can be used for sweet or savoury dishes. They can be frozen plain, or filled with a mixture such as creamed chicken, shellfish or mushrooms.

When tomatoes are plentiful I buy several pounds and reduce them to a thick purée, carefully seasoned and flavoured with fresh basil or marjoram. I store the resulting purée in half-pound cartons and use it as a sauce for noodles during the winter. Likewise, when cooking apples are falling off the trees, I make them into a purée and freeze in the same way, to eat with yoghourt or cream throughout the winter. Even in my small garden I sometimes have an excess of green vegetables: spinach, sorrel and lettuce. These I make into soups and freeze, adding cream either at this point or when re-heating.

At the end of the summer I freeze small bunches of tarragon and other favourite herbs in plastic bags. *Pesto* or *pistou*—the Mediterranean paste made from pounded basil, garlic and pine kernels—freezes well also; it is the most delicious addition to a minestrone-type soup or a dish of fettucine or spaghetti.

Last of all I come to my favourite use of the freezer; as a place to store treats. I find it sad that from the child's point of view the kitchen is no longer the exciting pleasurable place it once was. Few mothers, or aunts or grandmothers for that matter, have the time to make toffee and fudge, cookies and cakes for fun. In the United States most children are allowed to raid the icebox and there is often a giant jar of cookies for general use. In England our more puritan attitude has, I am afraid, made the kitchen almost out of bounds, at least as far as indiscriminate eating goes. I sympathize with both points of view; on the one hand I like the idea of children being free to help themselves, but I am the first to get annoyed when pounds of fruit vanish in an afternoon. For this reason I think the freezer makes a good compromise; it can be filled with delicious treats—ice-cream and sorbets, cookies, waffles and cakes—but it cannot be raided on impulse as the things need time to defrost.

1 *Peppermint ice-cream*
2 *Strawberry and raspberry sorbet*
3 *Plum ice-cream*
4 *Mocha ice-cream*
5 *Oatmeal, chocolate and Catherine wheel biscuits*
6 *Pancakes*
7 *Lemon sorbet*

pistou p106
green sauce p107
strawberry and raspberry sorbet p113
peppermint ice-cream p114
strawberry and raspberry ice-cream p114
plum ice-cream p114

A cook-out

Barbecuing is the most primitive of cooking methods, and somehow an excess of equipment and trimmings seems to spoil what is essentially a simple pleasure

1 *Skewered onions*
2 *Skewered tomatoes*
3 *Lobster*
4 *Brochettes of conger eel*
5 *Rosemary brush*
6 *Home-made bread*
7 *Skewered giant prawns*
8 *Clams*
9 *Lemon*
10 *Red mullet in hinged grill*

Barbecue cookery has two aspects, the one as appealing as the other is unattractive. In the beginning it was simply grilling raw food, usually meat or fish, over an open fire. Not only is this an attractive sight, it is also a delicious and wholesome method of cooking. Yet in recent years this simplicity has almost been lost under a plethora of modern equipment. Even ten years ago the barbecue department of New York stores used to fill me with dismay: cans of liquid "smoke flavour" jostled on the shelves with spray-on fire-lighters, and the barbecues themselves were almost as glossy and alarming as automobiles. These machines, with hoods and rotisserie attachments, seem to defeat their own purpose since they often need electricity, and there is something distinctly unaesthetic in yards of flex trailing through the garden.

To be fair, it must be remembered that many Americans are past masters at the art of outdoor eating and have made a feature of festive open-air meals, such as clam bakes and corn roasts, for hundreds of years. It is not only in the United States that barbecues have been vulgarized, for the comparable departments in some of our own large stores are enough to send me rushing back to the kitchen with relief. I am convinced that the nicest barbecues are home-made, whether a permanent feature in a corner of the garden or terrace or a temporary construction on the beach or camping site. These also solve the storage problem since many commercial barbecues take as much space to store as a lawn mower. Simple cast-iron grills can be bought, for laying on a base made with bricks. Sandwich-shaped wire grills with long handles are also available, for holding food while grilling. These facilitate the turning of such fragile foods as hamburgers and small flat fish. Fish-shaped wire baskets in various sizes can be found; small ones are useful for holding trout or small red mullet, while large ones hold bass or grey mullet, and stand on their own legs directly over the coals. Whole fish can, of course, be laid directly on the grill but turning is sometimes tricky. When barbecuing, care must always be taken to prevent the food becoming burned. If this threatens, it should be moved slightly farther from the heat than usual and watched like a hawk.

My favourite barbecue is one of seafood; more unusual than meat, they also have the advantage of quick cooking and are all cooked to the same degree. Lobsters are excellent cooked on a barbecue, either raw or par-boiled. Ideally they should be grilled raw, but this necessitates killing them with a knife, which I cannot bring myself to do. I drop them into boiling water as usual shortly before I am ready to barbecue them, and boil them only briefly. Lobster tails are also delicious barbecued, simply flattened and basted with butter and lemon juice. Giant prawns can be threaded on skewers or held between grills, either in their shells or simply with their tails left on for decorative effect. Firm white fish such as conger eel, monkfish and halibut can be cut into cubes, marinated in olive oil and lemon juice, then put on skewers and grilled, occasionally basted with the marinade. Clams can be sprinkled with water and wrapped in foil, nine or ten at a time, and steamed directly on the hot coals.

Meat-based barbecues are more conventional, but delicious none the less, and are generally more popular with children. A large piece of meat, either a two-inch-thick slice of rump or a whole leg of lamb, boned and slightly flattened, is excellent cooked in one piece, then cut in strips before serving. A heavy chopping board and a sharp knife are essential. Individual steaks cook more quickly, and can be served in heated buns with mustard. Pork and lamb chops are good, but should be trimmed of excess fat to prevent flare-ups. Sausages are always popular with children, and frankfurters only need heating through before slipping into hot rolls. Spareribs are best grilled in whole racks, basted with a sweet and sour sauce, then cut up in ribs. I like tender lamb cut in cubes and marinated, then threaded on skewers and grilled over dried twigs of rosemary, and served with hot flat bread. Chicken drumsticks are easily eaten in the fingers, but even more delicious are small spring chickens cut in half and flattened, marinated and basted with a teriyaki sauce.

Sauces and marinades play an important part in barbecue cookery, since the fierce heat threatens to dry out the meat. The only foods I prefer without sauce are steaks, hamburgers, sausages and a boned leg of lamb. In other cases I find the best sauce is dictated by the character of the food itself. Shellfish—and other fish—are best basted with melted butter and lemon juice, though the butter must be replaced with oil if the fish needs marinating, while small pieces of lamb, such as chops or skewers, are best basted with a mixture of olive oil and lemon, with chopped onion and added herbs. Pork, being a fat meat, needs little oil but is excellent in a sweet mixture of soy sauce and brown sugar or honey. Thin sauces can be applied with a bulb-type baster while thicker ones need a brush. I like to make my own brush from a bunch of rosemary twigs tied together.

The pleasures of the picnic

The open air whets the appetite and sharpens the senses, so eschew the sandwich in favour of outdoor food planned with imagination and served with flair

I find cooking for picnics a very rewarding task. For one thing it is a versatile meal with scope for a wide choice of dishes; also I find that people are less critical, more appreciative in fact, than usual, with better appetites. For a change the food is not the focal point; the weather, the view, the general surroundings, are all more important. The main thing is to have fun, and since the guests are usually mixed in ages, I like to make the food as varied as possible, so that there is something to please everybody.

One way of providing a large choice, yet giving an impression of unity, is by concentrating on one or two sauces, and providing a large number of different foods to eat with them. My fondness for Middle Eastern foods stands me in good stead here, since many such dishes make ideal picnic food. A variation on a Lebanese sauce is easily made by mixing equal parts of *tahini* (a sesame seed paste, not unlike peanut butter in consistency) with yoghourt and lemon juice; other good sauces can be made by combining cream cheese, buttermilk, garlic and fresh herbs in a food processor. These smooth thick sauces are easy to transport and they go well with a variety of good picnic foods, like joints of roast chicken, meatballs, tiny fried fish cakes, hard-boiled eggs, sausages, *crudités* of all sorts, potato crisps, small whole tomatoes, crisp leaves of cos lettuce, and tiny new potatoes, boiled or baked in their skins. Flat *pitta* bread, heated in the oven just before leaving and wrapped in foil, makes the ideal accompaniment. Cartons of *hummus* or *taramasalata* can be taken along for eating with the bread. Almost all these foods appeal to children of all ages, even if they don't particularly like the taste of the sauces.

An excellent Middle Eastern *meze*, or hors d'oeuvre, is a spread made of puréed aubergines and tomatoes with olive oil and lemon juice. Packed in a carton and spread, at the picnic, on small squares of rye bread or pumpernickel, this makes a delicious appetizer. Another good picnic food is stuffed eggs, but I find these so fragile to pack that I prefer to carry them separately, and only fill the whites at the last moment.

As an alternative to meatballs, I sometimes make a flat meat loaf of minced lamb under a thick tomato sauce; this hardens on cooling and can be cut in wedges and eaten in the fingers. For a pudding I recommend making a baking tin full of chocolate brownies and transporting them in the tin, covered with foil. Alternatively, a rich fruit cake can be taken, with wedges of hard cheese—Gruyère, Cheddar or Emmental. Apples, bananas and grapes are the best fruit for picnics, since they are easy to pack and to eat.

A totally different sort of picnic that occurs, though less frequently, in my life is the evening picnic. An expedition to Glyndebourne is a good example of this sort of occasion, and here it seems worth while to be more extravagant. I like to construct this sort of picnic as if it were a formal meal, served on china plates with proper silver and glass, taking a pretty tablecloth to spread on the grass. Several bottles of chilled white wine, or even better, still champagne, are almost obligatory. To start, perhaps home-made potted shrimps with small sandwiches of brown bread and butter, or giant prawns or crayfish, served with mayonnaise. Then possibly some small chicken pies, served warm; or a roll of flaky pastry enclosing a large spicy sausage served with a mustard sauce; or an enclosed quiche, like a shallow pie, filled with spinach and tomatoes, or mushrooms, fish and rice. An alternative menu might consist of a hot consommé madrilène or a bortsch served in small cups and followed by a cold main dish such as smoked chicken or turkey, cold duck, or a duck pâté with crusty French bread and a green salad. Slices of cold roast sirloin can be rolled round small heaps of freshly grated horseradish, or thick slices of rare fillet of beef can be served with a rich and creamy horseradish sauce.

During a spell of hot weather, a totally cold meal is quite acceptable: a first course of smoked trout, skinned and filleted for easy eating, or slices of smoked salmon rolled round a mousse of smoked mackerel, could be followed by a *chaudfroid* of chicken, with a dish of mixed vegetables in a light vinaigrette. For the dessert, I might make individual coffee mousses in *oeuf en cocotte* dishes, or a wine jelly; or I might simply take some of the best chocolate truffles I could find in my favourite shop.

1 Stuffed cucumbers
2 Chaudfroid of chicken
3 Bortsch en gelée
4 Salad of lettuce, spring onions, fennel
5 Grapes

61

Stocking up

Some foods take kindly to canning, some keep best when dried or pickled; the judiciously stocked larder means meals to be proud of at all times of the year

1 York ham
2 Pepperoni sausage
3 Side of bacon
4 Hams
5 Salamis
6 Garlic
7 String of onions
8 Dried herbs
9 Dry foods
10 Liquid foods
11 Mustard
12 Tinned foods
13 Olive and sunflower seed oils
14 Bottled fruits
15 Home-made preserves
16 Dried wild mushrooms
17 Cheeses
18 Eggs
19 Home-made wines
20 Potatoes
21 Veal and ham pie
22 Pickled eggs

clam chowder p66
celery hearts mornay p100
tomato and pepper
    sauce p103

Over the years, the larder has changed its character. Originally a cool room on the north-facing side of the house, with shelves of slate and netted windows, it was intended as a storage place for food that could be kept over a period of time: for hams and sides of bacon, root vegetables in sacks, and eggs pickled in brine or waterglass. It was at its fullest in the autumn, when it would be stocked to capacity with food to last through the winter. In America in the nineteenth century, vegetables such as potatoes, onions, cabbages, turnips and squash were stored in a pit dug in the ground, while parsnips were kept frozen in the soil where they grew until they were needed.

The preserving of food by various methods had been going on for hundreds of years, and was a highly developed skill. After the invention of the tin can in 1812—bottling had been developed by a Frenchman a few years earlier—many of these skills fell into disuse and were forgotten. Elaborate methods of keeping food had been necessary, not just for the average household that had some fresh food to fall back on during the winter, but for the long sea voyages to America and to India. When the *Mayflower* landed off Cape Cod in 1620 its 100 passengers had been living for three months on a diet of hard tack, dried fish, cheese and beer. Two hundred years later, however, the preserving of food had become a much more finely developed art, and some live animals were usually taken on board to be killed during the trip. A lady travelling to India in 1850 took with her, for her own consumption, squares of soup made by boiling down chicken legs with veal bones to make a thick concentrate, salted duck potted with herbs, "kitted" chickens—an ingenious method of preserving whole chickens in a sort of vacuum pack of suet paste—condensed cream, fresh lemons, and a supply of fresh watercress to be grown in the cabin.

Nowadays, just as canning and freezing have ousted the old ways, so the larder has been superseded by the store cupboard, at least in urban areas. The original feeling of the passing year has been lost, for tins know no seasons.

I find the most successful tins fall into three categories; first, the fish products: tinned tunny fish, sardines, anchovy fillets, cod's roe and minced clams are all delicious and unfailingly useful. Second, the vegetables: Italian plum tomatoes, condensed tomato paste, and sweet red peppers; haricots, *flageolets* and red kidney beans; chick-peas and petits pois, sweet-corn, celery hearts and endives; red cabbage and sauerkraut to combine with fresh or tinned frankfurters for a sustaining meal. Lastly, the juices: my favourite is a mixed vegetable juice from America which is excellent drunk with ice, or as a substitute for tomato juice in a Bloody Mary, heated as a soup, mixed with yoghourt or sour cream as a sauce, or used as an ingredient for cooked dishes such as *navarin* of lamb. Straight tomato juice is also good, as is clam juice, which can be drunk chilled with a squeeze of lemon juice as an appetizer, heated as a consommé, or used as the base for a delicious fish sauce. Fruit juices are good, too, preferably unsweetened, as are many tinned fruits, but these I regard as a luxury and seldom buy. I like some tinned soups but I prefer to make my own whenever possible. There is a good clam chowder for instance, but you can make a better one with a tin of minced clams, some bacon, potatoes and a pint of milk. Jellied consommé and consommé madrilène in tins are useful, either chilled as cold soups, or used as a substitute for aspic in cold dishes, or chopped as a garnish. One can buy Greek tins of *dolmades*, but much better results are obtained by simply buying the vine leaves, in tins or in brine, and making the stuffing with fresh ingredients. Tinned *tortillas* are good for serving with *guacamole* and other cold vegetable dishes in oil. Bottled prune juice is useful for making prune jellies quickly, while an American chocolate syrup, also in tins, is very popular with children when poured over vanilla ice-cream.

When stocking up my country larder for a definite period of time, like the summer holidays, I think the most important things to have are the minor things, the spices and flavourings, which are so hard to find in country shops and which I have come to rely on for so many dishes. I usually make a special trip to stock up, before leaving, with things like risotto rice, saffron, dried mushrooms, good French mustard, feta cheese packaged in brine, Danish mozzarella for pizza, pine kernels, plenty of good olive oil, white wine vinegar, French or Belgian cooking chocolate, and a whole Italian salami.

No larder is complete without at least a few home-made foods. A few jars of home-made jams or sauces, bottled fruits, even a few dried herbs from the garden, or wild mushrooms strung on a knotted string and hung in a warm place to dry, will transform the larder into a place of character and individuality.

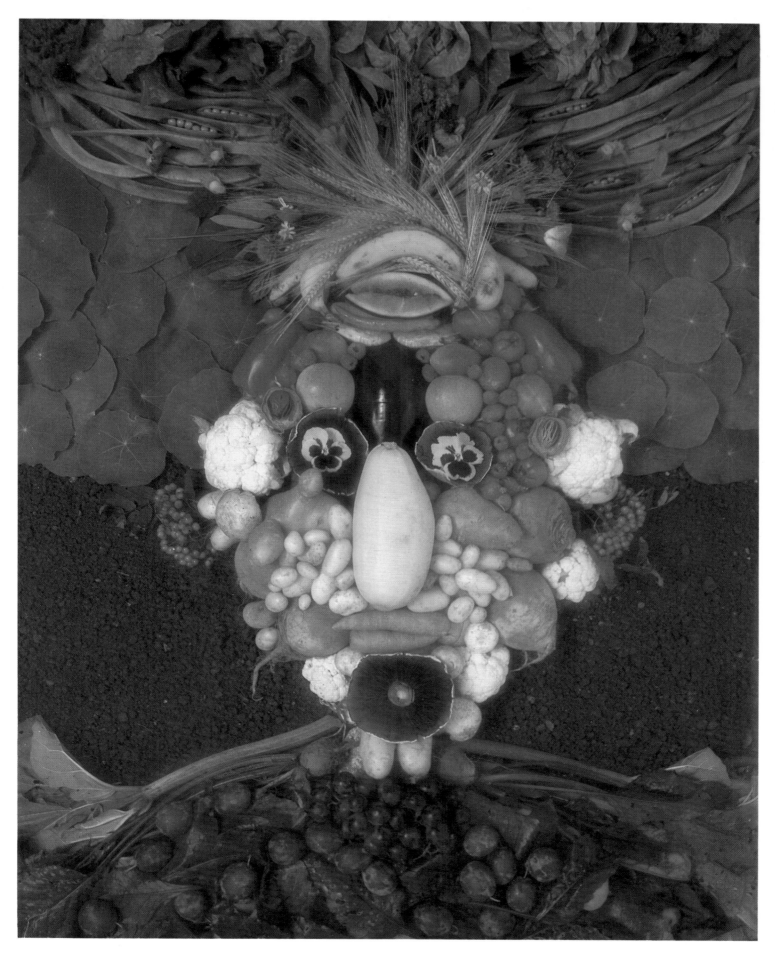

Summer recipes

In this book all metric equivalents are approximate (weights have been rounded up and volume measures have been rounded down, for convenience). Tablespoons and teaspoons are standard measure; amounts given are for level spoonfuls. Oven temperature conversions are those recommended by the Metrication Board.
The number of people each recipe serves is indicated wherever appropriate.
In all recipes requiring salt, sea salt is recommended, but only specified when necessary.

Soups/chowder and consommé

shellfish soup

1–2 pints/6dl–1 litre shellfish such as mussels, clams or cockles, or 4–6 scallops

2 leeks

1 stalk celery

2 potatoes

1½ oz/45g butter

1 pint/6dl milk and cream, mixed

pinch of saffron, or 2 tablespoons parsley

black pepper

SERVES 4–5

Wash the shellfish (except the scallops) thoroughly and put, still in their shells, into a heavy pan with ½ pint/3dl water. Bring to the boil, lower the heat and cook for a few minutes, uncovered, until they open. With a slotted spoon take out each one as it opens; remove from their shells and keep warm. If scallops are included, these will need to be removed from their shells and then poached gently in the shellfish stock for 3–4 minutes, before being lifted out and kept warm. Strain the stock and reserve. Wash the leeks well and slice finely. Chop the celery and peel and thinly slice the potatoes. Melt the butter in a heavy saucepan and sauté the leeks. Add the celery and potatoes and ½ pint/3dl hot water. Bring to the boil, lower the heat and simmer for about 25 minutes with the lid partially covering the pan, until the vegetables are soft. Heat the milk until almost boiling and add. Reheat the fish stock, adding the saffron (if used), and stir into the soup. At this stage the soup may be put in a blender for a smoother texture; I prefer the coarser version, however, which is more like a chowder. Cut the large shellfish in pieces and add to the soup. Keep just below simmering point for 4–5 minutes, until all is well heated, and serve, after tasting again for seasoning, and adding parsley (if using instead of saffron).

clam chowder

3 oz/90g streaky bacon

2 oz/60g butter

1 large onion

2 potatoes

one ½ lb/240g tin minced clams

1 tablespoon flour

1 pint/6dl milk

2 tablespoons chopped parsley

black pepper

SERVES 4–5

Cut the bacon and fry slowly until crisp, adding 1oz/30g butter to stop it sticking. Chop the onion and add it to the bacon when crisp. Fry gently until the onion is golden, stirring frequently. Peel and dice the potatoes and add to the pan; pour on enough hot water barely to cover them. Bring to the boil and simmer for 15–20 minutes, until the potatoes are soft. Add the minced clams and their juice, bring back to the boil and simmer for another 2–3 minutes. Mix the flour and a little of the milk to a paste; add to the pan and stir until smooth. Bring the rest of the milk almost to the boil and immediately pour into the clam mixture. Stir in the remaining butter, add plenty of black pepper, sprinkle the chopped parsley on top and serve.

beetroot and fennel soup

½ lb/240g raw beetroot

1½ pints/9dl chicken stock

1 lb/0.5 kg fennel

4 tablespoons sour cream

salt and black pepper

SERVES 5–6

Peel the beetroot and chop it finely by hand or in a food processor. Put into a heavy pan, add the stock and bring to the boil. Reduce the heat and simmer gently for 30 minutes.

Meanwhile chop the fennel finely. Add to the soup and simmer for another 30 minutes, covered. Add water or stock during cooking if it seems too thick. Cool slightly. Put in the liquidizer and blend briefly. Return to the pan, stir in the sour cream and adjust the seasoning to taste.

jellied bortsch

2 lb/1 kg raw beetroot
½ Spanish onion
2 packets gelatine
1 pint/6 dl chicken stock
2–3 tablespoons lemon juice
salt

SERVES 6–8

A day in advance, scrub the beetroot, then peel and chop in a food processor, or by hand. Put it into a pressure cooker with 1⅓ pints/8 dl very lightly salted water. Bring to the boil and cook for 30 minutes under pressure. Strain and measure the stock; you should have about 1 pint/6 dl. Discard the beetroot. Slice the onion finely and add to the stock; refrigerate overnight. Strain again. Melt the gelatine in the chicken stock and add to the beetroot stock. Add lemon juice to taste. If there are any lumps, strain the mixture. Refrigerate until set. To serve, roughly chop the aspic and spoon into cups.

consommé madrilène

1 large piece knuckle of veal (about ¾ lb/360 g)
2–3 lb/1–1.5 kg beef bones
½ lb/240 g shin of beef
1 onion
½ lb/240 g carrots
½ lb/240 g turnips
4 stalks celery
1 lb/0.5 kg tomatoes
1 bay leaf
4 stalks parsley
½ lb/240 g raw beetroot
juice of 1 lemon
salt and black pepper

SERVES 8–10

Put the meat and bones into a large pot. Cover with about 3 quarts/3 litres water and bring to the boil extremely slowly. It should take about 45 minutes to boil. Skim off the scum as it rises to the surface. Meanwhile chop the onion, carrots, turnips and celery. Peel and cut up the tomatoes, discarding the seeds. When the stock is boiling, and clear, add the chopped vegetables and the bay leaf and parsley. Bring back to the boil and simmer for 6 hours, covered. Pour through a strainer or colander lined with a double layer of butter muslin. When it is cool, put into the refrigerator and leave overnight, or for several hours, long enough to solidify the fat. Remove and discard the solid fat from the surface. Taste the soup—if the flavour is weak, or if the consommé is not firm enough to form a jelly, bring to the boil and simmer for about 15 minutes, to reduce and strengthen it. Peel and chop the raw beetroot and drop into ¾ pint/4.5 dl boiling salted water. After 20 minutes strain off the juice and add to the soup, to colour it. Add salt, pepper and lemon juice to taste. Strain again; allow to cool and finally chill before serving. Besides being served as a jellied consommé this can be used as an aspic, perhaps turned out of a ring mould and filled with prawns or lobster meat, or from individual moulds filled with lightly cooked vegetables such as green peas. It can also of course be served as a hot clear soup.

soupe au pistou

Pistou also makes a delicious sauce for
noodles or spring vegetables, and freezes very
well (see recipe, page 106)

1 *onion*
2 *small leeks*
2 *small carrots*
2 *courgettes*
6 *oz*/180 *g string beans*
¾ *lb*/360 *g tomatoes*
½ *lb*/240 *g shelled fresh, or* ¼ *lb*/120 *g dried*
haricot beans
2 *oz*/60 *g wholemeal elbow macaroni*
2 *oz*/60 *g basil leaves*
2 *cloves garlic*
4 *tablespoons pine kernels*
2 *oz*/60 *g grated Parmesan cheese*
6 *fl oz*/180 *ml olive oil*

SERVES 8

Chop the onion, leeks and carrots. Cut the
courgettes in ½-inch/1 cm slices and the green
beans in 1-inch/2.5 cm pieces. Peel the
tomatoes, discard the seeds and chop coarsely.
Heat 2 tablespoons olive oil in a broad, heavy
pan and sauté the onion and leeks gently until
pale golden. Add the carrots and haricot beans
and 2 pints/1 litre hot water. (If they are dried
the haricot beans should be precooked for
30 minutes.) Bring to the boil, add salt and
simmer for 45 minutes. Add the courgettes,
string beans and tomatoes to the soup and
simmer for another 30 minutes. Add the
macaroni and cook for another 12–15 minutes
until tender. Meanwhile prepare the pistou:
chop the basil leaves and pound them in a
mortar. Add the chopped garlic and the
chopped nuts. Pound all together into a
smooth paste, then add the grated cheese.
Continue to pound until smooth and blended;
then beat in the remaining oil very gradually,
pounding all the time, until you have

obtained a creamy paste like thick butter. Put
this paste into the bottom of a heated soup
tureen and add the boiling soup, one spoonful
to begin with, then the rest. Mix well and
heat gently in a barely warm oven.

tarragon soup

This recipe is also good with dill or chervil in
place of tarragon

2 *tablespoons fresh tarragon, chopped, plus*
3 *sprigs left whole*
1 *oz*/30 *g butter*
2 *tablespoons flour*
1½ *pints*/9 *dl good hot chicken stock*
1 *egg yolk*
1 *tablespoon lemon juice*
salt and black pepper

SERVES 3–4

In a large, heavy pan, melt the butter, stir in
the flour and cook for 1 minute. Add the hot
stock and stir until blended. Simmer gently
for 3 minutes. Add the sprigs of tarragon, and
salt and pepper, and turn off the heat. Cover
the pan and leave for 30 minutes. Taste, and
if the flavour seems faint, reheat until almost
simmering and turn off again. Strain into a
clean pan and reheat until almost boiling. Beat
the yolk of egg with the lemon juice in a small
mixing bowl. Stir in one ladleful of the hot
soup, mix and pour back into the pan. Stir
over a very low heat for about 1 minute. Add
the chopped tarragon and serve.

crème Sénégal

This is a most delicious and unusual soup
which can be served hot or cold. If preferred,
the chicken meat may be omitted

1 *oz*/30 *g butter*
1½ *teaspoons light curry powder*

2 tablespoons flour
1½ pints/9 dl strong chicken stock
juice of ½ lemon
¼ pint/1.5 dl single cream
¼ lb/120g breast of chicken, chopped
salt and black pepper

SERVES 4–5

Melt the butter in a saucepan over a medium heat and stir in the curry powder and then the flour. Cook gently for 3 minutes, stirring often. Heat the stock and add, a little at a time, stirring as it thickens. After 3–4 minutes, add the lemon juice, the cream and salt and pepper to taste. If you wish to serve this as a hot soup, the chopped white meat should be added at this stage and heated gently before serving. For a cold soup, cool quickly in a container half-full of cold water, stirring now and then to prevent a skin forming. When cool, refrigerate for 2–3 hours. Add the chopped chicken before serving.

chicken noodle soup

carcass of 1 chicken
3 small carrots
¼ lb/120g thin French beans
2 small leeks
2 small courgettes
2 small tomatoes
1 oz/30g star noodles
2 tablespoons chopped fresh tarragon, chervil, basil or dill
salt and black pepper

SERVES 3–4

Put the carcass into 2 pints/1 litre salted water and bring to the boil; reduce the heat and simmer for 1 hour. Strain the stock and remove the bones after salvaging any scraps of meat clinging to them; put these pieces of chicken back in the stock. Cut the carrots,

beans, leeks and courgettes in ½-inch/1cm slices. Peel and quarter the tomatoes, discarding the seeds. Bring some lightly salted water to the boil and add the carrots. After 5 minutes, add the beans, then the leeks, the courgettes and the tomatoes, at 5-minute intervals, in that order. Meanwhile reheat the chicken stock. When the vegetables are tender, lift them out with a slotted spoon and transfer them immediately to the chicken stock. Drop the noodles into the vegetable water, bring to the boil, lower the heat and simmer until tender. Drain, and add them to the soup. Season with salt and pepper to taste and stir in the chopped herbs. Stand for 5 minutes before serving. Have a bowl of Parmesan on the table.

kitchen garden soup

1 bunch watercress
½ cucumber
2 potatoes
½ lettuce
1½ oz/45g butter
1½ pints/9 dl hot chicken stock
¼ pint/1.5 dl single cream
salt and black pepper

SERVES 5–6

Chop the watercress coarsely, stalks and all. Peel the cucumber, and chop in small pieces. Peel the potatoes and slice them fairly thickly. Shred the lettuce. Melt the butter in a heavy pan and add all the vegetables. Sauté gently for 5–8 minutes. Add the stock, bring to the boil, lower the heat and simmer, covered, for 30 minutes, adding salt and pepper to taste. Mash the vegetables roughly with a fork and adjust the seasoning. Add the cream, stir in over low heat just until heated through and serve as soon as possible.

gazpacho

Everyone has a favourite recipe for gazpacho; this is the one I usually make. It can be made more quickly in a blender, but I prefer this version, in which each ingredient is chopped separately. A food processor can be used for chopping everything except the tomatoes (for these are reduced to a pulp too quickly)

½ cucumber
1 lb/0.5 kg tomatoes
1 Spanish onion
1 large green pepper
2 cloves garlic
2 slices dry wholemeal bread
½ pint/3 dl V8 mixed vegetable juice or tomato juice
½ pint/3 dl chicken stock
4 tablespoons olive oil
2 tablespoons wine vinegar
salt and black pepper
SERVES 6–8

Peel the cucumber and skin the tomatoes, chop them, and remove the seeds from the tomatoes. Finely chop the onion and green pepper and put them with the cucumber and tomatoes into a large bowl. Crush the garlic and add. Remove the crusts from the bread, cut it in small dice and stir into the mixture. Add the tomato or vegetable juice, the chicken stock and oil and vinegar. Add salt and pepper to taste. Chill in the refrigerator for several hours or overnight. About 1 hour before serving, add 6–8 ice cubes and taste for seasoning. If necessary, thin the soup with iced water or more stock.

courgette soup

2 lb/1 kg large courgettes or marrow
1 medium onion
2 oz/60 g butter
1 medium potato
1¾ pints/1 litre chicken stock
4 tablespoons double cream
3 tablespoons chopped basil
salt and black pepper
SERVES 6–8

Chop the onion. Melt the butter in a heavy pan and sauté the chopped onion until pale golden. Cut the courgettes in chunks and add to the pan. Cook gently for about 8 minutes, stirring often. Peel and slice the potato and add to the pan. Gradually add the stock, stirring, and salt and pepper; cover the pan and simmer for 25 minutes. Cool slightly, then pour into a blender and purée. Reheat, adding more salt and pepper if required. Stir in the cream and sprinkle with the chopped basil (if available). Let the soup stand for a few minutes before serving.

mangetout soup

This soup is also good served chilled
½ lb/240 g potatoes
1½ pint/9 dl chicken stock
1 small onion
½ lb/240 g mangetout peas
1½ oz/45 g butter
pinch of sugar
¼ pint/1.5 dl single cream
salt and black pepper
SERVES 6

Peel the potatoes, slice and put into a pan with the stock. Bring to the boil and simmer for about 20 minutes, until soft. Meanwhile chop the onion finely; cut the ends off the peas and cut each pod in two or three pieces.

Melt the butter in a sauté pan and add the onion and then the peas. Cook gently for 5 minutes, stirring occasionally. Add to the potatoes, bring back to simmering point and cook gently for another 5 minutes, not longer or the peas will spoil. Cool slightly and sieve. Reheat the purée gently, adding the sugar and cream, and salt and pepper to taste.

broad bean soup

1 lb/0.5 kg broad beans, frozen or fresh
1 pint/6 dl chicken stock
½ pint/3 dl milk
¼ pint/1.5 dl single cream
2 tablespoons very finely chopped lean ham
salt and black pepper
SERVES 6

Cook the beans in the stock until soft. Heat the milk and cream together. Put the beans into a blender with the stock and add the milk and cream. Blend. Pour into a clean pan, add salt and pepper to taste and reheat gently. Serve at once, with a little chopped ham on top of each bowl of soup.

cold watercress soup

1 bunch watercress
1½ oz/45 g butter
¾ pint/4.5 dl hot chicken or beef stock
1 pint/6 dl buttermilk
SERVES 4

Wash and chop the watercress, stalks and all. Melt the butter in a saucepan and add the watercress; sauté gently, stirring occasionally, for about 8 minutes. Pour on the stock. Simmer for 20 minutes, then cool. Put in a liquidizer with the buttermilk and blend. Chill before serving.

sorrel soup

¼ lb/120 g sorrel
¼ lb/120 g watercress
2 oz/60 g butter
1 medium potato
1¼ pints/7.5 dl hot chicken stock
½ pint/3 dl buttermilk
SERVES 4–5

Chop the sorrel and the watercress and stew them gently in the butter in a heavy pan for about 5 minutes. Peel and slice the potato. Add to the pan, and stir in the stock. Cover and simmer for 35 minutes or until the potato is mushy. Cool slightly, then pour into the blender. Blend well and then pour into a bowl. Stir in the buttermilk. Chill before serving. For a hot soup, substitute a half-and-half mixture of milk and cream for the buttermilk, and reheat gently before serving.

cold cucumber soup

½ cucumber
¾ pint/4.5 dl chicken stock
¾ pint/4.5 dl buttermilk
2 tablespoons chopped fresh mint, or a dash of Tabasco
salt and black pepper
SERVES 6

Peel the cucumber and cut in chunks. Put the stock, which must be free from all fat, into the blender with the buttermilk. When blended, add the cucumber. Blend again until it is in fine pieces but not yet entirely smooth. Add salt and pepper to taste. Chill for 2–3 hours before serving, then garnish every bowl with fresh mint, or stir in a dash of Tabasco.

Soups/vegetable

tomato and cucumber soup

I love this soup, which has a very light fresh
taste; it is like a gazpacho but more subtle

1 lb/0.5 kg tomatoes
1 cucumber
5 or 6 spring onions
1 oz/30 g butter
1½ pints/9 dl hot chicken stock
4 tablespoons sour cream
juice of ½ lemon
salt and black pepper
SERVES 4–5

Peel and cut the cucumber in small chunks.
Cut the spring onions in thin slices. Melt the
butter in a heavy pan and sauté both gently for
5 minutes. Add the hot stock and simmer for
20 minutes. Pour into the liquidizer and blend
briefly. Return to the clean pan and then
season with lemon juice, salt and pepper. Peel
the tomatoes, discarding the seeds, and chop
them finely; stir into the soup. Add the sour
cream and serve either hot or cold. If cold:
chill well before serving. If hot: heat only
once for a few minutes after adding the sour
cream, just before serving.

carrot and tomato soup

This is a totally raw soup, to be served cold

1 lb/0.5 kg carrots
1 lb/0.5 kg tomatoes
juice of 1 small orange
¼ pint/1.5 dl yoghourt
SERVES 3–4

Peel the carrots and tomatoes and cut up,
discarding the tomato seeds. Put into the
liquidizer with the orange juice. Blend, and
stir in the yoghourt. Serve immediately.

tomato soup

This is a hot soup, but is also very good chilled

1½ lb/0.75 kg tomatoes
1 pint/6 dl chicken stock
1 teaspoon sugar
1 tablespoon lemon juice
2 tablespoons chopped basil, chervil or dill
salt and black pepper
SERVES 4–5

Peel the tomatoes and cut in quarters. Heat
the stock in a large pan and when it is nearly
boiling, drop in the tomatoes. Add salt,
pepper and sugar and bring back to the boil;
simmer for 5 minutes, then remove from the
heat. Press through a medium-mesh sieve and
return to the pan. Reheat, adding the lemon
juice and more salt and pepper if needed.
Serve in cups and sprinkle the chopped herb
over the top of the soup.

cold lentil soup

An unusual cold soup that is quite substantial
without being heavy

½ lb/240 g continental lentils
1 lb/0.5 kg frozen chopped spinach
1 pint/6 dl buttermilk
juice of 1 lemon
SERVES 6

Cover the lentils with plenty of cold, lightly
salted water. Bring slowly to the boil, lower
the heat and simmer until soft, about 45
minutes. Drain. Meanwhile cook the spinach
briefly and drain; put it into the blender with
the buttermilk. Blend well and pour into a
bowl. Stir in the whole lentils. Add lemon
juice to taste and chill.

72

Eggs/first and main course dishes

eggs with watercress

6 eggs
2 bunches watercress
1 pint/6dl hot chicken stock
1½ oz/45g butter
2 tablespoons flour
¼ pint/1.5dl cream
2 tablespoons grated Parmesan cheese
salt and black pepper
SERVES 6

Wash the watercress and chop it coarsely, stalks and all. Cook in about ¾ pint/4.5dl of the stock, just simmering, for 5 minutes. Pour into a liquidizer and blend to a purée. Melt 1oz/30g butter and add 1 tablespoon flour; stir over medium heat. Add the watercress purée and stir until well mixed. Simmer for a few moments, then add 1 tablespoon cream. Season with salt and pepper and set aside to keep warm. Cook the eggs in boiling water for 5 minutes exactly; cool them under running water just enough so they can be shelled. Put them in a shallow dish and keep warm. Melt the remaining butter and add the rest of the flour. Cook, briefly, stirring, then add the remaining stock and stir until thickened and smooth. Cook gently for 2–3 minutes, then add the rest of the cream and stir in the grated cheese. Stir until melted and add salt and pepper to taste. Pour the hot watercress purée over and around the eggs and dribble the sauce over the top.

eggs with purslane

5 eggs
1 bunch purslane
1½ oz/45g butter
salt and black pepper
SERVES 2

Use only the tender part of the purslane, probably the top 2 inches/5cm of the stalk. Wash and dry well and chop. Melt the butter in a frying pan and add the purslane. Cook briskly until wilted, 3–4 minutes. Meanwhile beat the eggs and season them with salt and pepper. Pour into the pan on top of the purslane. Cook like an omelette but without trying to fold it over. Serve immediately the moment it is cooked on a flat platter.

oeufs à l'estragon

4 eggs
¼ pint/0.5dl double cream
3–4 sprigs tarragon
salt and pepper
SERVES 4

Preheat oven to 325°F (170°C, Gas Mark 3). Heat the cream until nearly boiling. Add the sprigs of tarragon, reserving four nice leaves for garnish. Cover the pan and set aside for about 15 minutes in a warm place. Break the eggs into buttered cocotte dishes, add salt and pepper and put in the oven. After about 8 minutes, when almost set, pour the cream through a strainer, dividing it between the 4 eggs. Lay a tarragon leaf on top of each, return to the oven to warm for about 2 more minutes and serve at once.

Eggs/first and main course dishes

eggs in green peppers

4 eggs
4 green peppers
5 oz/150 g rice
1 medium onion
1½ oz/45 g butter
salt and black pepper
SERVES 4

Cook the rice in plenty of boiling salted water until tender; drain well. Preheat the oven to 350°F (180°C, Gas Mark 4). Drop the peppers into a large pan of boiling water and cook for 10 minutes. Lift out carefully, drain and cool slightly. Cut off the tops, scoop out the seeds and discard. Chop the onion. Melt the butter and sauté the onion until golden. Add the rice and mix well, and add salt and pepper to taste. Spoon into the green peppers and break an egg into each. Sprinkle the top with salt and pepper and bake for 12 minutes or until the whites of the eggs are just set. Serve with tomato sauce I (see recipe, page 103).

eggs and potatoes with yoghourt

4 eggs
2 lb/1 kg potatoes
1 oz/30 g butter
¼ lb/120 g shelled peas (or ½ lb/240 g in pods)
¼ pint/1.5 dl yoghourt
salt and black pepper
SERVES 4

Boil the potatoes and drain well; mash them with the butter and plenty of salt and pepper. Cook the peas in boiling water until just tender. Lift them out with a slotted spoon and add them to the potatoes with the yoghourt, stirring to mix thoroughly. Poach the eggs in lightly simmering salted water; drain. Spoon the potato mixture into heated bowls and put a poached egg in each one.

eggs with sausage and peppers

4 eggs
1 onion
1 green pepper
1 oz/30 g butter
1 clove garlic
1 chilli pepper or a dash Tabasco
one 12 oz/360 g tin tomatoes, roughly chopped
one 6 oz/180 g tin red peppers, chopped
pinch of sugar
2 kabanos (or other spicy Polish sausage)
salt and black pepper
SERVES 4

Chop the onion and green pepper. Melt the butter in a heavy pan and sauté the onion gently. Crush the garlic and add with the green pepper. Finely mince the chilli pepper (if used) and add it or the Tabasco, and tomatoes and red peppers. Simmer gently for 30 minutes, covered, stirring occasionally. Add salt and pepper and a pinch of sugar. Cut the sausage in thin slices and add for the last 5 minutes of cooking. Meanwhile fry the eggs in butter. Spoon the pepper mixture into a serving dish and lay the eggs on top.

stuffed eggs

6 eggs
2 tablespoons sour cream
4 tablespoons chopped herbs: tarragon, chervil, dill, chives
salt and black pepper
SERVES 4–6

Boil the eggs for 12 minutes, cool them quickly and shell. Cut them in half lengthwise. Scoop out the yolks into a bowl; mash to a paste with a fork, adding the sour cream and salt and pepper to taste. Fold in the chopped herbs. Spoon the mixture into halved egg whites just before serving.

egg croquettes

7 eggs
1 small onion
2 oz/60g butter
½ pint/3 dl milk
½ bay leaf
pinch of mace or nutmeg
2 tablespoons flour
2 tablespoons chopped parsley or ham
dry breadcrumbs

SERVES 3–4

Hard boil 6 eggs; let cool, shell and chop finely. Chop the onion. Melt 1 oz/30g of the butter and gently sauté the onion. Heat the milk with the bay leaf and mace or nutmeg, but not to boiling point. When the onion is soft and lightly coloured, stir in 2 tablespoons of flour and add the warm milk (after removing the bay leaf). Mix well. Add the chopped eggs and parsley or ham and mix again; season to taste with salt and pepper and pour into a lightly greased shallow dish. Cool, then cover and refrigerate for several hours or overnight. The next day shape the mixture into oval (egg-like) shapes; roll each one first in flour, then dip into beaten egg, then in dry breadcrumbs. Fry in the remaining 1 oz/30g of butter, turning on all sides, until heated through and browned. Serve with tomato and pepper sauce (see recipe, page 103).

eggs with potatoes and leeks

4 eggs
1½ lb/0.75 kg potatoes
1 lb/0.5 kg leeks
2 oz/60g butter
½ pint/3 dl milk
salt and black pepper

SERVES 4

Peel the potatoes and boil in salted water until tender; drain well. Meanwhile wash the leeks well and chop them coarsely. Melt the butter in a sauté pan and add the leeks. Cook gently for 8–10 minutes. Heat the milk, and pour about half of it over the leeks. Cover the pan and cook for another 10 minutes or until the leeks are soft. Mash the potatoes, and stir in the leeks with their juices and enough of the remaining milk to make a fairly thin purée. Season to taste with plenty of salt and pepper. Keep hot while you poach the eggs. Pour the potato-leek mixture into four warmed bowls and place a poached egg in the centre of each.

baked eggs with cheese

6 eggs
6 slices bread
6 oz/180g Cheddar, Gruyère or Emmenthal cheese
1 oz/30g butter
salt and black pepper

SERVES 3–6

Preheat oven to 400°F (200°C, Gas Mark 6). Cut the crusts off the bread. Butter the bottom of a baking sheet large enough for the six slices to be laid flat, close together. Cut the cheese in thin slices and lay them on the bread. Break the eggs over the cheese; sprinkle with salt and pepper. Bake for 15 minutes or until the whites have just set. Cut into pieces and serve with a green salad.

Eggs/quiches

herb quiche

8 oz/240 g plain flour
3 oz/90 g grated Cheddar cheese
3 oz/90 g butter
1 egg yolk
¼ lb/120 g spinach
¼ lb/120 g sorrel leaves
1 bunch watercress
5 or 6 spring onions
2–3 tablespoons chopped parsley
1 tablespoon each chopped tarragon, chervil, dill
2 eggs
½ lb/240 g Jockey cheese
¼ pint/1.5 dl double cream
salt and black pepper
SERVES 4–8

Mix the flour, grated cheese and a pinch of salt with the fingertips; cut the butter in with the blade of a knife. Sprinkle the mixture with 4 tablespoons iced water. Blend lightly; add more water if necessary to unite the ingredients. Chill for 30 minutes before using. Preheat oven to 400°F (200°C, Gas Mark 6). Roll out and line a 10-inch/25 cm flan ring. Prick with a fork in several places. Brush with beaten egg yolk and bake for 10 minutes. Reduce heat to 350°F (175°C, Gas Mark 4). Remove from the oven. Wash the spinach, sorrel, watercress and spring onions and drop into boiling salted water. After 4 minutes, drain well, squeeze out all moisture and chop, with the herbs. Beat the eggs, mix with the cream and Jockey cheese and add salt and pepper to taste. Stir in the greens and mix lightly. Pour the mixture into the pastry shell and return to the oven. Bake for 30 minutes.

spinach and cheese quiche

This quiche is best eaten hot, but it is also quite good cold for a picnic
½ lb/240 g pastry (see recipe, page 126)
2 eggs + 1 yolk
1½ lb/0.75 kg fresh spinach
½ oz/15 g butter
¼ lb/120 g ricotta or cream cheese
¼ pint/1.5 dl single cream
4 tablespoons grated Parmesan cheese
salt and black pepper
SERVES 4–5

Make the pastry and line a 9-inch/23 cm quiche pan with it. Chill. Preheat oven to 375°F (190°C, Gas Mark 5). Beat the yolk. Brush the cold pastry with beaten egg yolk, prick with a fork and bake for 10 minutes. Wash and chop the spinach; put it into a saucepan with the butter and stew gently until soft. Drain well, squeezing out as much moisture as possible. Add salt and pepper to taste and spoon into the pre-baked pastry shell. Beat the two eggs and add the ricotta or cream cheese gradually, as you beat. When the mixture is smooth, stir in the cream and add most of the grated Parmesan. Stir well and pour over the spinach. Scatter the reserved Parmesan evenly over the top, and bake for a further 30 minutes at the same temperature.

Salads/shellfish and chicken

shellfish salad

1 lb/0.5 kg hake or other firm white fish
6 scallops
6 crawfish tails or giant prawns
½ lb/240g prawns or shrimps
juice of 3 lemons
1 crisp lettuce, Webb's or Iceberg
1 large green pepper
1 cucumber, peeled
4 hard-boiled eggs
6 tablespoons olive oil
½ pint/3 dl mayonnaise (see recipe, page 104)
salt and black pepper
SERVES 6

Poach the fish gently and leave to cool in its court bouillon. Remove the skin and bones and break in large flakes. Pour the juice of 1 lemon over the fish flakes and leave for about 30 minutes. Poach the scallops for 5 minutes in the same court bouillon; cool, then marinate in lemon juice also. Shell the giant prawns or crawfish tails and shrimps or prawns, and soak for 10 minutes in a bowl of very cold salted water. Wash the lettuce and break up the leaves in neat pieces. Cut the pepper in strips and the peeled cucumber in sticks. Put the lettuce into a large salad bowl and cover with the pepper and cucumber. Pile the white fish in the centre and arrange the shellfish over the top. Surround with the halved hard-boiled eggs and pour over a vinaigrette made with 6 tablespoons olive oil and 2 tablespoons lemon juice, salt and pepper. Mix the salad at the table and hand the mayonnaise around separately.

chicken salad

1 chicken
1 crisp lettuce, Webb's or Cos
1 cucumber
1 large green pepper
1 head fennel
1 bunch watercress
4 stalks celery
4 tablespoons lemon juice
3–4 tablespoons sunflower seed oil
salt and black pepper
SERVES 6

Place the chicken in boiling salted water to cover and poach gently for 60 minutes; leave to cool in its stock. Remove from the liquid and cut the chicken meat in pieces, removing skin and bones. Sprinkle the chicken pieces with 3 tablespoons lemon juice. Shred the lettuce. Peel the cucumber and cut in chunks. Cut the green pepper in thin strips. Slice the fennel. Chop the watercress, reserving the best leaves. Slice the celery and reserve any leaves. Mix all together and dress with the oil and remaining tablespoon of lemon juice, and salt and pepper to taste. Serve with herb sauce (see recipe, page 105) using the reserved leaves for a garnish.

Salads/leaf vegetables

oriental salad

1 bunch radishes
1 bunch spring onions
1 curly endive
1 tablespoon lemon juice
3 tablespoons sunflower seed oil
pinch of sugar
black pepper
SERVES 4

Start the day before. Cut the tops from the radishes and, using a small sharp knife, cut from the bottom of the radish upwards in thin slices to resemble a flower. Trim all but the freshest part of the green leaves off the spring onions and treat them in the same way as the radishes. Put the radishes and spring onions in a bowl of cold water and refrigerate for several hours or overnight. The next day the cut parts will have curled back into fantastic flower-like shapes. Drain and pat dry with paper towels. Remove the green outer leaves of the endive and use the pale inner part only. Separate it in small lacy leaves; wash and dry, and lay in a shallow bowl or dish with the radishes and spring onions in the centre. Mix the lemon juice, oil, sugar and pepper, and sprinkle over.

wild green salad

a good bundle of mixed wild green leaves: sorrel, dandelion, watercress, etc. (garden lettuce and spinach can be added as needed)
3 tablespoons sunflower seed or nut oil
1 tablespoon lemon juice
a handful of cobnuts or a few wild primroses
salt and black pepper
SERVES 3–4

Mix the greens in a large salad bowl, leaving them whole. Dress with the oil and lemon juice, salt and pepper. Scatter the nuts or the primroses (only use the flowers) over.

mixed salad

1 lb/0.5 kg tomatoes
½ Spanish onion
1 bunch watercress
juice of 1 lemon
black pepper
SERVES 4

Skin the tomatoes and cut them in slices. Slice the onion finely. Put the tomatoes into a salad bowl and scatter the sliced onion over them. Add the tender sprigs of watercress, discarding the tough parts, and toss with the tomato and onion. Scatter with pepper and squeeze over the lemon juice. Toss so that it is well mixed and serve.

avocado, tomato and mozzarella salad

This is best served alone as a salad course rather than as an accompaniment to other main course dishes

2 avocados
1 lb/0.5 kg tomatoes
2 mozzarella cheeses
juice of ½ lemon
6 tablespoons olive oil
2 tablespoons white wine vinegar
1 teaspoon oregano
salt and black pepper
SERVES 6–8

Peel the avocados, halve them to remove the stones and cut them in slices. Squeeze the lemon juice over them to prevent discolouring. Skin and slice the tomatoes and cut the mozzarella in slices. Arrange the three ingredients in a shallow dish and sprinkle them with salt and pepper. Mix the oil and vinegar and pour this dressing evenly over the salad. Sprinkle the oregano over all and serve.

garden thinnings salad

This delicate salad is best served with very mild simple foods such as scrambled eggs, omelettes, or poached fish

about 4 handfuls of young leaves of lettuce, sorrel, spinach, rocket, dandelion, mustard or similar greens

½ tablespoon lemon juice

2 tablespoons sunflower seed oil

pinch of sugar

freshly ground black pepper

SERVES 4

Wash and dry the leaves. Pile them into a salad bowl and scatter the sugar over them, and a few turns of the peppermill. Mix the lemon juice and the oil and add. Toss the leaves lightly before serving.

watercress and orange salad

This is particularly good with cold game or roast duck

2 bunches watercress

3 small oranges

2 tablespoons chopped shallots

1 tablespoon lemon juice

1 tablespoon orange juice

4 tablespoons olive oil

salt and black pepper

SERVES 4

Pinch the tender sprigs off the watercress, wash and shake dry. Pile into a salad bowl. Peel the oranges with a sharp knife, removing all the pith. Divide them carefully in sections and mix with the watercress. Scatter the chopped shallot over all. Mix the lemon and orange juice, olive oil and salt and pepper. Pour over the salad and toss well.

dandelion salad

This salad is best as a separate course, either as an hors d'oeuvre or after a light main course. It is also very good when made with young spinach leaves or sorrel, or with a mixture of the two

1 large bunch dandelion leaves (about 6 oz/180g)

¼ lb/120g bacon

2 slices dry white bread

1 oz/30g butter

1 clove garlic

3 tablespoons olive oil

1 tablespoon white wine vinegar

salt and black pepper

SERVES 4

Wash the dandelion leaves and dry. Cut them across in slices and pile them lightly into a salad bowl. Cut the bacon in small pieces and fry slowly until crisp; drain and cool. Remove the crusts from the bread and cut the bread in cubes. Add the butter to the remaining bacon fat in the frying pan and fry the cubes of bread, with the peeled clove of garlic, stirring them around until evenly coloured a light golden brown. Mix together the olive oil and vinegar and add salt and pepper; pour this dressing over the leaves. Toss well. Discard the garlic and scatter the croûtons and bacon pieces over the leaves and mix lightly. Serve this salad as soon as possible.

fennel and tomato salad

This Italian salad makes a good hors d'oeuvre

2–3 *heads fennel*

1 *lb/0.5 kg ripe tomatoes*

2 *tablespoons olive oil*

½ *tablespoon lemon juice*

½ *tablespoon white wine vinegar*

salt and black pepper

SERVES 3–4

Wash the fennel and cut very thinly in horizontal slices, reserving the leaves. Put the slices into a bowl of cold water in the refrigerator for an hour or two to become crisp. Drain and dry well before using. Peel and slice the tomatoes. Arrange the fennel and tomato slices on each side of a large dish. Sprinkle salt and pepper over them. Mix the oil, lemon juice and vinegar well and spoon over the vegetables. Chop the reserved leaves of fennel and scatter over the top.

spinach, bacon and mushroom salad

½ *lb/240 g spinach*

½ *lb/240 g small mushrooms*

juice of ½ lemon

¼ *lb/120 g streaky bacon rashers*

2 *slices dry bread*

½ *oz/15 g butter*

1 *clove garlic (optional)*

6 *tablespoons olive oil*

2 *tablespoons white wine vinegar or lemon juice*

salt and black pepper

SERVES 4

Wash the spinach and drain well. Discard the stalks and cut the leaves across in thin strips. Wipe the mushrooms, remove the stalks and slice the caps. Squeeze the lemon juice over them. Fry the bacon slowly until crisp, drain on soft paper and break in small pieces. Remove the crusts and cut the bread in small cubes. Melt the butter and fry the croûtons until golden brown, with the whole peeled clove of garlic. Mix all together in a bowl after discarding the garlic. Add salt and pepper to taste and dress with the oil and vinegar, or use lemon juice instead of vinegar.

pitta salad

1 *cucumber*

1 *lb/0.5 g tomatoes*

1 *green pepper*

1 *piece pitta bread*

¼ *lb/120 g feta cheese*

6 *tablespoons olive oil*

3 *tablespoons lemon juice*

salt and black pepper

SERVES 4

Peel the cucumber and cut it in strips like thick matchsticks. Peel the tomatoes, slice them thickly and cut in similar strips, discarding the seeds and juice. Cut the pepper in strips likewise. Toast the pitta briefly. (It can be cut in half and put in an electric toaster.) Cool, then tear in pieces. Mix all together in a bowl and season with salt and pepper. Crumble the cheese roughly and scatter over the salad. Dress with oil and lemon juice, and serve.

orange and almond salad

Like all salads with orange, this is excellent with cold duck, goose or game

1 *Cos lettuce*
1 *bunch watercress (optional)*
2 *medium oranges*
1 oz/30 g *flaked almonds*
1 *tablespoon chopped shallot*
1 *tablespoon orange juice*
3 *tablespoons lemon juice*
3 *tablespoons olive oil or nut oil*
pinch of sugar
salt and black pepper
SERVES 4–5

Cut the lettuce across in 1-inch/2.5 cm pieces. Pinch the tender part of the watercress, if used, in sprigs. Put with the lettuce into a salad bowl. Peel the oranges carefully, removing all the pith; cut them in half lengthwise, and then in slices, saving any juice. Lay the orange slices over the green salad and scatter the flaked almonds over them. Mix the fruit juices, shallots, oil, salt, pepper and sugar. Pour over and mix well.

pine kernel salad

This pretty green, pink and white salad is delicious with cheese

1 *cucumber*
1 *green eating apple*
1 *heart of crisp lettuce*
1 *bunch watercress*
1 *bunch radishes*
2 oz/60 g *pine kernels*
2 *tablespoons sunflower seed oil*
1 *tablespoon lemon juice*
salt and black pepper
SERVES 4

Peel the cucumber and cut it in small dice. Peel and core the apple. Chop the lettuce heart, the apple and the watercress, stalks and all. Slice the radishes finely and mix all together in a large bowl. Scatter in the nuts and season with salt and pepper. Dress lightly with the oil and lemon juice.

potato and vegetable salad

1 *round lettuce*
½ lb/240 g *new potatoes*
3 or 4 *new carrots*
¼ lb/120 g *shelled peas or broad beans*
1 *small cauliflower*
½ lb/240 g *small tomatoes*
5 or 6 *spring onions*
4 *hard-boiled eggs*
4 *tablespoons olive oil*
2 *tablespoons white wine vinegar*
4 *tablespoons single cream*
3 *tablespoons chopped chervil*
salt and black pepper
SERVES 4

Wash the lettuce. Cook the unpeeled potatoes and the carrots, peas or beans and cauliflower separately until just tender; leave to cool. Before they are completely cool, peel the potatoes and slice them thickly. Mix them with the other cooked vegetables in a bowl and pour half the oil and vinegar over them. Put the lettuce leaves into a salad bowl; add the peeled tomatoes, left whole if they are small, or quartered if larger, and the spring onions, bulbs only. Add the cooked vegetables and the remaining oil and vinegar. Season with salt and pepper and mix lightly, without breaking the ingredients. Pour on the cream and mix again. Shell the eggs, cut them in half and lay them around the edge of the bowl. Scatter the chervil over and serve.

Fish/freshwater and seafish

grilled trout

4 trout
2 oz/60 g butter
1 tablespoon lemon juice
1–2 lemons
salt and black pepper
SERVES 4

Preheat the grill. Make two or three small diagonal cuts on each side of the fish; sprinkle with salt and pepper. Heat the butter with the lemon juice until melted. Lay the fish on the grill pan and cook under the grill, basting with butter and lemon juice. Cook for 5 minutes on each side quite close to the flame, then for 4–5 minutes farther away. To serve, lay the fish on a flat dish, pour the basting juices over them and garnish with cut lemons. Serve with boiled or steamed new potatoes.

baked trout with cucumber

6 trout
2 oz/60 g butter
juice of 1 lemon
a few sprigs fresh tarragon, chervil or dill, or
1 tablespoon finely chopped parsley
1 medium cucumber
½ pint/3 dl single cream
1 tablespoon finely chopped parsley, tarragon, chervil or dill
SERVES 6

Preheat oven to 375°F (190°C, Gas Mark 5). Have the trout cleaned but with their heads and tails left on. Lay them in a well-buttered ovenproof dish and pour the lemon juice over them. Add salt and pepper and the fresh sprigs of herbs. Cover the dish with a buttered piece of aluminium foil and bake for 10 minutes. Meanwhile peel the cucumber and cut in sticks like thick matchsticks. Melt 1 oz/30 g butter and sauté the cucumber sticks

for 2–3 minutes, stirring. Add the cream and bring to the boil while stirring to mix with the cucumber sticks. Remove the fish from the oven and uncover. Pour the cucumber-cream mixture over the trout. Cover and return them to the oven for a further 5 minutes, then remove the sprigs of herbs, garnish with the chopped fresh herbs and serve.

trout fillets in oatmeal

4 trout
a little milk
coarse oatmeal
2 oz/60 g butter
1 lemon
salt and black pepper
SERVES 4

Cut off the heads and tails of the fish; lift each side carefully from the central bone, leaving the skin on. Sprinkle each fillet with salt and pepper, dip in milk, then in oatmeal. Fry them in butter, or alternatively put under the grill dotted with the butter cut in small pieces. In either case, turn the fish carefully, trying to avoid knocking off the oatmeal. When nicely browned on both sides, serve with cut lemons and grilled tomatoes.

trout en gelée

4 trout
2 or 3 cloves
1 onion
1 carrot
1 stalk celery
1 bay leaf
3 stalks parsley
½ pint/3 dl dry white wine
2 teaspoons coarse salt and 6 black peppercorns
SERVES 4

82

The day before, make the court bouillon. Stick the cloves in the onion. Put the onion, carrot, celery, bay leaf, parsley, salt and peppercorns into a narrow pan with the wine and 1 pint/6 dl water. Bring to the boil, lower the heat, cover and simmer for 25 minutes. Meanwhile clean the trout but leave the heads and tails on. Add to the simmering court bouillon and poach very gently for 7–8 minutes, until the trout are cooked. Lift them out carefully; cut off the heads and tails and remove the skin, and put heads, tails and skins back into the pan. Lay the fish on a shallow dish. Boil up the stock to reduce it until you have about ½ pint/3 dl of liquid. Strain. Cut the cooked carrot in thin slices and lay three or four on each fish. Pour about a third of the cooled fish stock over them and chill. When it has set, repeat the process twice. When the third layer has been added, refrigerate overnight. Either serve in the same dish or cut each fish out and surround with the cubed jelly. Serve with curry sauce (see recipe, page 107).

poached rainbow trout

4 rainbow trout	
1 onion, stuck with 3 cloves	
1 carrot	
1 stalk celery	
1 leek	
3 stalks parsley	
1 bay leaf	
1 small bundle fresh herbs: lovage, burnet, tarragon, chervil and dill	
¼ pint/1.5 dl dry white wine or vermouth or 4 tablespoons white wine vinegar	
1 tablespoon salt	
10 black peppercorns	

SERVES 4

Cut the onion, carrot, celery and leek in large pieces and put them into a fish kettle or large pan. Add the bay leaf, fresh herbs, salt, peppercorns and the wine or vinegar. Add enough cold water to cover the fish and bring to the boil. Reduce the heat and simmer, covered, for 20–30 minutes. Lower the trout into the simmering court bouillon; bring back to the boil and then adjust the heat so that it barely simmers. Poach the fish for 7–8 minutes, until just cooked. Lift out carefully and drain. Serve with shallot sauce (see recipe, page 105), or easy hollandaise sauce (see recipe, page 108).

cold poached bass

one 2½ lb/2.25 kg bass	
1 carrot	
1 onion	
2 stalks celery	
1 bay leaf	
6 black peppercorns	
2 tablespoons white wine or white wine vinegar	

SERVES 4

In advance prepare a court bouillon by cutting the carrot, onion and celery in large pieces, and putting them into a heavy pan with the bay leaf, peppercorns, the wine or wine vinegar and enough water barely to cover the fish. Bring to the boil, reduce the heat, cover and simmer for about 30 minutes. Leave to cool before using. Put the bass in the court bouillon and bring to the boil. Lower the heat and poach very gently for about 20 minutes, then turn off the heat. When it is cool, lift the fish from the court bouillon and remove the skin. Slide it on to a platter and serve with tomato mayonnaise (see recipe for mayonnaise, page 104).

baked stuffed carp

one 2–2½ lb/1 kg–1.25 kg golden carp
1 oz/30 g buckwheat
1 small onion
2½ oz/75 g butter
4 tablespoons chopped parsley
2 shallots
4 tablespoons sour cream
4 tablespoons lemon juice
salt and black pepper

SERVES 4–5

Heat 2 fl oz/60 ml very lightly salted water until boiling. Put in the buckwheat and bring back to the boil. Boil hard for 1 minute, then lower the heat as much as possible, cover the pan and leave to simmer very slowly for 10–12 minutes, until all the water is absorbed. Do not stir. Leave to cool. Chop the onion and cook in 1 oz/30 g butter until golden. Stir in the cooked buckwheat and mix well. Add salt and pepper to taste, stir in the chopped parsley, reserving a tablespoon, and allow to cool before using. Preheat oven to 350°F (180°C, Gas Mark 4). Fill the carp with buckwheat stuffing. Thickly butter the bottom of an ovenproof dish. Chop the shallots very finely and scatter over the butter. Lay the fish on the shallots and sprinkle with salt and pepper. Dot the remaining butter in small pieces over the surface of the fish. Lay a piece of foil over the fish and bake for 40 minutes. Mix the sour cream and lemon juice, and pour over the fish. Put the fish back into the oven, without the foil, and bake for another 10 minutes, or until the fish flakes easily when pierced with a fork. Scatter with chopped parsley and serve.

anguilles au vert

2 lb/1 kg small freshwater eels, skinned and cut in 2-inch/5 cm chunks
4 shallots
3 tablespoons olive oil
½ lb/240 g sorrel, spinach and watercress
leaves from 2 heads of celery
2 tablespoons chopped parsley
1 tablespoon chopped chervil
1 tablespoon chopped tarragon
½ pint/3 dl fish stock (or water)
½ pint/3 dl dry white wine
1 bay leaf
salt and black pepper

SERVES 4–5

Chop the shallots and cook gently in the oil in a heavy pan until soft. Wash and chop all the green leaves except the bay leaf, and add to the shallots. Cook slowly for about 10 minutes, stirring often. Add the pieces of eel, and enough fish stock mixed with an equal amount of white wine to barely cover the eel. (If too much is used the sauce will not set to a jelly.) Add the bay leaf, salt and pepper and cover the pan. Bring to the boil and boil hard for 1 minute. Reduce the heat to the lowest possible and simmer for 20 minutes. Remove the bay leaf and serve immediately, in soup plates. Accompany with a dish of boiled potatoes. Alternatively, it can be served as a cold dish. Leave to cool, then refrigerate overnight; the liquid will set to a thick green jelly. Serve with brown bread and butter.

sole with watercress sauce

2 large Dover sole, plaice, or lemon sole, filleted, with their bones

1 onion

1 carrot

1 stalk celery

1 bay leaf

3 stalks parsley

2 tablespoons white wine vinegar

2 oz/60 g medium-fat cream cheese

6 tablespoons watercress leaves

salt, pepper and peppercorns

SERVES 4

Cut the onion, carrot and celery in large pieces and put into a pressure cooker with the fish bones. Add the bay leaf, parsley, salt and 6 peppercorns. Add 1½ pints/9 dl cold water and the vinegar. Bring to the boil and cook for 15 minutes under pressure. Reduce the pressure and remove the lid. Cool slightly, then put in the fillets and poach gently (not under pressure) for 5 minutes. Lift the fillets out and lay them on a serving dish; keep warm. Strain ¼ pint/1.5 dl of the cooking liquid and put into a blender with the cream cheese and the watercress leaves. Blend, then pour into a small pan and reheat, adding salt and pepper as needed. Pour some of the sauce over the fillets and serve the rest separately in a small jug.

goujons of sole

2 Dover sole, filleted

2 egg yolks

2 tablespoons olive oil

3 tablespoons dry breadcrumbs

1 tablespoon nut oil

SERVES 3–4

Skin the fillets and cut them in diagonal strips, about ¾ inch/1.9 cm wide. Pat dry with paper towels. Beat the egg yolks with the olive oil and 2 tablespoons water. Dip each fish piece in this mixture, then in dry breadcrumbs. Shake off excess. Heat the nut oil in a sauté pan until very hot but not smoking. (A small cube of bread should sizzle immediately on being dropped in.) Cook the *goujons* quickly, turning on all sides until golden brown, for not more than 3 minutes. Drain briefly on paper towels and serve with tomato sauce 2 (see recipe, page 103) or horseradish sauce (see recipe, page 107).

baked cod

2½–3 lb/2.25–2.5 kg cod on the bone

juice of 2 lemons

¼ lb/120 g butter

3–4 tablespoons dry breadcrumbs

salt and black pepper

SERVES 4–6

Preheat oven to 350°F (180°C, Gas Mark 4). Place the fish in a fireproof dish and pour the lemon juice over it. Dot with the butter and add salt and pepper. Cover with a buttered piece of aluminium foil and put in the oven to bake for about ½ hour. Take the dish from the oven, remove the foil and skin the top side of the fish. Baste with butter and lemon, then cover with a thick layer of breadcrumbs. Return to the oven and bake for another ½ hour, basting two or three times more.

Fish/seafish and shellfish

fish in aspic

3 fillets plaice
1 carrot
1 onion
1 stalk celery
1 bay leaf
2 tablespoons white wine or white wine vinegar
¼ lb/120g frozen petits pois
2 tomatoes
1 or 2 sprigs fresh tarragon
1–2 tablespoons lemon juice
¼ oz/7.5g powdered gelatine
salt and 6 black peppercorns
SERVES 3

Skin the fillets and cut each one in half. Put the skins into a pan with the carrot, onion, celery, bay leaf, salt and peppercorns. Cover with cold water and add the wine or wine vinegar. Bring to the boil and simmer for 30 minutes. Cook the peas briefly in a little boiling salted water; drain and cool. Skin the tomatoes and chop finely, discarding seeds and juice. Strain the fish stock and bring back to the boil. Roll the fillets and drop them into the stock. Add a sprig of tarragon, after reserving six good leaves for garnish. Poach very gently for about 5 minutes, then lift out the fish and drain. Taste the stock, and if it seems weak, boil for a few minutes to reduce it. Strain again and measure ½ pint/3 dl. Flavour with lemon juice. Dissolve the gelatine in 1 tablespoon water and stir into the measured stock. Strain again and pour a thin layer into each of six *oeufs en gelée* moulds. Put into the refrigerator to set. When firm, lay one leaf in each mould, then a rolled fish fillet and finally the peas and tomatoes, dividing them evenly among the six moulds. Cover with the rest of the fish stock and return to the refrigerator to set. Turn out and serve with a light curry sauce (see recipe, page 107).

smoked haddock with eggs

2 medium smoked haddock
4 eggs
½ pint/3 dl milk
1 oz/30g butter
1½ tablespoons flour
¼ pint/1.5 dl single cream
1 tablespoon finely chopped parsley
black pepper
SERVES 4

Cut the fish in large pieces and put them into a broad, shallow pan. Pour the milk over them, and enough water to barely cover the fish. Bring to the boil, cover the pan and remove from the heat. Leave for 15 minutes. Lift out the fish and strain the stock. Boil this until sufficiently reduced and well flavoured. Take care it does not get too salty. When cool, flake the fish, removing all skin and bone. Put into a serving dish and keep warm. Melt the butter, blend in the flour, add ¼ pint/1.5 dl reduced fish stock and the cream. Stir over a low heat until blended, seasoning to taste with pepper, and simmer for 3 minutes. Meanwhile poach the eggs in salted boiling water, drain carefully and place them on the fish. Pour the sauce over the eggs and sprinkle with parsley.

barbecued lobster

2 medium lobsters
barbecue sauce 1 (see recipe, page 108)
SERVES 4

Drop the lobsters into boiling salted water; after 10 minutes, lift them out and cool slightly. Cut each in half with a sharp knife, and lay them, shell side down, on the grill. Cook them for 5 minutes, basting the exposed flesh side with the sauce. Turn over and cook the inside for another 5 minutes.

potted shrimps

2 lb/1 kg cooked shrimps in the shell, or
¾ lb/360 g shelled cooked shrimps
½ lb/240 g butter
½ bay leaf
pinch of ground mace
coarsely ground black pepper

SERVES 4

Cut the butter in pieces and melt it in the top of a double boiler, or in a large bowl standing over a saucepan of simmering water. Add the bay leaf and mace and leave for 5 minutes. Add the shrimps and some freshly ground black pepper. Stir gently, then cook for 10 minutes, stirring now and then. Spoon the shrimps into a china dish that holds roughly ¾ pint/4.5 dl. Add enough butter mixture to come level with the shrimps but not cover them completely. Cool, then refrigerate for 24 hours. In this form they should be eaten within two days. Alternatively, cover the shrimps completely with a second layer of melted seasoned butter, in which case they will keep for two weeks, although you will lose the fresh, juicy flavour. (They can even be stored in the freezer for up to two months, but in this case they will taste no better than the commercially produced variety.) Serve with small sandwiches of thin brown bread and butter, or freshly made toast.

barbecued prawns

1½ lb/0.75 kg giant prawns, uncooked
barbecue sauce 1 (see recipe, page 108)

SERVES 4

Either leave the prawns in their shells, or peel them, leaving the tails on. Thread them on four skewers and grill slowly, basting continuously with the sauce, for about 4 minutes on each side. Serve with cut lemons.

curried shellfish

¾ lb/360 g (weight without shells) cooked shellfish such as scallops, crabs, crawfish tails, shrimps, prawns
1½ oz/75 g butter
2 onions
2 cloves garlic
½ teaspoon ground turmeric
½ teaspoon ground coriander
½ teaspoon ground cumin
¼ teaspoon ground chilli pepper
2 oz/60 g ground almonds
1 pint/6 dl fish, chicken or vegetable stock
juice of 1 lime or ½ lemon
1 tablespoon red currant jelly
4 tablespoons desiccated coconut
salt and black pepper

SERVES 4

If you do not have stock, make it by simmering the shells of the shellfish in lightly salted water. To make coconut milk, put half the stock aside with the desiccated coconut soaking in it, for 30 minutes. If the shellfish include scallops they should be poached gently for 4 minutes in slightly salted water and drained. Chop the onions. Melt the butter in a heavy pan and sauté the onions until pale golden. Crush the garlic and add to the pan. Stir in the four ground spices and cook gently for another 4 minutes. Add the ground almonds and cook for another 2–3 minutes. Pour on half the heated stock. Warm the jelly and press it through a sieve. Add it with the lime (or lemon) juice to the pan. Strain the coconut from the stock and put the liquid into the pan; stir well to blend. Taste for seasoning, adding salt and pepper or more spices as required. Add the shellfish to the pan. Heat all together gently; pour into a serving dish. Serve with plain boiled rice.

Poultry/chicken

pot-roasted chicken

one 3–4 lb/1.5–2 lb chicken

2 oz/60g butter

juice of 1 lemon

sprigs of fresh herbs: marjoram, tarragon, chervil, thyme, basil, dill

SERVES 4–6

Preheat oven to 300°F (160°C, Gas Mark 2). Heat the butter in a covered casserole and brown the chicken all over. Pour the lemon juice over the chicken and add the herbs, still on their stalks. Cover and bake for 1½ hours, turning the chicken occasionally. To serve, throw away the herbs, carve the bird and pour the juices over it. Serve with rice, noodles, or boiled potatoes and a green salad.

chicken with grapes

one 3–4 lb/1.5–2 kg chicken

3 oz/90g butter

juice of 1 lemon

juice of ½ orange

3–4 shallots

½ lb/240g grapes, mixed black and white, halved and seeded

SERVES 4

Preheat oven to 300°F (160°C, Gas Mark 2). Heat 2 oz/60g butter in a heavy casserole and brown the chicken all over. Pour the lemon and orange juice over the chicken. Cover and bake for 1½ hours. Meanwhile, chop the shallots and sauté in 1 oz/30g butter until browned. Add the unpeeled grapes to the sauté pan and cook gently for 5 minutes, stirring now and then until they are hot and coated with fat. Serve the chicken on a serving dish surrounded by the grapes and shallots, with the juices in a separate jug.

grilled chicken skewers

1 medium roasting chicken, jointed

2 oz/60g butter

juice of 1 lemon

2 cloves garlic, finely chopped

SERVES 4

Take the uncooked chicken off the bones, and cut in neat squares. (Save the bones and scraps for soup.) Thread the chicken pieces on small skewers. Melt the butter and add the lemon juice and garlic; use this to baste the chicken while grilling. Baste frequently during grilling as the meat is lean and has no skin to protect it. Grill for about 12–14 minutes turning almost constantly. Serve on a bed of rice with the basting juices poured over. Accompany with avocado relish (see recipe, page 104), cucumber and yoghourt sauce (see recipe, page 104).

chicken on a spit

This recipe is for those whose kitchen equipment includes a revolving spit

1 medium chicken

Dijon mustard

juice of 1 lemon

1–2 tablespoons olive oil

salt and black pepper

SERVES 4

Paint the chicken all over with the mustard and squeeze the lemon juice over it. Sprinkle with salt and black pepper and leave for 1 hour. Preheat the grill. Put the chicken on the spit and pour the olive oil over it. After a couple of minutes' cooking, reduce the heat and then cook for 1 hour, basting with oil and lemon juice frequently. Serve with rice and a lettuce salad, with the juices in a jug.

chaudfroid of chicken

one 3½ lb/1.75 kg roasting chicken
1 onion
1 carrot
1 stalk celery
3 stalks parsley
½ bay leaf
2½ oz/75 g butter
4 tablespoons flour
1 packet gelatine
½ pint/3 dl double cream
2–3 sprigs of fresh tarragon
1 small bunch chives
salt and 5 or 6 black peppercorns

SERVES 5–6

Poach the chicken for 1 hour in simmering water with the onion, carrot and celery, cut in pieces, and the parsley and bay leaf, salt and peppercorns. Lift out the chicken and strain the stock, discarding the vegetables. Cool the stock until the fat has solidified on top. Remove every particle of fat and boil up the stock until it is reduced to 1 pint/6 dl. Melt the butter, blend in the flour and cook for 2 minutes, stirring. Add ¾ pint/4.5 dl of the stock gradually, stirring until smooth, and simmer for 15 minutes, stirring occasionally. Meanwhile dissolve the gelatine in the remaining stock and add it to the sauce when it has finished cooking. Stir until smooth, then add the cream. When all is blended, adjust the seasoning and pour into a bowl; leave to cool until tepid and on the point of setting. Carve the chicken into neat joints, removing all skin. Lay the pieces on a large dish not touching each other. Spoon the sauce over them, allowing it to run smoothly of its own accord, guiding with a spatula dipped in hot water where necessary. Keep the sauce warm over a pan of hot water, to prevent it setting in the bowl, while the first coating

sets. Then make a second layer and leave to set again. Decorate with the tarragon leaves and the chives, cut in short lengths. Chill in the refrigerator for a couple of hours. Cut round each piece carefully and lift with a palette knife on to a flat serving dish.

marinated chicken

6 chicken breasts, with wings attached
1 tablespoon Dijon mustard
¼ pint/1.5 dl sunflower seed oil
¼ pint/1.5 dl yoghourt
1 small piece (½ oz/15 g) fresh green ginger
½ teaspoon cumin seeds (whole or ground)
½ teaspoon coriander seeds (whole or ground)
½ teaspoon ground turmeric
juice of 1 lemon
1 green chilli pepper

SERVES 6

Put the mustard in a bowl and add the oil, drop by drop, whisking. When all is absorbed, beat the yoghourt until smooth and stir in. Chop the ginger and put in a mortar with the coriander, cumin seeds and turmeric. Pound to a powder. Add the lemon juice and stir to form a paste. Stir into the yoghourt mixture. Finely mince the chilli pepper and add. Alternatively all this can be done very quickly in a food processor. Make small cuts all over the chicken joints with the tip of a sharp knife. Cover with the marinade mixture. Leave for 6–24 hours in the refrigerator. Preheat oven to 400°F (200°C, Gas Mark 6). Lay the chicken pieces in an oiled baking tin and bake for 35 minutes. Re-arrange the pieces from time to time so that they brown evenly all over. This is good served with boiled rice, cucumber and yoghourt sauce (see recipe, page 104), or avocado relish (see recipe, page 104).

Poultry/chicken

chicken pâté

3½ lb/1.75 kg chicken
¾ lb/360 g belly of pork, minced
¾ lb/360 g unsalted streaky bacon, minced
½ lb/240 g bacon fat
1 medium onion
pinch of mace
4 tablespoons brandy
1 large egg
sea salt and black pepper
SERVES 10–12

Start two days in advance. Cut the uncooked chicken off the bones and chop it. (Reserve the carcass to make excellent stock.) Cut a few long thin strips of bacon fat and reserve; chop the rest in small dice. Chop the onion finely. Add the pork and bacon and mix all together, adding lots of sea salt and black pepper and a pinch of mace. Stir in the brandy. Fry a tiny ball of the mixture to test for seasonings. Lightly beat the egg and stir in. Line a fireproof dish or tin mould with the strips of bacon fat and fill with the mixture. Preheat oven to 325°F (170°C, Gas Mark 3). Cover the pâté with foil and stand in a baking tin with enough hot water to come halfway up the sides of the meat loaf dish. Put in the oven and leave for 2 hours 10 minutes, or until the pâté has shrunk away from the sides of the dish. Cool for 1 hour, then put a 3 lb/1.5 kg weight on top and leave until completely cold. This pâté will keep for eight or nine days under refrigeration and longer if re-sealed with a layer of fat or clarified butter. This quantity can be cooked in 2 containers, in which case allow 1¾ hours cooking time.

chicken mould

one 3½–4 lb/1.75–2 kg chicken
1 onion
1 carrot
1 stalk celery
3 stalks parsley
½ bay leaf
1 packet gelatine
¼ pint/1.5 dl double cream
3 sprigs tarragon
salt and 5–6 black peppercorns
SERVES 4–6

Start 36 hours in advance. Barely cover the chicken with highly salted hot water and poach it gently for 1 hour with the flavouring vegetables, and black peppercorns. Lift out the chicken and strain the stock. Cool it, then chill overnight in the refrigerator. The next day, remove every trace of fat and boil up until reduced to ½ pint/3 dl. Dissolve the gelatine in a little of it and mix with the rest. Stir in the cream and add salt and pepper to taste. Pour into a bowl and leave to cool, stirring often to prevent a skin forming. Carve the chicken into neat fillets, free from skin and bone. Lay them in a shallow dish that fits them nicely. When the sauce is cool and about to set, pour it over the chicken. Cool, then chill in the refrigerator until it is set. Decorate with leaves of tarragon.

Meat/lamb

braised lamb with vegetables

1 *shoulder of lamb*
1 *Spanish onion*
¾ *lb/360g carrots*
¾ *lb/360g leeks*
6 *stalks celery*
2 *small turnips*
3 *oz/90g butter*
1½ *tablespoons flour*
1 *egg yolk*
4 *tablespoons single cream*
2 *tablespoons chopped parsley*
salt and black pepper

SERVES 6

Be sure that you have a pot with a lid big enough to hold the shoulder. If in doubt, ask the butcher to cut off the bone to make it less bulky. Chop the vegetables. Heat 2oz/60g butter in the casserole and cook the vegetables in it for 5 minutes, stirring often. Take out the vegetables and brown the lamb on all sides. Put back the vegetables and pour on enough very hot water to come level with the surface of the lamb. Cover and simmer gently for 2 hours, either on top of the stove or in a low oven. When it is cooked, take out the meat and keep hot. Pour the vegetables and the liquid into a strainer over a bowl. Keep the vegetables hot but leave the stock to cool slightly while you carve the meat. Lay the slices in a large, shallow dish and surround with the vegetables. Cover with foil and return to the warm. Skim off all the fat from the surface of the stock and measure 1 pint/6dl. Melt the remaining butter in a small pan, stir in the flour, then blend in the stock. Add seasonings and beat the egg yolk with the cream and stir in a little of the sauce. Return to the rest of the sauce in the pan and stir over a very low heat until slightly thickened. Stir in the parsley and serve.

navarin d'agneau

1 *small leg of lamb, boned, or ½ a large leg*
1 *oz/30g beef dripping or butter*
½ *pint/3dl chicken or beef stock*
½ *pint/3dl white wine*
½ *pint/3dl V8 vegetable juice*
½ *lb/240g small new potatoes*
½ *lb/240g very small onions*
½ *lb/240g small carrots*
½ *lb/240g tiny turnips*
½ *lb/240g courgettes*
½ *lb/240g string beans or ½ lb/240g shelled broad beans and ¼ lb/120g shelled peas*
1½ *oz/45g butter*
3 *tablespoons flour*
4 *tablespoons chopped parsley*
salt and black pepper

SERVES 4–5

You will need about 2½lb/1.25kg lean lamb without bone. Cut it in neat cubes. Melt the dripping or butter in a heavy casserole and brown the meat in it. Mix the stock, wine and vegetable juice and heat in a separate pan. Pour over the meat and stir until simmering. Cover the pan and cook gently for 1 hour. Add the whole peeled potatoes, onions, carrots and turnips. Bring back to simmering point, cover the pan and simmer for another 30 minutes. Add the courgettes, cut in thick chunks, and the string beans or the broad beans and the peas. After 30 minutes mix the flour and butter to a paste and drop into the pot in small bits, stirring until each one is amalgamated. Add salt and pepper to taste and sprinkle with the chopped parsley. Serve with French bread.

Meat/lamb

skewers of lamb

½ leg of lamb, boned
barbecue sauce 3 (see recipe, page 108)

SERVES 4–6

The day before, or at least 6 hours before cooking time, cut the lamb in neat evenly sized rectangles, fairly small. Put them in a bowl and pour the sauce over them. Leave them overnight, or for several hours, turning now and then. Thread the lamb pieces on to skewers, being careful not to crowd them. Grill them slowly, basting with the remaining sauce until well browned on the outside but still slightly pink within. Serve with hot pitta bread and a green salad, or fried rice.

meat loaf

2 lb/1 kg minced lamb
1 Spanish onion
1 teacup full of chopped parsley
one ¾ lb/360g tin Italian peeled tomatoes
pinch of sugar
sea salt and black pepper

SERVES 4–5

Finely chop the onion and parsley. Mix the minced meat with these and season with plenty of sea salt and freshly ground black pepper. Try out a tiny ball in a frying pan for seasoning. Spread the mixture in a shallow layer in a square baking tin. Preheat the oven to 350°F (180°C, Gas Mark 4). Pour the tinned tomatoes into a bowl with their juice. Cut them up roughly with a palette knife. Add sea salt and black pepper to taste and a pinch of sugar. Pour over the meat and bake for 1 hour. When it is ready, the meat will have shrunk away from the sides of the tin and there will be a lot of juice. Extract this with a baster and pour into a jug. Cut the meat loaf in sections and serve with its gravy.

carré d'agneau

1 best end neck of lamb trimmed
and tied (with the chine bone removed)
1 glass red wine

SERVES 3

Preheat the oven to 375°F (190°C, Gas Mark 5). Lay the carré on a rack in a roasting tin and cover loosely with a piece of foil. Cook for 1 hour in all. After 30 minutes remove the foil and pour a glass of red wine over the meat. Lower the heat to about 350°F (190°C, Gas Mark 4) and baste two or three times during the remainder of the cooking time. Leave in a warm place for 10 minutes before carving into cutlets. Serve the juices in a sauce boat.

Irish stew

2½ lb/1.25 kg middle neck of lamb
2 lb/1 kg potatoes
1 lb/0.5 kg mild onions, sliced
2 tablespoons chopped parsley
salt and pepper

SERVES 4–5

Trim excess fat off the meat and leave the meat on the bone. Peel and slice the onions and potatoes, cutting about half the potatoes in thicker slices and the rest in fine slices. Put the thinly sliced potatoes in the bottom of a heavy casserole, in layers with the sliced onions and the meat, seasoning each layer with salt and pepper. Use the thicker potato slices in the upper layers. Pour over ¾ pint/4.5 dl hot water and bring to the boil. Lower the heat to a simmer, cover and leave for 2–2½ hours, or place in an oven at 300°F (160°C, Gas Mark 2) for the same length of time. At the end of cooking, the thinly sliced potatoes should have dissolved to thicken the sauce, while the thicker-cut ones should retain their shape. Sprinkle with parsley.

yogurtliya

This dish is quickly assembled and made, but should not be kept waiting. It is a Turkish dish which I first ate in Istanbul. Like many Middle Eastern dishes, it is eaten warm rather than hot

½ lb/240g lean tender lamb

1 tablespoon sunflower seed or arachide oil

1½ oz/45g butter

2 pieces pitta bread

1 lb/0.5 kg tomatoes

½ pint/3 dl yoghourt, at room temperature

1 oz/30g pine kernels

2 tablespoons chopped parsley

sea salt and black pepper

SERVES 4

Half a leg of lamb will give the best sort of meat for this dish; the quantities are not vital. Cut the meat in small neat cubes and sauté until cooked through in a mixture of the oil and 1 oz/30g of the butter. Keep hot. Split the pitta and cut in triangles; toast lightly under the grill until pale golden. Peel the tomatoes and chop coarsely. Sauté them very briefly in the remaining ½ oz/15g butter, stopping as soon as they are softened but before they have turned into a mush. Beat the yoghourt and season to taste with sea salt and black pepper. Lay some of the bread pieces on a large flat dish and pour the tomatoes over them with their juices. Pour most of the yoghourt over the tomatoes, reserving a little. Drain the meat of its cooking juices and lay over the top, surround with more triangles of bread, and sprinkle with the pine kernels and chopped parsley. Serve with a lettuce salad.

barbecued leg of lamb

1 small leg of lamb, boned but not rolled

olive oil

sea salt and black pepper

SERVES 5–6

Ask the butcher to cut the lamb so as to give you a rectangular piece of meat of roughly even thickness. Sprinkle with freshly ground black pepper and lay it, fat side down, facing the heat, on the grill. Cook for about 12 minutes, then brush a little olive oil over the uncooked side, turn and grill for 12–15 minutes more. To serve lay on a board and cut in thick slices. It should still be quite pink inside. Serve with sea salt.

spicy meatballs

1½ lb/0.75 kg minced lamb

1 medium onion

1 teaspoon ground coriander

1 teaspoon ground cumin

½ teaspoon ground chilli

4 tablespoons very finely chopped parsley

1 tablespoon oil

½ oz/15g butter

sea salt and black pepper

SERVES 4

Mince or finely chop the onion and mix it with the meat. Add a good quantity of sea salt and freshly ground black pepper and stir in the spices. Mix in the finely chopped parsley and form into very small balls, using a large teaspoon as a measure. Lay the balls on a floured surface until ready to cook. Heat the oil and butter in a heavy pan and when very hot, put in as many of the balls as you can cook at one time without crowding. Turn on all sides until evenly brown, then drain on soft paper and keep hot while you cook the rest. Serve with yoghourt and a mixed salad.

Meat/beef and pork

grilled sirloin with garnishes

A good dish for dieters

1 *sirloin steak about 1½ inches/3.5 cm thick*

2 oz/60g *tiny onions*

¼ lb/120g *button mushrooms*

½ *bunch watercress*

4 *small tomatoes*

1½ *lemons*

SERVES 4

Cook the steak in an iron grill pan, or under the grill, until well browned outside but still red within. Cool. Peel and cook the onions in boiling water until tender. Drain and cool. Slice the raw mushrooms. Divide the watercress into tender sprigs and wash. Slice the tomatoes. Cut the cold beef in diagonal slices and divide between four plates, garnishing with the cooked onions, sliced mushrooms, watercress sprigs and sliced tomatoes. Squeeze the lemon juice over the vegetables and serve with horseradish sauce (see recipe, page 107).

barbecued spareribs

This amount is enough for 4 people as part of a larger meal, but as a main course you will need 1lb/0.5kg per person. Racks of ribs can be cooked on a spit by threading them on concertina fashion or spread out on baking trays in a hot oven for 1 hour.

2 lb/1 kg *spareribs*

barbecue sauce 2 (see recipe, page 108)

SERVES 4

Keep the spareribs whole, in racks; brush them with the sauce and leave for 1 hour before cooking. Grill gently, basting often with the sauce, being careful not to let them get too burnt, for 15–20 minutes on each side. Cut up into ribs for serving.

skewered bacon and plums

Serve with grilled pork chops, grilled sausages, grilled chicken, roast turkey or goose, or roast game birds

6 *large ripe plums or 12 small ones*

6 *thin rashers streaky bacon*

SERVES 4

Stone the plums, cutting them in half if they are large. Cut each rasher of bacon in half and wrap around a plum, or half a plum according to size. Thread 3 on each of 4 small skewers and grill slowly, turning often, until the bacon is crisp—about 10 minutes.

barbecued gammon steaks

4–6 *gammon steaks, cooked or uncooked, about ½ inch/1 cm thick*

barbecue sauce 5 (see recipe page, 108)

SERVES 4

Paint the steaks on each side with the sauce, and leave for 1–2 hours before grilling. Cook gently, basting often with the sauce. Uncooked steaks will take 5–6 minutes on each side; cooked steaks need only 3–4 minutes on each side.

spinach and meat loaf

1½ lb/0.75 kg *spinach*

¾ lb/360g *pure pork sausage meat*

½ lb/240g *pastry (see recipe, page 126)*

1 *egg yolk*

salt and black pepper

SERVES 3–4

Cook the spinach briefly, drain well, then squeeze out as much moisture as possible and chop. Make the pastry; wrap in cling-film wrap and refrigerate for 30 minutes. Roll it out on a floured surface to form a rectangle. Form the sausage meat into a fat roll a little

smaller than the size of the pastry. Spoon the spinach on to the pastry in an even layer. Sprinkle with salt and pepper. Lay the sausage roll on the spinach and roll up the pastry and spinach around it. Seal the edges with a little water. Beat the egg yolk and brush it on to the pastry. Use the pastry trimmings to decorate the loaf. Preheat the oven to 350°F (180°C, Gas Mark 4). Lift the pastry encased loaf carefully on to a buttered baking tray and bake for 45 minutes, then reduce heat to 325°F (170°C, Gas Mark 3) and bake for a further 30 minutes. If it seems to be getting too brown, cover loosely with a piece of foil. This is at its best hot with mustard sauce (see recipe, page 106), but it can also be eaten cold.

grilled loin of pork with sesame seeds

one 3–3½ lb/1.5–1.75 kg loin of pork, boned but not rolled
2 tablespoons soy sauce
2 tablespoons vermouth or sherry
1 tablespoon finely chopped shallots
2 teaspoons sesame seeds
black pepper
SERVES 4–6

Make a marinade by mixing the soy sauce with the vermouth or sherry and stirring in the chopped shallots and some black pepper. Remove the crackling from the loin and detach the fillet. Cut the loin in neat thin slices. Brush the slices on both sides with the marinade and leave for 1–2 hours. Lay them on the grill and scatter over half the sesame seeds. Grill slowly until well browned, about 5 minutes. Turn and scatter the remaining sesame seeds over them. Grill for 4–5 minutes.

barbecued pork chops

4–6 pork chops
barbecue sauce 5 (see recipe, page 108)
SERVES 4

Coat the chops on both sides with some of the sauce. Leave them to marinate for at least 1 hour before cooking. Baste with more of the sauce while grilling, being careful not to let them become too blackened; they should be cooked slowly and thoroughly. Serve with sea salt and mustard.

grilled pork with ginger marinade

1 pork fillet
6 tablespoons pineapple juice
3 tablespoons soy sauce
2 tablespoons clear honey
1 piece preserved ginger
SERVES 3–4

Mix the fruit juice with the soy sauce and the honey. Wash the ginger briefly to remove the syrup, then chop it finely and stir into the marinade. Cut the pork fillet in slices about ½ inch/1 cm thick and lay between 2 pieces of cling-film wrap. Beat them out with a mallet until very thin. Lay in a shallow dish and pour the marinade over them. Leave for 1 hour. Heat the grill and lay them on the grid. Remove the little pieces of ginger from the marinade and reserve them. Grill the pork gently, brushing with extra marinade once or twice, for about 4 minutes on each side. Lay the slices in a serving dish, with the ginger scattered over them. Serve with boiled rice and a green salad.

mushrooms in sour cream

1 lb/0.5 kg flat mushrooms
2 oz/60g butter
½ pint/3 dl sour cream
juice of ½ lemon
2 tablespoons chopped chervil or dill (optional)
salt and black pepper

SERVES 4

Wipe the mushrooms and cut off the stalks. Slice the caps and stew gently in the butter in a sauté pan. When they have softened, after about 8 minutes, stir in the sour cream and mix well, adding salt, pepper and a little lemon juice to taste. Stir until reheated and serve with noodles or boiled rice. If you wish, chopped fresh chervil or dill can be added at the last moment before serving.

stuffed mushrooms

8 flat mushrooms about 4 inches/10 cm across
1 medium onion
¼ lb/120g streaky bacon rashers, chopped
1½ oz/45g butter
1 small clove garlic, crushed
2 oz/60g coarse dry breadcrumbs
3 tablespoons chopped parsley
2 tablespoons olive oil
salt and pepper

SERVES 4 AS A FIRST COURSE

Wipe the mushrooms, and chop the stalks, leaving the caps whole. Chop the onion and bacon finely. Melt the butter in a sauté pan and cook the onion until pale golden. Add the chopped bacon, then the mushroom stalks, and brown again. Add the minced or crushed garlic and the breadcrumbs and continue to cook gently, stirring often, until all is well mixed and lightly coloured. Remove from the heat and stir in the parsley and salt and pepper to taste. Cool before using, if possible.

Preheat oven to 350°F (180°C, Gas Mark 4). Lay the mushroom caps upside down on a large flat dish, lightly buttered. Divide the filling between them, spreading it with a palette knife to cover each mushroom. Pour a teaspoon of oil over each and bake for 25 minutes or until cooked and well coloured.

mushroom koulibiac

2 oz/60g rice
4 eggs + 1 yolk
¾ lb/360g mushrooms
5 oz/150g butter
juice of ½ lemon
2 packets frozen puff pastry
salt and black pepper

SERVES 6

Cook the rice in plenty of boiling salted water until tender—you should have 6 oz/180g cooked rice. Hard boil the eggs, shell and chop them. Wipe the mushrooms and slice them thickly. Heat 2 oz/60g butter and sauté the mushrooms for about 2 minutes. Add the lemon juice, cover the pan and cook gently another 10 minutes. Roll out the pastry in two rectangles or squares on a floured surface. On one piece, spread a layer of half the rice, mixed with the remaining butter, melted, and seasoned with salt and pepper. Sprinkle over half the chopped hard-boiled eggs, then the mushrooms, drained of their juice. Cover with the remaining eggs, then the rest of the rice. Cover with the second piece of pastry and seal the edges firmly. Preheat oven to 400°F (200°C, Gas Mark 6). Beat the egg yolk and brush the pastry with it. Bake for 25 minutes, until golden brown. Serve with herb sauce (see recipe, page 105).

mushroom pudding

This unusual suet pudding is absolutely
delicious when served with stewed beef,
carrots and onions

½ lb/240g self-raising flour
¼ lb/120g suet
¾ lb/360g small button mushrooms
1 oz/30g butter
juice of ½ lemon
¼ pint/1.5 dl game or chicken stock
salt and pepper
SERVES 4

To make the pastry: sift the flour, add a pinch
of salt and mix in the shredded suet. Add
enough iced water to make a thick paste. Cut
in two uneven pieces and roll out the larger
one thinly to line a 1½-pint/9dl pudding
basin. Wipe and trim the mushrooms, and put
them whole into the basin with the butter cut
in small pieces. Add salt and pepper, then
pour over the lemon juice and the stock. Roll
out the remaining paste to form a lid, lay over
the top and trim and seal the edges. Cover
with a greased piece of aluminium foil and tie
with string. Place in a large pan half-full of
boiling water and steam for 2½ hours.

mushroom sandwich

2 thin slices wholemeal bread
1 oz/30g mushrooms
1 lettuce leaf
juice of 1 lemon
2 rashers streaky bacon
black pepper
SERVES 1

Cut the bread thinly and lightly spread with
butter. Wipe the mushrooms, remove the
stems, and slice them. On one slice put the
lettuce leaf, and top with the mushrooms.
Sprinkle with a few drops of lemon juice and
some black pepper. Fry the bacon slowly until
crisp and drain on soft paper. Cut each slice of
bacon in half and lay the slices on top of the
mushrooms. Cover with the remaining bread
and press well together.

stuffed Chinese cabbage

1 Chinese cabbage
¼ lb/120g rice
1 bunch spring onions
4 tablespoons chopped herbs: chervil, parsley,
tarragon, dill
6 hard-boiled eggs
1 pint/6 dl chicken stock
salt and black pepper
SERVES 6 AS A MAIN COURSE

Separate the leaves of the cabbage and choose
the six best ones. Make sure that they are
large but tender. Cut the rest in strips. Put
the whole leaves into a large pan of boiling
water and boil for 1 minute; drain. Throw the
rice into boiling water and cook for 5 minutes;
drain. Slice the spring onions and mix with
the rice, adding the chopped herbs and salt
and pepper to taste. Spread out each leaf
carefully and put a mound of rice on each one.
Lay a whole egg in the centre and wrap the
leaves up carefully. Place a layer of shredded
cabbage in a broad, shallow pan and lay the
stuffed leaves on it. Heat the stock and pour
over. Bring to boiling point, cover the pan and
simmer for 30 minutes. They can be served
hot: with the extra leaves and moistened with
their juice, or cold: lifted out of the pan and
laid on a flat dish to cool. Moisten with some
of the juice after cooling, and use the rest of
the cabbage and juice to make a delicious
soup. In either case, serve with cut lemons.

cabbage timbale

1 *small green cabbage*

1 *lb*/0.5 *kg potatoes*

2 *oz*/60 *g butter*

4 *eggs*

salt and black pepper

SERVES 4–5

Cut the cabbage in pieces, wash well and throw into boiling water. Cook until tender, drain well and chop finely with a long knife. Boil the potatoes, then put them through the coarse mesh of a food mill to make a purée. Dry out by stirring over gentle heat. Beat in the butter in small pieces while the potato is still hot, and add salt and pepper to taste. Stir in the chopped cabbage and taste again for seasoning. Separate the eggs, beat the yolks lightly and stir in. Beat the whites until stiff and fold in. Preheat the oven to 325°F (170°C, Gas Mark 3). Spoon the mixture into a buttered soufflé dish (a bread tin makes a good alternative) and place in a baking tin half-full of hot water. Bake for 40 minutes until lightly coloured and firm. Serve with tomato sauce 1 (see recipe, page 103).

lettuce purée

This delicious purée can be served with roast chicken, grilled cutlets, poached or grilled fish or poached eggs

2 *large lettuces*

1 *bunch spring onions, or ½ medium onion*

3 *oz*/90 *g butter*

2 *tablespoons flour*

½ *pint*/3 *dl single cream*

mace or nutmeg

salt and black pepper

SERVES 3–4

Cut the lettuces in quarters, wash well and throw into boiling water for 5 minutes. (Allow 5 minutes for Cos and Webbs, 4 minutes for round soft lettuces.) Drain well and chop finely. Dry out by stirring over gentle heat for a few moments in a heavy pan. Slice the spring onions (or chop the half-onion) and stew gently in 1 oz/30 g butter in a small covered pan for 5 minutes. Melt the remaining 2 oz/60 g butter, stir in the flour, and add the heated cream. Stir until blended, adding salt and pepper to taste, also a little mace or nutmeg. Stir in the spring onions and the chopped lettuce, and season.

vegetable fritters

1 *small aubergine*

2 *courgettes*

2 *tomatoes*

¼ *lb*/120 *g flour*

2 *tablespoons sunflower seed oil*

¼ *pint*/1.5 *dl soda water*

1 *egg white*

salt

SERVES 4 AS A FIRST COURSE

Cut the unpeeled aubergine and courgettes in thin diagonal slices. Cut the tomatoes vertically also in thin slices. (The tomatoes should be firm, not too juicy.) Make the batter. Sift the flour with a pinch of salt into a mixing bowl. Stir in the oil and the soda water (ordinary water may be used). You should have a batter consistency of fairly thick cream. Fold in the stiffly beaten egg white and use immediately. Dip the vegetable slices into the batter, and shake off any excess. Drop them into a pan of deep oil, heated to 360°F (185°C), and turn them over as soon as they are golden brown on one side. They should be done in small batches. As soon as they are brown on both sides, drain them and serve with skordalia (see recipe, page 104).

spiced courgettes

This is especially good with lamb and pork dishes

¾ lb/360g courgettes
1 oz/30g butter
1 tablespoon sunflower seed oil
½ lb/240g tomatoes
½ teaspoon ground cumin
½ teaspoon ground coriander
salt and black pepper

SERVES 4

Cut the unpeeled courgettes in ½-inch/1cm slices. Heat the butter and oil in a sauté pan. Put in the courgettes and stew gently with the lid on for 8 minutes, stirring now and then. Add the peeled and roughly chopped tomatoes, salt and pepper and the spices. Cover again and cook for another 8 minutes. Leave the courgette mixture for 5 minutes in a warm place before serving.

cucumber stuffed with green rice

Green rice also makes an excellent stuffing for cold tomatoes

1 large cucumber
3 oz/90g long grain rice
1½ tablespoons olive oil
½ tablespoon white wine vinegar
3 tablespoons chopped herbs: parsley, chives, tarragon, chervil, dill
salt and black pepper

SERVES 4

Cook the rice in plenty of boiling salted water until tender, then stir in the oil and vinegar. Cool, then stir in the chopped herbs. Peel the cucumber and cut in half lengthwise. Cut across in 2-inch/5cm pieces, then shape each one roughly to form a sort of boat, hollowing out the interior and rounding the ends. Sprinkle the interiors with salt and stand upside down to drain for 30 minutes. Pat dry with soft paper and fill each one carefully with the green rice.

stuffed aubergines

4 medium aubergines
2 oz/60g butter
1 medium onion
1 clove garlic
1½ lb/0.75 kg minced lamb
3 tomatoes
1½ tablespoons flour
½ pint/3 dl milk
2 oz/60g grated cheese
salt and black pepper

SERVES 4

Bake the aubergines for 30 minutes at 350°F (180°C, Gas Mark 4). Cool slightly, then cut a thin sliver off the top surface. Scoop out the inside with a small teaspoon, trying not to break through the skin. Keep the pulp for another dish. Chop the onion and cook gently in 1 oz/30g of the butter until pale golden. Add the minced garlic and the meat and stir around until nicely browned on all sides. Season highly with salt and black pepper. Leave to cool slightly, then spoon into the aubergines. Peel the tomatoes, slice them thinly and lay over the meat. Make a cheese sauce. Melt 1 oz/30g butter, add the flour and cook, stirring, for 1 minute. Add the milk, stirring as the sauce thickens. Add the cheese and stir in. Season to taste. The sauce should be very thick. Spoon over the aubergines in their baking dish. Bake for 10–15 minutes at 375°F (190°C, Gas Mark 5), until well browned. These are very filling and only need a green salad as accompaniment.

aubergine spread

Serve as a snack with drinks
1½ *lb*/0.75 *kg aubergines*
1 *small onion*
4 *tablespoons olive oil*
1 *clove garlic*
½ *lb*/240 *g tomatoes*
pinch of sugar
1–2 *tablespoons lemon juice*
salt and black pepper
SERVES 6–8

Preheat oven to 400°F (200°C, Gas Mark 6). Bake the aubergines whole until soft, 45–60 minutes. Test by piercing with a skewer. When soft, take them out and leave to cool. Chop the onion and cook in half the oil in a sauté pan until lightly coloured, adding the finely chopped garlic halfway through. Put to one side. Skin and finely chop the tomatoes. Cut open the aubergines and scrape out the inner pulp; put into a bowl and mix with the tomatoes and the fried onion. Add salt and black pepper to taste, and a pinch of sugar. Heat the remaining 2 tablespoons oil in the sauté pan and cook the aubergine mixture gently for 30 minutes, stirring now and then. By the end of the cooking time it should be quite thick. Remove from the heat and stir in lemon juice to taste. Cool, and chill in the refrigerator for several hours before serving. Spread generously on small squares of rye bread or pumpernickel.

celery hearts mornay

1 *large tin celery hearts or endives*
8 *slices ham*
1½ *oz*/45 *g butter*
2½ *tablespoons flour*
¾ *pint*/4.5 *dl chicken or vegetable stock*
¼ *pint*/1.5 *dl single cream*
¼ *lb*/120 *g grated Gruyère cheese*
salt and black pepper
SERVES 4

Divide the celery hearts (or endives) in 8 pieces and wrap each one in a slice of ham. Lay the rolls in a buttered fireproof dish and make the sauce. Melt the butter, stir in the flour and gently blend with the chicken or vegetable stock. When blended, add the cream and season with salt and pepper. Shake in the cheese, keeping a little for the top. When smooth and blended, pour the sauce over the rolls. Preheat the oven to 350°F (180°C, Gas Mark 4), scatter the remaining cheese over the top, and bake for 30 minutes.

potato cake with onions

1½ *lb*/0.75 *kg freshly mashed potatoes*
2 *large onions*
2 *oz*/60 *g butter*
salt and black pepper
SERVES 4

Slice the onions in thin rings and cook them in 1½ oz/45 g butter until soft and well browned, even slightly burnt in places. Stir into the hot mashed potato and season with plenty of salt and black pepper. Melt the remaining ½ oz/ 15 g butter in a frying pan. When hot, spread the potato and onion mixture evenly over the whole surface of the pan. Cook gently for about 25 minutes, then turn out on to a platter. Cut in wedges and serve with bacon and eggs or cold meat and salad.

potato purée with chervil

This is good with roast or grilled chicken, escalopes of veal, poached trout or poached eggs

1½ lb/0.75g potatoes
¼ pint/1.5dl milk
2oz/60g butter
2 tablespoons cream
4 tablespoons chervil
salt and black pepper

SERVES 4

Boil the potatoes as usual, drain and dry out slightly over a low heat. Push through the medium mesh of a food mill, or put into a food processor to make a dry purée. Put the milk into a small pan with the butter, cream and plenty of salt and pepper. Heat until the butter has melted. Add chopped chervil and beat gradually into the potato purée over gentle heat. When all is absorbed you should have a smooth creamy purée flecked with green. Pour into a serving dish.

potato pancakes

These are best served with cold meat, bacon and eggs, or ham. Do not prepare them in advance as the mixture will discolour if kept waiting. They should be eaten as soon as possible after cooking

1 lb/0.5kg potatoes
1 onion
2 eggs
2 tablespoons flour
sunflower seed oil, or nut oil
salt and black pepper

SERVES 4–6

Grate the raw potatoes quite finely, so that they form thin strips. Grate the onion. Beat the eggs and mix with the potato and onion in a large bowl. Stir in the sieved flour and add salt and pepper to taste. Heat a thin layer of oil in a large frying pan or very hot griddle. When it is very hot put in three large spoonfuls of the mixture, flattening with a palette knife to form round shapes. They will take about 5 minutes cooking on each side; do not let them brown too quickly as the raw potato must have time to cook.

chasse

This is an old-fashioned English breakfast dish, but makes a good high tea or light supper dish. It is delicious when served with poached eggs on top

1 large onion
1½ oz/45g butter
¾ lb/360g tomatoes
1 thick 5–6oz/150–180g slice ham, diced
½ lb/240g potatoes
2 tablespoons chopped parsley
salt and black pepper

SERVES 3–4

Chop the onion and cook in the butter in a sauté pan until it starts to colour. Skin and chop the tomatoes, and add, with the ham. In the meantime, cook the potatoes in boiling salted water until just tender, then drain and chop them. After the tomatoes have cooked for a few moments, add the chopped potatoes and about 4 tablespoons boiling water. (If the tomatoes are very juicy, the water may not be needed.) Cook for about ten minutes more, until the potatoes are completely soft and the liquid almost evaporated. Sprinkle with the chopped parsley and serve, with or without poached eggs on the top.

Vegetables/peas and beans

fresh pease pudding

Serve with hot or cold ham, gammon, roast
pork or sausages

2½ lb/1.25 kg old peas, in the pod
pinch of sugar
2 tablespoons chopped mint
1½ oz/45 g butter
salt and black pepper

SERVES 3–4

Shell the peas and put them into a bowl lined
with cheesecloth. Add salt and pepper and a
pinch of sugar. Stir in the chopped mint and
tie up the cheesecloth with a piece of string.
Bring a large pan of stock or water gently to
the boil and lower in the pudding. Cover the
pan and boil for 1 hour. Lift out the pudding
and stand in a colander. Cool for a few
minutes, then untie the cloth. Put the
contents into a food processor, or push
through a coarse food mill until it is a dry
purée. Tip back into the cloth and re-form
into a round ball. Turn out on to a shallow
serving dish. Heat the butter and pour over.
This is also good served cold, without the
melted butter; in this case turn on to a flat
dish and cut in slices.

lentils and buttermilk

½ lb/240 g continental lentils
1½ pints/9 dl chicken stock
1 pint/6 dl buttermilk
juice of ½ lemon
salt and black pepper

SERVES 4–5

Put the lentils into the cold stock, bring to the
boil and simmer for about 45 minutes until
tender, adding salt and pepper to taste at the
end of cooking. Pour the cold buttermilk into
a bowl, and stir in the whole lentils with their
liquid. Add lemon juice to taste. I like to eat
this immediately, with the contrast of the hot
lentils and the cold buttermilk, but it is also
good after cooling. To make an unusual cold
soup, purée in the blender and thin with a
little extra stock, as required.

barbecued corn on the cob

Method 1: fold back the outer husks and
leaves of the corn and remove the silky inner
covering. Wash in cold water and pat dry in a
cloth. Spread each ear with softened butter
and replace the outer leaves. Lay on the grid
and cook for 15–20 minutes, turning
frequently. Serve with extra butter.

Method 2: remove outer and inner coverings,
and wash and dry in a cloth. Spread the
kernels with softened butter and wrap in a
double thickness of foil. Lay directly on the
coals and cook for 15–20 minutes, turning
several times. Serve with extra butter.

a vegetable hors d'oeuvre

½ lb/240 g string beans
¾ lb/360 g tomatoes
½ lb/240 g mushrooms
2 tablespoons olive oil
2 teaspoons white wine vinegar
salt and black pepper

SERVES 4

Peel and slice the tomatoes. Wipe and slice
the mushrooms. Cut the ends from the beans
and put them into boiling salted water. Cook
briefly and drain. While the beans are still
warm, arrange them with the tomatoes and
mushrooms on a large serving dish or on three
separate dishes. Mix the oil and vinegar with
salt and pepper and pour over all.

tomato sauce 1

one ¾–1 lb/360g–0.5 kg tin peeled tomatoes
½ oz/15g butter
pinch of sugar
dash of Tabasco
salt and black pepper

Put the tomatoes and their juice into the blender. Pour resulting purée into a pan and heat. Add a little salt and black pepper, a pinch of sugar and a dash of Tabasco. When boiling point is reached, add the butter and remove from the heat.

tomato sauce 2

This is good served with goujons of sole and other fish dishes
½ lb/240g tomatoes
2 tablespoons sour cream
juice of ½ lemon
dash of Tabasco

Skin the tomatoes and put into the blender. Blend briefly, then add the sour cream and blend again. Add lemon juice to taste, and a dash of Tabasco. Pour into a small dish and freeze for 1½ hours, beating once or twice. It should be served slightly thickened and very cold without being frozen solid.

tomato sauce 3

Serve with crudités such as cucumber, fennel, celery, or spring onions
¼ pint/1.5 dl mayonnaise
¼ pint/1.5 dl sour cream
2 tablespoons condensed tomato purée
2 tablespoons lemon juice

Mix the mayonnaise and sour cream together, then beat in the tomato purée, and stir in the lemon juice until well blended.

tomato and pepper sauce

Serve hot with noodles and egg croquettes
1½ oz/45g butter
1 small chopped onion
1 teaspoon flour
one ½ lb/240g tin Italian plum tomatoes
one ¼ lb/120g tin red peppers
½ teaspoon sugar
1 tablespoon chopped basil or marjoram, or a handful chopped chives
salt and black pepper

Melt the butter and sauté the finely chopped onion until golden. Add the flour, the tomatoes and their juice. Chop them roughly with the edge of a palette knife. Chop and drain the peppers and after 4 minutes add them to the tomatoes. Simmer for about 8 minutes, adding salt and black pepper to taste, also a pinch of sugar and some chopped fresh herbs such as basil, chives or marjoram.

tomato chilli sauce

3 oz/90g cream cheese
¼ pint/1.5 dl buttermilk
½ tablespoon lemon juice
one 2¼ oz/67.5g tin condensed tomato purée
a few dashes of Tabasco
salt and pepper

Put the cheese in the blender with the buttermilk. Blend until smooth, then add the lemon juice and salt and pepper to taste. Add the tomato purée and blend again. Then add the Tabasco, a drop at a time, until the desired degree of hotness is reached.

mayonnaise

2 egg yolks, *at room temperature*
pinch of salt
pinch of mustard powder
½ *pint*/3 *dl olive oil*
1½ *tablespoons white wine vinegar*
½ *tablespoon lemon juice*

Break the egg yolks into a large bowl, firmly anchored on a damp cloth so that it will not slide around. Add the salt and mustard powder and start to beat the eggs with a wooden spoon. Put the oil in a jug and add it, literally drop by drop. Beat all the time and, after a moment or two the mixture will start to take on an emulsified appearance, like a thick ointment. Now you can begin to add the oil a little more quickly, in a thin stream, stopping between each addition and beating constantly with the other hand. When half the oil is absorbed, you can add the remainder in a thin steady stream. If it gets too thick, add a teaspoon of the vinegar from time to time. When all the oil is used up and what is left of the vinegar, add the lemon juice. If the sauce separates, start again in a clean bowl either by breaking in a fresh egg yolk, or a teaspoon of Dijon mustard. Add the separated sauce, drop by drop, and the remaining oil and vinegar. The sauce can be lightened by folding in a little whipped cream. Chopped herbs should be stirred in at the last minute.

For garlic mayonnaise, mix 2 crushed cloves of garlic with a pinch of salt and the yolks before adding the oil.

For tomato mayonnaise, add to the mayonnaise ½ lb/240g tomatoes, puréed in a blender, a teaspoon of mustard, a dash of Tabasco, 2 tablespoons chopped chives and lemon juice to taste.

cucumber and yoghourt sauce

Serve with grilled, barbecued or tandoori chicken

½ *pint*/3 *dl yoghourt*
½ *large cucumber*
dash of Tabasco
salt and black pepper

Beat the yoghourt until smooth. Peel the cucumber and cut it in small cubes. Stir into the yoghourt, adding salt and black pepper and a dash of Tabasco.

avocado relish

This makes a good accompaniment to chicken, and any plain fish dish

2 *avocados*
juice of ½ *lemon*
½ *lb*/240g *tomatoes*
1 *bunch spring onions*
2 *tablespoons sunflower seed oil*
juice of 1 *lime*
black pepper

Skin the avocados and cut in dice. Sprinkle them with a squeeze of lemon juice. Skin and chop the tomatoes, discarding seeds and juice. Mix with the avocado. Slice the spring onions and mix in. Add black pepper to taste. Dress with the sunflower seed oil, and the lime and lemon juice, mixed.

skordalia

Serve with vegetable fritters

4 *large cloves garlic*
1 *large potato*
2 *slices slightly stale bread*
¼ *pint*/1.5 *dl olive oil*
juice of ½ *lemon*

Crush the garlic and pound in a mortar. Boil and mash the potato, add it to the garlic and

pound again. Cut the crusts off the bread and soak for 10 minutes in water. Squeeze it between your hands and add to the potato. Pound again till reduced to a smooth pulp. Add the oil drop by drop, beating it in with a wooden spoon. Be careful not to let it separate. When all is absorbed, add lemon juice to taste. Alternatively this can all be quickly done in a food processor.

herb sauce

This is good with crudités, new potatoes, baked potatoes or oeufs mollets

one 3 oz/90g *Philadelphia cream cheese*
¼ *pint*/1.5 *dl buttermilk*
juice of ½ lemon
4 *tablespoons chopped herbs: chervil, tarragon, dill, chives*
salt and pepper

Put the cheese into the blender with the buttermilk and blend until smooth. Add the lemon juice, and salt and pepper to taste. Stir in the herbs and serve cold.

Tabasco sauce

Serve with any kind of crudité except perhaps tomatoes

¼ *pint*/1.5 *dl yoghourt*
4 *tablespoons mayonnaise*
1 *tablespoon condensed tomato purée*
generous dash of Tabasco

Mix the yoghourt and mayonnaise until smooth and well blended. Stir in the tomato purée and add Tabasco to taste.

ricotta sauce

Serve this delicious thick sauce with crudités such as tomatoes, celery, cauliflower or turnips

¼ *lb*/120g *ricotta cheese*
¼ *pint*/1.5 *dl yoghourt*
1½ *tablespoons lemon juice*
2 *tablespoons grated Parmesan cheese*
2 *tablespoons chopped parsley*
black pepper

Mix the ricotta with the yoghourt until smooth. Add the lemon juice to taste, then stir in the grated Parmesan and chopped parsley. Add plenty of black pepper to taste.

shallot sauce

Serve with poached freshwater fish, such as trout, pike, or grayling

2 *tablespoons chopped shallots*
3 *tablespoons chopped parsley*
¼ *pint*/1.5 *dl white wine*
1 oz/30g *butter*
1 *tablespoon flour*
½ *pint*/3 *dl fish stock*
2 *tablespoons cream*
salt and black pepper

Put the chopped shallots and 2 tablespoons of the chopped parsley into a small pan with the wine. Bring to the boil and simmer, covered, for 8 minutes. Melt the butter in a clean pan, stir in the flour and cook for 1 minute, stirring. Add the heated fish stock and blend. Simmer for 3 minutes, stirring frequently. When smooth and blended, add the shallot mixture, then the cream. Add salt and pepper to taste, and sprinkle the remaining tablespoon of chopped parsley over the top.

Sauces/herb, spice and shrimp

tahini parsley sauce

Serve with cooked vegetables, crudités, chicken or white fish. Tahini is available from some delicatessens

¼ pint/1.5 dl tahini
¼ pint/1.5 dl lemon juice
¼ pint/1.5 dl yoghourt
1 teaspoon Dijon mustard (optional)
4 tablespoons chopped parsley

Tip the tahini into a bowl and beat until smooth with a wooden spoon. Add the lemon juice gradually, beating all the time. Then beat in the yoghourt, which you can thin with a tablespoon of cold water if necessary. Add the mustard, if used, and stir in the parsley.

pistou

This version of the Mediterranean sauce, with tomato instead of pine nuts, is delicious served with young vegetables, freshly cooked and still warm: courgettes, small onions, new potatoes, broad beans, carrots, artichoke hearts

½ pint/3 dl fresh basil leaves
2 cloves garlic
2 oz/60 g grated Parmesan cheese
1 large tomato
⅓ pint/2 dl olive oil

Chop the basil finely and pound in a mortar. Add the crushed garlic and pound again. Then add the grated cheese and continue to pound until a smooth paste. Cut the tomato in half and grill under a fierce heat until almost blackened on the cut surface. Cool, remove the skin and chop. Add to the pistou and beat in. When smooth, start adding the oil, as if making a mayonnaise, drop by drop.

salsa verde

Serve with hot or cold boiled beef or bollito misto

1 egg yolk
1 tablespoon Dijon mustard
1 teaspoon sugar
2 cloves garlic, crushed
½ Spanish onion, finely chopped
½ pint/3 dl chopped fresh herbs: parsley, chives, chervil, tarragon, dill
3 tablespoons white wine vinegar or lemon juice
¼ pint/1.5 dl olive oil
2 hard-boiled eggs
salt and black pepper

Break the egg yolk into a large bowl and beat with a wooden spoon until smooth, adding the mustard, sugar, salt and pepper. Then add the crushed garlic, the finely chopped onion, and the chopped herbs. Stir in the vinegar, or use lemon juice if you prefer, then the oil. Lastly stir in the chopped hard-boiled eggs. Alternatively, the whole sauce can be made in a food processor, which gives a much smoother and finer texture.

mustard sauce

Serve with cooked or raw vegetables, hard-boiled eggs, beef, chicken or fish salads

1 teaspoon Dijon mustard
1 tablespoon sour cream
¼ pint/1.5 dl yoghourt
1–2 teaspoons lemon juice
black pepper

Put the mustard into a bowl and beat in the sour cream. Add the yoghourt, beat until blended, and add lemon juice to taste and a little black pepper.

horseradish sauce

This is good served with hot or cold beef or with fish, particularly smoked

4 *tablespoons yoghourt*

2 *tablespoons sour cream*

1 *tablespoon grated horseradish*

2 *tablespoons white wine vinegar*

black pepper

Mix the yoghourt with the sour cream, stir in the grated horseradish and vinegar, and a little black pepper to taste.

green sauce

Serve with raw or cooked vegetables, especially cauliflower, string beans, tomatoes, new potatoes, cucumber or celery

1 *medium onion*

½ *oz/15g parsley*

1 *teaspoon Dijon mustard*

1 *teaspoon sugar*

1 *soft-boiled egg*

6 *tablespoons olive oil*

1 *tablespoon white wine vinegar*

1 *tablespoon lemon juice*

salt and black pepper

Chop the onion and parsley very finely, stirring in the salt and pepper, mustard and sugar. Cook the egg for exactly 5 minutes, then cut it in half and stir the yolk into the sauce. Chop the white and add it also. Stir in the oil, vinegar and lemon juice, adding more vinegar if needed. Alternatively, the sauce can be made very quickly in a food processor. Simply process the solid ingredients first, then add the oil, vinegar and lemon juice through the hole in the lid.

shrimp sauce

Serve with poached white fish, poached fish balls or hard-boiled eggs

1 *pint/6dl fresh shrimps, cooked*

¾ *oz/22.5g butter*

1 *dessertspoon flour*

¼ *pint/1.5dl single cream*

1 *tablespoon finely chopped parsley*

black pepper

Shell the shrimps and put the shells in a pan with cold water or fish stock to cover. Simmer for 15 minutes, half-covered, then strain and measure ½ pint/3dl. Melt the butter, blend with the flour and pour on the strained stock. Simmer until smooth and blended, stirring often, then add the cream. Blend again, add black pepper to taste and the shrimps. Keep just below simmering point for 3–4 minutes, until the shrimps are well heated, then sprinkle in the chopped parsley and serve.

curry sauce

Serve with freshwater fish such as cold poached trout or pike, or trout en gelée

¼ *teaspoon curry powder*

1 *egg yolk*

¼ *pint/1.5dl olive oil*

1 *dessertspoon white wine vinegar*

4 *tablespoons double cream*

pinch of salt

Make a mayonnaise, adding the curry powder and salt to the egg before adding the oil drop by drop until amalgamated, then in a very thin stream. Thin the mayonnaise with the vinegar, as needed, then whip the cream and fold it in to make a light, foamy sauce.

Sauces/hollandaise and barbecue

easy hollandaise sauce

This delicious sauce is time consuming and tricky to make by traditional methods, but can be made quickly and simply with a food processor. It can be made into sauce mousseline by adding 4 tablespoons whipped cream at the last moment

3 *egg yolks*
¼ *lb*/120g *butter*
1 *tablespoon lemon juice*
pinch of salt

Warm the container of the food processor by filling it with very hot water and leave it to stand for 2–3 minutes, then drain and dry it. Break in the egg yolks and add the salt. Turn on the processor, heat the butter in a small pan until bubbling, add the lemon juice and pour the mixture slowly through the hole in the lid of the food processor. As soon as all the butter is amalgamated, stop processing. Spoon into a warm bowl and either serve immediately or, if it must be kept for a few moments, stand it over a pan of hot water.

barbecue sauce 1

Use to baste all sorts of shellfish and other fish
¼ *lb*/120g *unsalted butter*
2 *tablespoons lemon juice*
coarsely ground black pepper

Melt the butter, add the lemon juice and season with freshly ground black pepper.

barbecue sauce 2

Use to marinate and baste spare ribs
1 *tablespoon Dijon mustard*
2 *tablespoons white wine vinegar*
3 *tablespoons brown sugar*
3 *tablespoons grapefruit or pineapple juice*

Mix all the ingredients together thoroughly.

barbecue sauce 3

Use as a marinade and basting sauce for lamb
¼ *pint*/1.5dl *olive oil*
4 *tablespoons lemon juice*
2 *tablespoons finely chopped onion*
2 *tablespoons finely chopped parsley*
coarsely ground black pepper
dash of Tabasco (optional)

Mix the olive oil and lemon juice and stir in the chopped onion and parsley. Add some freshly ground black pepper and a dash of Tabasco to taste.

barbecue sauce 4

Use as a marinade and basting sauce for chicken
4 *tablespoons arachide oil*
4 *tablespoons soy sauce*
4 *tablespoons vermouth*
1 *tablespoon finely chopped fresh ginger or* 1 *piece washed and finely chopped preserved ginger*
2 *teaspoons finely chopped orange rind*
dash of Tabasco

Mix the oil with the soy sauce and the vermouth. Add the ginger and the orange rind with a dash of Tabasco.

barbecue sauce 5

Use for marinating and basting pork
4 *tablespoons soy sauce*
2 *tablespoons brown sugar*
1 *tablespoon olive oil*
1 *large clove garlic*
1 *teaspoon fresh ginger, grated or chopped*
black pepper

Mix the soy sauce with the sugar then stir in the oil. Crush or mince the garlic and add with the chopped or grated ginger. Add some coarsely ground black pepper and mix well.

Jams, relishes and pickles

plum jam

4 lb/2 kg plums

4 lb/2 kg preserving sugar

Put the whole plums, stalks removed, in a large pot with a lid and add 1 pint/6 dl water. Cover the pot and cook in a low oven for 2 hours. Alternatively, put them in a slow cooker, and cook for 6–8 hours at setting no. 1. Warm the sugar and put it in a heavy pan. Add the cooked plums and their juice and bring slowly to the boil. Boil fast for about 7–8 minutes, until setting point is reached. Skim, pour into hot jars, cool and cover.

rhubarb and ginger jam

This jam is especially good with home-made white bread and butter. A cheaper version of ginger can be made by substituting 2 oz/60 g root ginger for the preserved ginger, well crushed and bruised and tied in a muslin bag. This should be added at the start of cooking and removed before bottling

4 lb/2 kg rhubarb

3 lb/1.5 kg preserving sugar

3–4 lemons

3 tablespoons syrup from the preserved ginger

2 oz/60 g (about 4 pieces) preserved ginger

Cut the rhubarb in small pieces and put in layers in a large dish, alternating with layers of sugar. Leave until the next day. Put in a heavy pan with all the juice, adding the rind and juice of the lemons (I pare the rind with a potato peeler and cut it in thin strips). Add the ginger syrup (or the root ginger) and bring slowly to the boil. Stir frequently until the sugar has dissolved, then boil rapidly for 15–20 minutes, until it sets. Skim, stir in the finely sliced preserved ginger (if used), and spoon into warm jars. Leave to cool, cover with greaseproof paper and screw on the lids.

four fruit jam

This makes a very beautiful jam with the dark cherries glowing through the red juice

1 lb/0.5 kg red currants

4 lb/2 kg preserving sugar

1 lb/0.5 kg dark red cherries

1 lb/0.5 kg raspberries

1 lb/0.5 kg strawberries

juice of 2 lemons

Take the currants off their stalks. Put them in a heavy pan with 1 pint/6 dl water. Bring to the boil and simmer for 20 minutes. Strain, pushing the currants against the sieve with a wooden spoon. Warm the sugar in a heavy pan. Add the stoned cherries, the raspberries and strawberries, the red-currant juice and the juice of 2 lemons. Stand for 1 hour, stirring occasionally. Bring slowly to the boil, stirring frequently until the sugar has completely dissolved. Boil rapidly for 20–30 minutes until setting point is reached, skim, and pour into warm jars. Leave to cool, then cover with greaseproof paper and screw-on lids.

red-currant jelly

A good jelly for eating with bread and butter, rather than meat dishes, can be made by substituting 1½ lb/0.75 kg raspberries for half the red currants in this recipe

3 lb/1.5 kg red currants

approx 1½ lb/0.75 kg granulated sugar

Take the currants off the stalks and put in a heavy pan with 1½ pints/9 dl water. Simmer for about 15 minutes, until mushy. Pour into a jelly bag and leave overnight. Next day measure the juice and allow 1 lb/0.5 kg granulated sugar to each 1 pint/6 dl of juice. Warm the sugar in the pan, add the juice and boil until setting point is reached. Skim and pour into warm jars. Cool before covering.

Jams, relishes and pickles

apple and quince jelly

This makes a good alternative to red-currant jelly for serving with lamb

6 lb/3 kg apples

2 lb/1 kg quinces

approx 5 lb/2.5 kg granulated sugar

3 lemons

Wash the apples and quinces and cut them in quarters. Put in a large pan and add water to come level with the fruit. Bring slowly to the boil and boil for 30 minutes, until the fruit is soft and pulpy. Pour into a jelly bag and leave to drip overnight, The next day measure the juice and put it in a large pan with 1lb/0.5kg granulated sugar to every 1 pint/6dl of juice, the rind of 1 lemon, and the juice of 3. Boil up, skim until clear and simmer till setting point is reached – about 20 minutes. Skim again, pour into hot jars and leave to cool before covering.

crab-apple jelly

3½–4 lb/1.75–2 kg crab apples

approx 2 lb/1 kg granulated sugar

2 lemons

Pick over the fruit carefully; wash and put the whole apples in a heavy pan with 2 pints/ 1 litre water. Bring to the boil and simmer for 30 minutes. Pour into a jelly bag and leave overnight to drip, without disturbing. Next day measure the juice and boil up in a clean pan, adding 1lb/0.5kg sugar for every 1 pint/ 6dl of juice. Add the pared rind and juice of the lemons. Boil for 20–30 minutes, until setting point is reached. Skim, removing the rind, pour into warm jars and cool before covering them.

cranberry relish

Serve with hot or cold roast turkey, ham, goose, pork or duck

1 lb/0.5 kg cranberries

½ pint/3 dl red wine vinegar

1 lb/0.5 kg soft brown sugar

2 teaspoons cinnamon

1 teaspoon salt

½ teaspoon ground cloves

1 teaspoon ground allspice

Put the cranberries in a pan with ½ pint/3 dl water and the vinegar. Bring to the boil and simmer for 6 minutes, until they start to burst. Push them through a sieve into a saucepan. Stir in the sugar, cinnamon, salt, cloves and allspice. Boil the mixture for 10–15 minutes, stirring, until it has slightly thickened. Pour into jars and seal.

chow chow

1 small cauliflower

1 lb/0.5 kg small tomatoes

1 red pepper

1 green pepper

6 oz/180 g string beans

½ lb/240 g sweetcorn kernels, when available

sea salt

1 pint/6 dl white wine vinegar

3 oz/90 g soft brown sugar

½ oz/15 g mustard powder

1 tablespoon mustard seed

1 teaspoon turmeric

Cut the cauliflower into sprigs, skin the tomatoes and cut them in quarters. Cut the peppers in strips, after removing all the seeds. Trim the beans and cut in 1-inch/2.5 cm chunks. Put all together in a large bowl with the corn kernels and scatter over plenty of salt. Leave for 24 hours, then drain off the water and put the vegetables in a heavy pan.

Heat the vinegar with the sugar, mustard and turmeric and, when boiling, pour over the vegetables. Bring back to the boil and simmer, covered, until they are just tender – about 15 minutes. Spoon into sterilized jars and seal. Keep for at least two weeks before opening and eating.

mango chutney

Serve with curries of all sorts

2 green mangoes
1½ oz/45 g sea salt
½ pint/3 dl white wine vinegar
½ lb/240 g soft brown sugar
2 cloves garlic, crushed
1 oz/30 g root ginger, chopped
1 teaspoon ground chilli
one 2-inch/5 cm piece cinnamon stick
2 oz/60 g almonds, chopped
2 oz/60 g raisins

Skin the mangoes and remove the stones. Chop the flesh and put in a bowl. Sprinkle with sea salt and pour over 1¾ pints/10.5 dl water; leave for 24 hours, then drain. Boil the vinegar with the sugar until it has dissolved, then add the crushed garlic, chopped ginger, chilli powder and cinnamon stick. Boil for 5 minutes, then add the chopped mango and continue to boil gently until thick, about 15 minutes, adding the chopped almonds and raisins for the last 5 minutes. Cool and discard the cinnamon stick before spooning into jars. Keep for at least two weeks before eating.

piccalilli

approx 3 lb/1.5 kg vegetables, for example:
1 small cauliflower
½ lb/240 g small tomatoes
½ cucumber
6 oz/180 g string beans
6 oz/180 g pickling onions
coarse salt
1 pint/6 dl + 2 tablespoons white wine (or cider) vinegar
1 tablespoon mustard seed
1 tablespoon ground ginger
1 teaspoon turmeric
1 large clove garlic
2 oz/60 g soft brown sugar
1 tablespoon flour

Cut the cauliflower into sprigs, skin the tomatoes and cut in quarters. Slice the unpeeled cucumber thickly, then divide each slice in four. Trim the beans and cut in 1-inch/2.5 cm chunks, peel the onions and leave whole. Put all the vegetables in a broad shallow dish and scatter over plenty of salt. Leave for 24 hours, then pour off the water, rinse in fresh water, and drain. Heat 1 pint/6 dl vinegar in a heavy pan with the crushed mustard seed, ginger, turmeric, crushed garlic and sugar. When it boils, add the drained vegetables. Bring back to the boil and simmer until they are tender, about 15 minutes, covered. Put the flour in a small bowl and mix to a smooth paste with the remaining 2 tablespoons vinegar. Add to the pan and simmer for 4 minutes, stirring. Spoon into hot sterilized jars and seal. Keep for at least two weeks before eating.

Jams, relishes and pickles

pickled beetroot

In my opinion this is the best of all pickles for eating with bread and cheese

1¾ lb/0.75 kg beetroot

1 medium onion

¾ pint/4.5 dl red wine vinegar

1½ tablespoons mustard powder

½ teaspoon sea salt

½ lb/240g sugar

Scrub the whole beetroot and cook them in a pressure cooker with plenty of water until soft – about 20–30 minutes. Cool slightly, reserving the cooking water, then skin and slice them. Slice the raw onion and arrange the beetroot and onion alternately in broad jars. Measure ½ pint/3 dl of the reserved cooking water and add the vinegar in a pan. Bring to the boil, then add the mustard, salt and sugar and boil again for 3 minutes. Cool slightly, then pour through a strainer into the jars to cover the beetroot and onion well. Close tightly. (Any extra juice can be used for pickling hard-boiled eggs, turning them pink.) Keep for two weeks before opening.

pickled red cabbage

1 small red cabbage (about 1 lb/0.5 kg)

1 tablespoon sea salt

1 pint/6 dl red wine vinegar

1 tablespoon soft brown sugar

1 tablespoon pickling spice

Shred the cabbage and put it in a bowl. Sprinkle with salt and leave for 24 hours. Drain off the water, rinse the cabbage and drain again. Pack it lightly into broad jars. Boil the vinegar with the sugar until it has dissolved, add the pickling spice and boil for another 5 minutes. Cool, pour over the cabbage in the jars and seal tightly. Keep for two weeks before opening.

pickled onions

1 lb/0.5 kg pickling onions

6 oz/180g salt

1 pint/6 dl white wine vinegar

1 tablespoon soft brown sugar

1 tablespoon pickling spice

Cut the tops and bottoms off the onions, leaving on the skin. Put them in a deep bowl. Dissolve the salt in 3 pints/1.5 litres boiling water and leave to cool. Strain it, and pour half over the onions. Leave for 24 hours, then peel the onions and cover with the remaining fresh brine. Weigh the onions down with a plate to keep them submerged. Leave for 48 hours. Put the vinegar in a pan with the sugar and spice and boil gently for 5 minutes; cool. Lift the onions out of the brine and pack into jars. Pour the spiced vinegar over them and seal tightly. Keep for at least two weeks before opening and eating.

pickled eggs

12 small eggs

1¾ pints/10.5 dl white wine vinegar

2 teaspoons black peppercorns

2 teaspoons whole allspice

2 teaspoons root ginger, chopped

1 teaspoon sea salt

Boil the eggs for 12 minutes; cool, shell and pack in broad jars. Put the vinegar in a pan and add the salt and spices tied in a piece of muslin. Bring to the boil and simmer for 20 minutes, covered. Leave to cool for 2 hours, then remove the muslin bag. Pour the cold spiced vinegar over the eggs and seal tightly. Keep for two weeks before opening.

Desserts/sorbets

elder-flower sorbet

Mint sorbet and geranium leaf sorbet can be
made with the same recipe by substituting
either mint leaves or scented geranium leaves
for the elder flowers

6 *young elder flowers*

¼ *lb*/120*g sugar*

juice of 1 *lemon*

1 *egg white*

SERVES 3

Wash the elder flowers and leave to drain.
Make a thin syrup by boiling the sugar with
½ pint/3 dl water until melted. Add the elder
flowers, cover the pan and leave the mixture
to infuse for 20–30 minutes. Strain, add the
juice of a lemon and freeze in an ice-cream
machine or ice trays covered with foil in the
freezer. After 45 minutes, beat the egg white,
fold it in and continue freezing. To serve,
spoon into quite small glasses and lay a tiny
sprig of mint on top of each one, or garnish
with red currants or *fraises des bois*.

grapefruit sorbet

2 *large grapefruit*

2 *oz*/60*g sugar*

1 *egg white*

SERVES 3–4

Squeeze the grapefruit and strain the juice.
You should have about ½ pint/3 dl. Boil the
sugar and ¼ pint/1.5 dl water together until
the sugar has melted, then cool. Mix with the
grapefruit juice and put into an ice-cream
machine, or alternatively ice trays covered
with foil in the freezer. After 45–60 minutes,
when it is still mushy, beat the egg white until
stiff and fold it in. Continue freezing until set.
Serve in small glasses.

black-currant leaf sorbet

6 *oz*/180*g sugar*

24 *young black-currant leaves*

juice of 1 *lemon*

1 *egg white*

SERVES 3–4

Make a syrup by boiling the sugar with
½ pint/3 dl water until the sugar has melted.
Wash the leaves, add them to the syrup, cover
the pan and leave for 20 minutes off the heat.
Strain, add the lemon juice and freeze in an
ice-cream machine, or alternatively in ice
trays, covered with foil in the freezer. After
45 minutes, stiffly beat the egg white, fold in,
and freeze again.

strawberry and raspberry sorbet

This is delicious when accompanied with
little biscuits or meringues

1 *lb*/0.5 *kg strawberries*

¾ *lb*/360*g raspberries*

3 *oz*/90*g sugar*

1 *egg white*

SERVES 4–5

Hull the berries, then put them in a blender
and rub them through a nylon sieve. Make a
thin syrup with the sugar and ¼ pint/1.5 dl
water; stir into the fruit purée and taste for
sweetness. Pour into an ice-cream machine
and freeze. Alternatively, if you do not have
an ice-cream machine, put the mixture in ice
trays covered with foil. After 1 hour, turn
out, beat the egg white and fold it in. Return
to the machine, or to the freezer, and freeze
again until set.

Desserts/ices and fools

black-currant ice-cream

1 *lb*/0.5 *kg black currants*

6 *oz*/180 *g sugar*

¾ *pint*/4.5 *dl double cream*

SERVES 6

Remove the currants from their stalks. Make a syrup by boiling ¼ pint/1.5 dl water with the sugar. When the sugar has melted, put in the currants. Simmer gently for 5 minutes. Sieve, or push through the fine mesh of a food mill. Cool, whip the cream until semi-thick and fold it in. Freeze either in an ice-cream machine or, if you do not have one, in ice trays covered with foil. In this case, beat with a fork once during freezing.

strawberry and raspberry ice-cream

2 *egg yolks*

3 *oz*/90 *g sugar*

1 *lb*/0.5 *kg strawberries*

½ *lb*/240 *g raspberries*

juice of ½ *a lemon*

½ *pint*/3 *dl double cream*

SERVES 4–5

Put the raspberries and strawberries in the blender, then through a nylon sieve. Beat the egg yolks with an electric beater or wire whisk while you cook the sugar with ¼ pint/3 dl water to form a thin syrup. Pour the syrup on to the egg yolks, continuing to beat. When thick and foamy, fold in the raspberry and strawberry purée. Lightly whip the cream and fold it in with the juice of half a lemon. Pour into an ice-cream machine and freeze. Alternatively, freeze the mixture in ice trays, covered in foil, beating once with a fork during freezing. The left-over egg whites can be made into meringues.

peppermint ice-cream

2 *eggs* + 2 *yolks*

2 *oz*/60 *g castor sugar*

½ *pint*/3 *dl milk*

½ *pint*/3 *dl double cream*

2 *tablespoons crème de menthe*

2–3 *drops green food colouring*

4 *tablespoons grated bitter chocolate*

SERVES 5–6

Beat the eggs and the yolks thoroughly. Add the sugar after a moment and continue to beat until it forms a smooth paste. Heat the milk until almost boiling, then pour on to the eggs, beating all the time. Stand the bowl over a pan of simmering water and stir for about 8 minutes, until slightly thickened. Strain into a clean bowl and stand in a basin of cold water until cool, stirring often to prevent a skin forming. When cool, whip the cream lightly and fold it in. Stir in the crème de menthe and the green food colouring, until it is a pretty pale green colour. Pour into an ice-cream machine and freeze until semi-frozen. Then stir in 3 tablespoons of grated chocolate and continue freezing as normal. To serve, spoon out into a glass bowl and scatter the remaining tablespoon of grated chocolate over the top. If you do not have an ice-cream machine, freeze the mixture in ice trays, covered with foil. Beat the mixture once during freezing.

plum ice-cream

1½ *lb*/0.75 *kg plums*

¼ *lb*/120 *g sugar*

juice of 1 *orange*

2 *egg yolks, beaten*

½ *pint*/3 *dl double cream*

SERVES 5–6

Cut the plums in thick slices, discarding the stones. Put them in a pan with 1 oz/30 g sugar,

the juice of 1 orange and 2 tablespoons of water. Simmer until soft, stirring often (the timing depends on the ripeness of the plums). Push the plums through the medium mesh of a food mill to get rid of the skins. Boil the juice up with 3oz/90g sugar, until reduced to about 6fl oz/180ml of thin syrup. Pour it while it is still boiling on to the beaten egg yolks. Continue to beat until frothy. Fold in the puréed plums. Leave to cool, then lightly whip the cream and fold it in. Freeze in an ice-cream machine or, if you do not have one, freeze in ice trays covered with foil, beating once with a fork during freezing.

strawberry fool with raspberry sauce

1½ lb/0.75 kg strawberries

3 oz/90g castor sugar

½ pint/3 dl double cream

sauce:

½ lb/240g raspberries, fresh or frozen

2 tablespoons castor sugar

1–2 tablespoons cream

SERVES 6

For a quick strawberry fool, put the berries together with the sugar and cream, which should be either half whipped, or if it is very thick, just as it is, in a food processor. The result can then be pushed through a sieve if you like. Chill very well in the refrigerator, or for an hour in the freezer, before serving. To make the sauce: put the raspberries in the blender, then through the fine mesh of a food mill. Add sugar to taste and a little cream to soften the acidity. Serve the fool in a glass bowl with the sauce in a jug.

raspberry fool

This semi-frozen fool is just as good as an ice-cream

1 lb/0.5 kg fresh or frozen raspberries

4 tablespoons sugar

½ pint/3 dl double cream

a few fraises des bois, when available

SERVES 6

Purée the raspberries in a blender, then rub them through a sieve or the fine mesh of a food mill. Add sugar to taste. Beat the cream until it is thick, but not too solid, and fold into the raspberry purée. Pour into a china dish and place in the ice compartment of a refrigerator for about 2 hours, stirring in the thickened parts at the edges of the dish once or twice. Serve in glasses and garnish with a few fraises des bois, if available.

orange Boodles fool

4 oranges

2 lemons

¾ pint/4.5 dl double cream

2–3 tablespoons sugar

¼ lb/120g slightly stale sponge cake or fingers

SERVES 4–5

Grate the rind of 2 oranges and 1 lemon. Squeeze the juice of the oranges and lemons. Half whip the cream, then strain the fruit juice into it, together with most of the grated rind. Mix. Add 2–3 tablespoons of sugar, to taste. Break the sponge cake or fingers into pieces and lay them in a soufflé dish. Pour the cream over them, pushing them down if they float to the surface. Chill in the refrigerator for 2–3 hours. Sprinkle with the reserved grated rind before serving.

plum brulée

1 *lb*/0.5 *kg ripe plums*
¼ *pint*/1.5 *dl double cream*
¼ *pint*/1.5 *dl sour cream*
castor sugar
squeeze of lemon juice
soft brown sugar
SERVES 6

Preheat the grill. Cut the plums in half, remove the stones and cut in chunks. Mix the two creams together and stir in the plums. Add castor sugar to taste and a little lemon juice. Pour into a shallow fireproof dish. Sieve an even layer of soft brown sugar on top, about ⅛ inch/1.25 cm thick. When the grill is very hot, place the dish under it. Turn it carefully so that the sugar melts evenly all over. Do not let it burn. Remove as soon as it is a fairly even golden brown and leave to cool. Chill before serving.

prune whip

¾ *lb*/360 *g prunes*
½ *pint*/3 *dl cold tea*
2 *tablespoons sugar*
2 *tablespoons lemon juice*
¼ *pint*/1.5 *dl yoghourt*
2 *egg whites*
SERVES 4

Soak the prunes overnight in the cold tea. The next day, cook them gently in the tea until soft, adding the sugar. Cut out the stones and put the prunes in a blender or food processor and purée. Beat the egg whites stiffly. Stir the lemon juice into the purée and fold in the yoghourt and the egg whites. Spoon into a dish and refrigerate for a couple of hours or until really cold.

apple snow

4 *medium Bramley apples*
sugar
2 *egg whites*
SERVES 4

Slice the Bramleys and cook with a very little water and sugar to taste until soft. Push them through the medium mesh of a food mill. Cool, then stiffly beat 2 egg whites, and fold them in. Pile into glasses and serve with cream and extra sugar if required.

blueberry slump

A good slump can also be made with a mixture of red and white currants and cherries; the cherries should be stoned and cooked for 5 minutes longer than the currants, which only need 2–3 minutes

1 *lb*/0.5 *kg blueberries*
2 *oz*/60 *g sugar*
5 *oz*/150 *g flour*
1½ *teaspoons baking powder*
1½ *oz*/45 *g butter*
a little milk
SERVES 4–5

Cook the berries gently in a broad heavy pan with the sugar and just enough water to cover the bottom of the pan. Stop when the juice starts to run, about 4–5 minutes. Sift the flour into a bowl with the baking powder and rub in the butter cut in small pieces, as if making pastry. Add enough milk very gradually to make a stiff dough, slightly more than you would use for pastry. (Alternatively, put flour, baking powder and butter in a food processor and add milk while mixing.) Pat out on a board until about ½ inch/1 cm thick. Cut into little squares or rectangles, roughly 1 inch/2.5 cm across. Reheat the blueberries until simmering, lay the dough squares on

top, cover with a lid and cook gently for 15 minutes. Pour into a glass dish and serve hot, accompanied by a jug of cream.

soft fruit compôte

½ lb/240g cherries, red and white mixed
½ lb/240g strawberries
½ lb/240g raspberries
½ lb/240g red currants, or red and white mixed
6 oz/180g sugar

SERVES 5–6

Prepare the fruit before making the syrup. Stone the cherries; halve the strawberries; hull the raspberries and pick the currants from their stalks. Make a syrup by heating the sugar with ¼ pint/1.5 dl water until the sugar has melted. Put in the cherries and simmer gently for about 4 minutes, until slightly softened. Put the other fruit in a large china bowl and pour the cherries and their syrup over them. Leave to cool. This compôte is delicious eaten warm or cooled, but is better not chilled. Serve with cream.

raspberry meringue

Strawberries or loganberries are also good used in this way; if frozen berries are used, only allow them to thaw for one hour before using, and place them on the cream at the moment of serving

3 egg whites
6 oz/180g castor sugar
½ pint/3 dl double cream
½ lb/240g raspberries

SERVES 6

Beat the egg whites until stiff, then spoon in the sugar gradually, continuing to beat until all is absorbed. Line a baking sheet with a piece of lightly oiled aluminium foil. Spread the meringue over it in a large circle and put in a very low oven. Leave for about 2 hours, watching now and then to make sure the oven is not too hot. The meringue should be a pale straw colour by the end of cooking time. Take it out of the oven and leave to cool before removing from the foil. Place it on a flat dish and cover with lightly whipped cream. Lay the raspberries all over the surface of the cream and serve immediately.

peaches on meringue

2 egg whites
¼ lb/120g castor sugar
2 large ripe peaches or nectarines
sauce:
½ lb/240g raspberries, fresh or frozen
2 tablespoons castor sugar
2 teaspoons brandy (optional)

SERVES 4

Prepare the sauce: purée the raspberries in a blender and rub through a nylon sieve, or the fine mesh of a food mill. Stir in 2 tablespoons sugar and a drop of brandy if you like. Chill until needed. Beat the egg whites until stiff, then add the sugar gradually, continuing to beat. When thick and smooth, spoon on to an oiled sheet of aluminium foil in four mounds. Flatten them slightly with a palette knife. Bake for 1½–2 hours with the oven at its lowest mark, until firm and slightly coloured. Cool before removing from foil. Lay the meringue nests on a platter and lay half a peeled peach on each one. Pour a little of the sauce over each peach before serving and hand round the rest in a small jug.

Desserts/tarts, pancakes and dumplings

vacherin of red currants

3 egg whites

6oz/180g castor sugar

¾ pint/4.5dl double cream, lightly whipped

½–¾ lb/240–360g red currants

SERVES 6–8

Cover a flat baking sheet with a lightly oiled piece of aluminium foil. Beat the egg whites until stiff, then fold in the castor sugar. Spoon the meringue mixture on to the baking sheet and smooth it into a round mass with a palette knife. Bake for 2 hours, with the oven at its lowest temperature, watching to see that it does not become any darker than a pale straw colour. When the time is up, switch off the oven and leave the meringue to cool. Later, take it off the paper carefully but do not despair if the meringue breaks. Cover with a thick layer of lightly whipped cream, then pile the currants on top. A mixture of red and white currants can be used, but the colour should be predominantly red to contrast with the white of the cream and meringue.

raspberry and red-currant tart

¾ lb/360g raspberries

½ lb/240g red currants

3oz/90g castor sugar

pastry:

½ lb/240g flour

¼ lb/120g butter

2oz/60g lard

½ teaspoon castor sugar

2 egg yolks

1 teaspoon lemon juice

about 3 tablespoons iced water

SERVES 6

Prepare the fruit and make the pastry as follows. Rub the butter and lard into the flour and add the sugar. Stir in 1 egg yolk and the lemon juice, then enough iced water to make a firm dough. Handle as little as possible, wrap in cling film and chill for 30 minutes in the refrigerator. Roll out and use it to line a large flan tin or china dish. Chill again for 30 minutes and preheat the oven to 400°F (200°C, Gas Mark 6). Brush the pastry with the remaining egg yolk. Bake for 10 minutes, then for a further 10 minutes at 350°F (180°C, Gas Mark 4). Lower the heat to 325°F (170°C, Gas Mark 3), pile the raspberries and currants mixed with castor sugar into the shell and return to the oven for 5 minutes. Serve immediately, or as soon as possible, with a bowl of whipped cream.

plum tart

¾ lb/360g short pastry (see recipe, page 126)

1 egg yolk

1 lb/0.5kg dark red plums

2 tablespoons castor sugar

4 tablespoons jelly: raspberry, crab apple, or red currant

Make the pastry: chill for 30 minutes, then roll out and line a large flan dish or tin. Preheat the oven to 400°F (200°C, Gas Mark 6). Brush the pastry with the beaten egg yolk and bake for 10 minutes. Cool slightly. Slice the plums thickly, removing the stones and retaining any juice that escapes. Lay them on the pastry. Sprinkle with the sugar and bake for 25 minutes at 350°F (180°C, Gas Mark 4). Put the jelly in a small pan and warm gently. When the tart is cooked, extract the juice from the plums with a baster and add 2 tablespoons of it to the jelly. Stir until blended, then spoon or brush over the surface of the plums. Best eaten within an hour of baking, this tart is also good cool, but should not be chilled. If it is to be eaten cool, brush

again with the glaze once or twice while cooling. If you have the patience, reduce the plum juice by boiling to strengthen the flavour. On no account use more than half the amount of juice in relation to jelly, or it will not thicken enough to use as a glaze.

blueberry pancakes

½ lb/240g *plain flour*
¼ teaspoon *salt*
½ teaspoon *castor sugar*
2 *eggs*
½ pint/3 dl *milk*
6–8 oz/180–240g *blueberries*
SERVES 6

If making the batter by hand, sift the flour into a bowl and make a depression in the centre. Break in the eggs and put the milk and water (½ pint/3 dl) in a jug. Start to beat the eggs with a wire whisk, gradually incorporating the flour from around the edges, at the same time pouring in the milk and water in a slow stream. When all the flour is amalgamated, the liquid should also be absorbed. Add the salt and sugar and continue to beat for a minute or two. Stand for an hour before using. Alternatively the batter can be made quickly in a food processor. Just before using the batter, fold in the berries. Heat the griddle or frying pan until very hot indeed. Pour on a large spoonful of the batter, with some blueberries in it, and cook for about 3 minutes, turning once. Serve with cream and sugar, and scatter with more uncooked blueberries if liked.

Austrian plum dumplings

10 oz/300g *self-raising flour*
½ teaspoon *salt*
¼ pint/1.5 dl *milk*
6½ oz/195g *butter*
1 *egg* + 1 *yolk*
10–12 *small ripe plums or* 5–6 *large ones*
1½ oz/45g *dry breadcrumbs*
2 tablespoons *poppy seeds*
SERVES 5–6

Sift the flour and salt into a large bowl. Heat the milk with 2 oz/60g of the butter until it reaches boiling point. Pour over the flour and mix well with a wooden spoon. Beat together the egg and the yolk and stir them in. Mix until smooth and well blended. Roll out in small circles about ¼ inch/0.5 cm thick. Put a stoned plum in the centre of each and seal the edges carefully round it. (If the plums are large, you can use half a plum for each one.) Poach for about 8 minutes in steadily boiling water. Drain carefully. Melt ½ oz/15g butter and fry the dry breadcrumbs to a golden brown. Mix with the poppy seeds. Roll each dumpling in this mixture. Melt the rest of the butter and serve it with the dumplings.

plums in yoghourt

1 lb/0.5 kg *ripe plums*
¼ pint/1.5 dl *double cream*
¼ pint/1.5 dl *yoghourt*
1 *egg white*
2 tablespoons *castor sugar*
SERVES 4

Chop the plums, retaining any juice. Beat the cream until fairly stiff and fold in the yoghourt. Stiffly beat the egg white and fold in with the castor sugar. Spoon the mixture over the plums and chill in the refrigerator.

floating island

4 *eggs*
6 *tablespoons vanilla sugar (see recipe, page* 126) *or* 7 *tablespoons castor sugar and* ½ *vanilla pod*
¾ *pint*/4.5 *dl milk*
¼ *lb*/120 *g granulated sugar*
SERVES 5–6

First make the caramel: put the ¼lb/120g granulated sugar in a heavy pan with 4fl oz/120ml water and bring very slowly to the boil. Continue to boil slowly and steadily until it starts to caramelize and turn a pale golden colour. Stop immediately at this stage for the colour turns very rapidly and it will burn within a matter of seconds. Pour it into a wet mould – either a tin cake mould or a fireproof glass or china bowl, holding about 1½ pints/9dl. Turn it quickly so that the inside is coated more or less all over with the golden caramel. Leave to harden while you make the meringue. Separate the eggs and beat the whites until stiff. Fold in 4 tablespoons vanilla sugar, or plain castor sugar if you have no home-made vanilla sugar. Pile the meringue into the caramel-lined mould and put in a baking tin half-filled with water. Stand in the oven and bake for 20 minutes at 325°F (170°C, Gas Mark 3). Meanwhile make the custard. Beat the egg yolks for several minutes with an electric beater until thick and creamy. Heat the milk with the remaining 2 tablespoons vanilla sugar until almost boiling, then pour on to the egg yolks, continuing to beat. (If you have no vanilla sugar, heat the milk with a piece of vanilla pod in it and leave to stand, covered, for 10 minutes to flavour it; remove the pod, reheat the milk until almost boiling and pour on to the egg yolks.) Stand the bowl in a saucepan over simmering water and stir continuously with a wooden spoon until very slightly thickened. Then remove and cool, stirring often, standing the bowl in a basin of cold water to accelerate the cooling. When both the meringue and the custard sauce are cool, chill them in the refrigerator for a couple of hours. Then turn out the meringue into the centre of a shallow dish (run a sharp knife round the edges of the dish), and pour the sauce around it.

caramel mousse

6 *oz*/180 *g sugar*
½ *pint*/3 *dl double cream*
½ *oz*/15 *g* (1 *packet) gelatine*
4 *egg whites*
SERVES 4

Put 4oz/120g of the sugar in a heavy pan with a scant ¼ pint/1.5dl water. Heat gently until a pale golden, then remove from the heat. While it cools, whip the cream until thick. When the caramel is just cool enough to allow you to dip your finger in it without pain, pour it on to the cream and stir it in. (If it forms into a hard toffee, lift out the solid parts with a slotted spoon and put back in the pan with some of the cream. Stir over gentle heat until melted and blended with the cream, then pour back into the rest of the cream and mix well.) Dissolve the gelatine in 2 tablespoons of cold water in a cup, then place in a shallow pan of simmering water to melt. Stir into the caramel cream. Beat the egg whites until stiff, then fold in. Pour into a soufflé dish and place in the refrigerator to set. Make extra caramel by heating 2oz/60g sugar with 4 tablespoons water until a pale golden colour, then pour into an oiled cake tin to set in a thin layer. When cold, break into little pieces and scatter over the top of the mousse before serving.

oeufs en neige

3 eggs

4 tablespoons vanilla sugar (see recipe, page 126)

¾ pint/4.5 dl milk

SERVES 4–5

Separate the yolks from the whites. Beat two of the whites until stiff and fold in half the vanilla sugar to make a meringue mixture. Put plenty of water in a large broad pan and heat it to simmering point. Drop in the tablespoons of the meringue mixture, a few at a time, so that they do not touch each other. Poach gently, barely simmering, for about 3 minutes, then turn them with a skimmer and poach for a further 2–3 minutes. Lift them out and drain on a cloth (paper will stick) while you poach the rest. When drained, lift them off the cloth on to a flat plate and place in the refrigerator. Beat the egg yolks with the remaining vanilla sugar. Heat the milk until almost boiling and pour on to the yolks. Place the bowl over a pan of boiling water and stir until slightly thickened, about 12 minutes. Cool quickly in a sink half-full of water, stirring to prevent skin forming. Refrigerate for a few hours. To serve, pour the custard sauce into a shallow dish and lay the meringues on it.

caramel junket

2 oz/60 g sugar

1 pint/6 dl milk

1–2 teaspoons rennet, according to directions

2 tablespoons double cream

SERVES 4–5

Melt 2 oz/60 g sugar in a heavy pan with 2 tablespoons of water until it becomes a pale golden colour. Meanwhile, bring ¼ pint/1.5 dl milk almost to boiling point, and as soon as the caramel is the right colour, pour in the hot milk gradually, stirring hard to blend the two. If they refuse to mix and the caramel forms into toffee, simply drain off the milk, reheat the toffee until soft and pour on the hot milk again. When amalgamated, pour into a bowl and leave to cool until lukewarm. Warm ¾ pint/4.5 dl of milk until tepid and stir in the caramel. Cool until 98°F/37°C (blood heat), then stir in the rennet. Pour into 4 or 5 small dishes to set, or 1 larger dish. When set, spread a generous spoonful of lightly whipped cream over each dish.

peaches in jelly

4 large peaches

6 oz/180 g sugar

juice of 2 lemons

¼ oz/7.5 g gelatine

SERVES 6

Peel the peaches, cut them in half and remove the stones. Put the sugar in a pan with 6 fl oz/180 ml water and heat until the sugar has dissolved and made a thin syrup. Put in enough of the halved peaches to fit comfortably in one layer and poach for a few minutes, turning once. Lift them out carefully and drain while you poach the rest. When all are done, squeeze the juice of the lemons into the syrup and measure it. With any luck you should have about ½ pint/3 dl; if not make it up to this measure with water or fruit juice. Melt ¼ oz/7.5 g gelatine in a couple of tablespoons of water and stir into the syrup. Lay the peaches in a round flat dish and pour the liquid over them through a strainer. Only half cover them so that the domed tops of the peaches rise above the pink jelly. Put in refrigerator until set.

orange jelly

5–6 *oranges*

1 *lemon*

¼ *lb*/120*g sugar*

½ *oz*/15*g gelatine*

SERVES 4

Take the rind off 2 of the oranges and half the lemon. Put in a bowl and squeeze the juice of all the fruit over it. Put the sugar in a small pan with ½ pint/3 dl of water; bring to the boil and simmer until the sugar has melted and the liquid has slightly reduced. Pour the fruit juice with the grated rind into the pan and bring back to the boil. Skim off any scum that rises to the surface, add a tablespoon of cold water and skim again. Dissolve the gelatine in 2 tablespoons of cold water and stir, standing it in a pan half-full of hot water, until melted. Add to the fruit juice, stir well, then pour through a strainer into a measuring jug. You should have about 1 pint/6 dl. Pour into a ring mould and cool, then chill in the refrigerator until set before serving.

lemon jelly

4 *large lemons*

6 *oz*/180*g sugar*

1½ *packets gelatine*

SERVES 4

Cut the rind off the lemons thinly, put it in a bowl and squeeze the juice. Boil the sugar with ½ pint/3 dl water until the sugar has melted, then pour it while still boiling over the lemon rind. Cover and stand for 20 minutes. Strain it and dissolve the gelatine in a little of it. Mix the strained syrup with the dissolved gelatine and the lemon juice. Measure it and make it up to 1 pint/6 dl by adding water if necessary. Strain into a ring mould and chill until set.

chocolate apple cream

Much loved by children, I always thought this recipe was special to our family, as I had never had it anywhere else. Not long ago, however, I came across what must have been the original recipe, published in 1923 in a book called *Caviare to Candy*, by Mrs Philip Martineau, long out of print

2 *lb*/1 *kg Bramley apples*

2 *oz*/60*g sugar*

½ *pint*/3 *dl double cream*

2 *oz*/60*g Menier, or any other good dark chocolate*

SERVES 4

Peel and slice the apples and cook them with the sugar and a little water. Push through the medium mesh of a food mill. When cool, spoon in a flat layer in the bottom of a serving dish. Whip the cream until thick but not solid and spoon over the apple. Grate the chocolate and sprinkle over the cream. Chill for 2–3 hours before serving.

apples with toffee sauce

6 *small Bramley apples*

3–4 *yellow plums*

3 *large slices dry bread*

¼ *lb*/120*g soft brown sugar*

2 *oz*/60*g butter*

4 *tablespoons double cream*

SERVES 6

Core the apples. Chop the plums, removing the stones. Cut the bread into six squares or round pieces. Butter a baking tin and lay the apples in it, each one on a piece of bread. Fill the centres with chopped plums. Preheat the oven to 400°F (200°C, Gas Mark 6) and mix the sugar and the slightly softened butter to a paste and dot around the dish. Bake for 30 minutes, basting the apples now and then

with the sugar and butter mixture. When done lift them out carefully on their pieces of bread and lay on the serving dish. Put the tin on a gentle flame and stir the cream into the toffee mixture. Pour into a jug and serve with the apples. If no plums are available, the apples can be filled simply with the butter and sugar paste (the bread will prevent it running out during the cooking). Or the bread can be fried separately when plums are used as a filling and put under the apples at the last minute before serving.

tuiles

To make the classic French *tuiles d'amandes* add 2 tablespoons coarsely grated almonds to the mixture before baking

2 oz/60g butter
2 oz/60g castor sugar
2 oz/60g flour

MAKES ABOUT 12 TUILES

Cream the butter and sugar together and stir in the flour. Make small round balls with a large teaspoon and flatten them with a wetted palette knife. Preheat the oven to 350°F (180°C, Gas Mark 4). Lay the tuiles on a lightly greased baking sheet, well spaced out and only 5 at a time. Bake for 6–8 minutes, until evenly spread out and pale golden with slightly darker edges. Take them out of the oven and wait for half a minute before attempting to lift them off the baking sheet with a fish slice. As soon as they can be moved without breaking, lay them over an oiled wine bottle to cool. If they cool and become stiff while still on the baking tray, replace them for a moment in the oven to soften them again. When cool and firm, slide carefully off the bottle and lay on a flat dish.

strawberry shortcake

shortcake:

½ lb/240g plain flour
2 teaspoons baking powder
½ teaspoon salt
1 tablespoon sugar
2 oz/60g butter
6 fl oz/180 ml milk and cream, mixed

filling:

½ pint/3 dl double cream
½ lb/240g strawberries
1 oz/30g castor sugar

SERVES 6

Sift the flour with the baking powder, salt and sugar. Cut in, then rub in, the butter; alternatively use a food processor. Add the creamy milk until the mixture becomes a soft dough. Knead lightly a couple of times on a floured board then divide into two unequal pieces. Roll or pat out into 2 rounds about ½ inch/1 cm thick, one bigger than the other. Lay on 2 oiled baking sheets and bake at 450°F (230°C, Gas Mark 8) for 12–15 minutes, until a pale golden brown. Cool on a rack for about 15 minutes. Lightly whip the cream. Take the strawberries, reserving a third for garnish, halve them, and mix them with the sugar. Spread the larger circle with lightly whipped cream and the halved strawberries. Place the smaller round on top, press lightly and decorate with the reserved whole berries and some of the cream, as liked. Eat within at least an hour of baking.

Biscuits/flapjacks and brownies

cheese scones

½ lb/240g plain flour

2 teaspoons baking powder

½ teaspoon salt

1 level teaspoon mustard powder

2 oz/60g grated Cheddar cheese

2 oz/60g butter or margarine

1 medium egg

½ pint/1.5 dl milk

2 tablespoons grated Parmesan cheese

MAKES 12 SCONES

Sift the flour with the baking powder and salt. Add the mustard powder, grated Cheddar and fat cut in small pieces. Rub in quickly, or use a food processor. Beat the egg with the milk and add enough to form a soft dough. Wrap in cling-film wrap and place in refrigerator for half an hour, preheat oven to 400°F (200°C, Gas Mark 6). Roll out dough to about ½ inch/ 1cm thick and cut into shapes with an oval or round cutter. Place on a buttered baking sheet, sprinkle with grated Parmesan cheese and bake near the top of the oven for 8–10 minutes, or until puffed up and golden. Serve immediately with butter.

cinnamon toast

4 large slices dry white bread

1 oz/30g butter

2 tablespoons castor sugar

½ teaspoon powdered cinnamon

SERVES 4

Toast the bread lightly and remove the crusts. Mix the sugar and cinnamon together in a cup and spread each slice of bread with butter on one side and sprinkle thickly with the mixed sugar and cinnamon. Place under the grill until the sugar has melted and turned a golden brown. Cut into triangles or strips and serve immediately.

brownies

¼ lb/120g plain chocolate

3½ oz/105g butter

4 eggs

10 oz/300g castor sugar

¼ lb/120g flour

¼ lb/120g walnuts (optional)

pinch of salt

Break the chocolate in small pieces and put with the butter in a bowl over a pan of boiling water. Preheat the oven to 350°F (180°C, Gas Mark 4). As they melt, mix them well and leave to cool. Later, beat the eggs thoroughly and stir in the salt and sugar. Stir in the cooled chocolate mixture then the sifted flour and the chopped nuts, if included. Mix lightly and quickly. Pour into a shallow well greased tin, about 10 inches/25cm square. Bake for 35 minutes or until lightly coloured. Brownies should be slightly soft in the middle, so be careful not to over-cook them. Cut in squares after cooling and serve with a bowl of lightly whipped cream.

flapjacks

3 oz/90g butter

3 oz/90g soft brown sugar

¼ lb/120g breakfast or rolled oats

MAKES 9 BISCUITS

Put the butter in a small pan and heat gently. As soon as it has melted stir in the sugar and remove from the heat. Preheat the oven to 350°F (180°C, Gas Mark 4). Mix the oats into the butter and sugar mixture and turn into a well-buttered shallow tin, about 8 inches/ 20cm square. Cook for about 15 minutes or until golden brown all over. Leave to cool before cutting.

Drinks

carrot and tomato juice

1 lb/0.5 kg carrots
1 lb/0.5 kg tomatoes
¼ pint/1.5 dl yoghourt (optional)
2 tablespoons lemon juice
1 tablespoon orange juice

SERVES 3–4

Put the carrots and tomatoes through a juice extractor. Mix the two juices together and stir in the yoghourt, if you want a more substantial mixture. Stir in the fruit juices and chill briefly in the refrigerator.

currant cordial

½ lb/240 g white currants
1 pint/6 dl brandy
pinch ground ginger
½ lemon
6 oz/180 g sugar

Pick the currants from their stalks and crush them in a china bowl. Pour over the brandy and add the thinly pared rind of half a lemon and a pinch of ground ginger. Stir well and cover the bowl with foil. Stand for 24 hours, stirring now and then. Strain through muslin and measure. Add 6 oz/180 g of sugar for every 1 pint/6 dl of liquid. Stir until melted and bottle.

cucumber and yoghourt drink

1 medium cucumber
1 pint/6 dl yoghourt
3 cracked ice-cubes
1 tablespoon chopped mint
pinch sea salt

SERVES 4

Peel the cucumber and cut it in chunks. Put in a blender with the yoghourt, salt, and the cracked ice-cubes. Blend, stir in the fresh mint and blend again. Chill before serving.

sorrel and buttermilk drink

½ lb/240 g sorrel
½ pint/3 dl buttermilk
½ pint/3 dl yoghourt

SERVES 4

Put the sorrel through a juice extractor. Put the juice in a blender or food processor with the buttermilk and yoghourt. Process, then chill briefly. If you do not have a juice extractor, use ¼ lb/120 g sorrel, 1 pint/6 dl buttermilk and ¼ pint/1.5 dl yoghourt. Put the leaves into a blender with the buttermilk and yoghourt, discarding the stalks.

buttermilk and watercress drink

1 pint/6 dl buttermilk
¼ pint/1.5 dl yoghourt
1 bunch watercress

SERVES 4

Put the buttermilk and yoghourt in a blender or food processor with the leaves of the watercress. Blend, chill, and pour into glasses.

mango and orange drink

1 ripe mango
1 oz/30 g sugar
½ pint/3 dl orange juice
6 tablespoons lime juice

SERVES 3–4

Skin the mango and cut the flesh off the stone, scraping off all the juicy parts into a blender or food processor. Heat ½ pint/3 dl water with the sugar, until the sugar has dissolved, to form a thin syrup. Cool. Blend the chopped mango with the sugar syrup and the fruit juices. Chill and serve poured over ice-cubes in glasses.

Basic recipes

basic white sauce

½ pint/3 dl liquid: milk, chicken, fish or vegetable stock
1 slice onion
2 cloves
¼ bay leaf
1½ oz/45g butter
2 tablespoons flour
pinch grated nutmeg
salt and black pepper

If no other flavouring is to be used in the white sauce, the milk (if used) should be infused before adding. Put it into a small pan with the onion, cloves and bay leaf. Bring slowly to the boil and immediately remove from the heat. Cover the pan and stand for 20 minutes, then strain before using. Melt the butter slowly in a heavy pan. Remove from the heat and shake in flour, stirring until amalgamated. Return to the heat and cook for 1 minute, stirring constantly. Remove from the heat again and add the heated milk or stock gradually, mixing until each new addition is blended. When all is absorbed, return to the heat and bring to the boil, stirring. Simmer gently for at least 4 minutes, stirring now and then. Add salt and pepper to taste and the grated nutmeg. Grated cheese or cream should be added at this stage, chopped herbs only at the last moment. This sauce can be served immediately or kept warm over a pan of hot water until needed; in this case beat well before serving.

vanilla sugar

3–4 vanilla pods
castor sugar

Half-fill a large glass jar with castor sugar and stick a few vanilla pods upright in the sugar. Fill up the jar with more sugar and close tightly. Leave for at least a week before using, if possible, to allow the flavour to permeate the sugar. Some people cut the pods in half lengthwise, which increases the flavour, but gives a sticky brown substance to the sugar, which I find unattractive. If required, a pod can be taken out of the sugar and used to flavour a dish, then carefully washed, dried and replaced in the jar. This is rarely necessary, however, as I do not often seem to need the flavour of vanilla without the sweetness of the sugar. As it is used up, the sugar can be replenished. The pods will only need replacing after a year or so.

short pastry

Where a recipe calls for ½ lb/250g pastry, use the quantities given here. Where a recipe calls for 6oz/180g pastry, make this quantity, reserving the leftovers for another use. Where a recipe calls for ¾ lb/360g, make double the quantity and reserve the rest. For a sweet dish, omit the salt and add a pinch of castor sugar and a squeeze of lemon juice

½ lb/240g flour
pinch of salt
¼ lb/120g butter
2 oz/60g lard
iced water

Make sure the fats are very cold indeed before starting. Sift the flour with the salt in a large bowl. Cut the fats in small pieces. Rub them into the flour very quickly, then add just enough iced water, mixing with the blade of a knife, to make a soft dough. Form into a ball, handling as little as possible, wrap in cling-film wrap and chill for 30 minutes in the refrigerator before using.

Index